INTO MY OWN

THE ENGLISH YEARS
OF
ROBERT FROST
1912–1915

Robert and Elinor Frost, fall 1911 at Plymouth, New Hampshire, a few months before leaving for England, taken by one of Frost's students at the Normal school. (Courtesy of James E. Newdick)

INTO MY OWN

THE ENGLISH YEARS
OF
ROBERT FROST
1912 – 1915

JOHN EVANGELIST WALSH

GROVE WEIDENFELD

NEW YORK

Published by Grove Weidenfeld
A division of Grove Press, Inc.
841 Broadway
New York, N.Y. 10003-4793

Library of Congress Cataloging-in-Publication Data

Walsh, John Evangelist, 1927–
    Into my own:the English years of Robert Frost, 1912–1915/John
Evangelist Walsh.—1st ed.
        p.   cm.
    Bibliography: p.
    Includes index.
    ISBN 0-8021-1045-2
    ISBN 0-8021-3292-8 (pbk.)
    1. Frost, Robert, 1874–1963—Homes and haunts—England.   2. Poets,
American—20th century—Biography.   3. Beaconsfield
(Buckinghamshire)—History.   4. England—Intellectual life—20th
century. I. Title.
PS3511.R94Z985   1988
811'.52—dc19   88–1705
                                                                        CIP

Manufactured in the United States of America

Printed on acid-free paper

Designed by Irving Perkins Associates

First Edition 1988
First Evergreen Edition 1991

10   9   8   7   6   5   4   3   2   1

Page viii constitutes a continuation of this copyright page.

For
TIMOTHY and BARBARA
and a welcome aboard
for their
ANDREW

Permission to quote from specific sources, published and unpublished, is hereby acknowledged with thanks:

Henry Holt & Co, Inc.: *Robert Frost: The Early Years*, by Lawrance Thompson, copyright © 1966; *Selected Letters of Robert Frost*, edited by Lawrance Thompson, copyright © 1964; *Robert Frost: the Trial by Existence*, By Elizabeth S. Sergeant, copyright © 1960; *Interviews with Robert Frost*, edited by Edward C. Latham, copyright © 1966; *The Poetry of Robert Frost*, edited by Edward C. Latham, copyright © 1975.

The State University of New York Press: *Newdick's Season of Frost: An Interrupted Biography of Robert Frost*, by William A. Sutton, copyright © 1976; *New Hampshire's Child, The Derry Journals of Lesley Frost*, edited by Lawrance Thompson and Arnold Grade, copyright © 1969.

The University of Oklahoma Press: *Robert Frost: Life and Talks-Walking*, by Louis Mertins, copyright © 1965.

The University of Massachusetts Press: *Robert Frost: A Living Voice*, edited by Reginald L. Cook, copyright © 1974.

Yale University Press: *The Pastoral Art of Robert Frost*, by John F. Lynen, copyright © 1960.

Harcourt Brace Jovanovich Inc.: *The Letters of Ezra Pound*, edited by D. D. Paige, copyright © 1950.

The Oxford University Press and David Higham Associates, London: *Edward Thomas: The Last Four Years*, by Eleanor Farjeon, copyright © 1958.

Viking Penguin Inc.: *Writers at Work, Second Series*, edited by Malcolm Cowley, copyright © 1963 by The Paris Review Inc., all rights reserved.

Materials from the following manuscript collections are used by joint permission of the Estate of Robert Frost, Alfred C. Edwards, Trustee, and the Collection named:

Dartmouth College Library for some forty letters to Frost from various correspondents (see the Notes), and for the excerpts in Appendix B from the Morrison Notebook.

The University of Virginia Library, Manuscripts Department, Robert Frost Collection (#6261) for the excerpts in Appendix B from the Cohn Notebook, and for various Frost family letters.

The Harry Ransom Humanities Research Center, The University of Texas at Austin, for the letters of Robert Frost to Frank Flint.

Boston University Library for the letters of Robert Frost to Gertrude McQuesten, and one letter of Nettie McQuesten to Frost.

The Huntington Library for an excerpt from an early draft of "To A Moth Seen In Winter," and an excerpt from "On the Sale of My Farm."

Princeton University Library for a letter of Robert Frost to Alfred Harcourt.

University College, Cardiff, for excerpts from several Robert Frost letters to Edward Thomas.

Plymouth State College Library for the notes and postcards of the Frost children to Bertha Huckins, and for the 1913 photograph of the Bungalow, Beaconsheld.

CONTENTS

ACKNOWLEDGMENTS

A NUMBER of kind people having in various ways aided my efforts with this book, it is my distinct pleasure to return them sincerest gratitude.

In the United States:

Timothy A. Walsh, University of Wisconsin, and Walt Bode, Grove Press, for incisive readings of the manuscript that frequently helped to refine thought and expression;

John C. Walsh, George Mason University, for invaluable research assistance, here and abroad;

James E. Newdick, for access to his father's Frost papers, as well as for pleasant hospitality; also Kristin Newdick;

Dan Lombardo of Jones Library, Donald Swanson of Wright State University, Philip Cronenwett and Barbara Krieger of Dartmouth College Library, Robert Fleming of Emerson College, Sarah Truher of Boston University Library, Helyn Townsend of Plymouth State College Library, Cathy Henderson of University of Texas Library, also, William A. Sutton and Howard Schmitt, all for prompt and unstinting response to requests for information, advice, documents, and other helps. Also the staffs of Princeton University Library, Amherst College Library, Houghton Library, the Huntington Library, and the Library of the University of Virginia; also Ann A. Walsh and Matthew O. Walsh, for helpful comment on the manuscript.

My wife Dorothy is hereby tendered a special measure of thanks, for much forbearance, and for making the Bungalow in Beaconsfield seem just like home.

In England and Scotland:

Mrs. Joan Clarence, Beaconsfield, for making the old Frost cottage available to me and my family, and for pleasant associations;

Mrs. Barbara Davis, Ryton, for able research assistance;

O. Flint, for use of his father's unpublished letters to Robert Frost, and for supplying an unpublished photograph of his father, Frank Flint;

Professor James Kenworthy, St. Andrews University, for generously making available both his knowledge and his time;

Henry Panton, for use of the unpublished letters of his grandfather, James Cruikshank Smith, to Robert Frost;

Myfanwy Thomas, for gracious permission to make use of her father's letters to Robert Frost;

Kari Dorme of Beaconsfield, for many courtesies; also R. G. Thomas, Dr. Ann Sanderson, Jane Powell, Kathleen Holden, Cissie Pitcher (now deceased), Kathleen Day, Mr. and Mrs. Gordon Churchill, Mr. and Mrs. Charles Churchill, Philip Churchill, Jill Churchill, Max Baker, O. Flint, Edith Clay, A. W. Taylor, Lyn Rodley, John Boardman, Bernard Ashmole, W. S. Philips, Ian Philips, Henry Panton, Marjorie Gwilt, Ann Gwilt, Mr. and Mrs. Catharine Swan, May Swan, Mr. and Mrs. Percy Halliday, Sarah Bowdeen, and the staff of the Public Records Office, Aylesbury. Also, the libraries of University College, Cardiff (B. Ll. James), the London School of Economics (Angela Raspin), and St. Andrews University, Fife.

My debt to all the many able and conscientious scholars who have been before me in the field is obvious from the bibliography and the citations in the notes. Whatever may have been their opinions and conclusions, I thank them for making my own studies so stimulating and rewarding. In this I specifically include the late Lawrance Thompson, whose work on Frost, if ultimately in some part flawed, was yet in its own way dedicated, as well as prodigious in extent.

How peculiar, how different from the interest which we grant to the ideas of a great philosopher, a great mathematician, or a great reformer, is that burning interest which settles on the great poets who have made themselves necessary to the human heart.

—DeQuincey
on Wordsworth

INTO MY OWN

THE ENGLISH YEARS
OF
ROBERT FROST
1912–1915

PROLOGUE

OVER THERE

WHEN Robert Frost died in a Boston hospital in January 1963, six weeks short of his eighty-ninth birthday, he closed a writing career notable, among other things, for its sheer length. His first published poem appeared in a New York periodical in 1894, his final volume of new poetry was issued only months before his death. Such an extended working life, quite apart from considerations of quality, must be among the lengthiest ever granted an artist. More remarkable yet, it was in the brief space of only two of those seventy years, or a little more than two, that he wrote and published much of the poetry on which his rank and reputation are at last to rest. During those two eventful years, moreover, he was living, with his wife and four children, not among the familiar sights of his own New Hampshire or Massachusetts, but in far-off England, for the most part in a well-populated suburb of London.

The crucial importance of this memorable interlude—stretching approximately from October 1912 to December 1914—for a full understanding of Frost's life and career has not, of course, been entirely lost on his biographers and critics. And yet, considering that it is now at least a half-century since he reached the height of his unequaled fame as America's uncrowned poet laureate, generating intense interest in every minutest facet of his life and work, it is surprising how little is known of the period. As a matter of fact, next to nothing has been added to the picture of Frost's English sojourn as it was drawn by Gorham Munson in 1927 and expanded by Elizabeth Sergeant in 1960, and by Lawrance

Thompson in 1965 in the first volume of his massive official biography. And all three of these treatments, it must be said frankly, are curiously limited and inadequate, especially in view of the rare opportunities given their authors for contact with Frost and his family.

Still more surprising, and even more to be regretted, is the fact that all descriptions to date of Frost's English years labor under a serious distortion. Following the lead of Sergeant and Thompson, all Frost's biographers and commentators dwell on and thereby emphasize the latter part of the period, the nine supposedly idyllic months he spent with his family in the Gloucestershire countryside, mingling happily with the small group now recalled as the Dymock Poets. As a result, the much more important year and a half that he spent living with his family in the London suburb of Beaconsfield has been neglected, throwing badly out of focus the whole story of his English stay.

It was while Frost was living in Beaconsfield that he quite unexpectedly brought his long struggle for poetic recognition to a triumphant close. With little help he managed to find a publisher for his first two books, and garnered reviews of those books at a time when such attention to poetry was by no means automatic or easy to earn. He also brought to fruition both the theory and, what is worthier, the practice of his highly original sound-of-sense ideas of poetic technique. In that same Beaconsfield period he wrote two of the best-known poems in American literature—"Birches" and "Mending Wall"—as well as most of the other poems in the epoch-making volume *North of Boston*. When Frost first entered the door of his rented Beaconsfield home he was virtually unknown to the world of literature, his name barely recognizable by the editors of a very few American magazines. When he left Beaconsfield for the move down to Gloucestershire he was well on his way to achieving lasting world fame.

One large reason for this slighting of the Beaconsfield period, and the English years generally, rests with the poet himself. In the earlier years of his fame especially, it is clear that Frost preferred to minimize and discourage any too close inspection of his time in England, not for any devious purpose, but for self-protection. The breakthrough he so suddenly achieved in London, with publication of his first two volumes, had left him feeling extremely sensitive to the charge—and it was quickly pressed—that in taking his work abroad he had deliberately scorned his own country to seek something he valued more, a British reputation.

In addition, while he made no very strenuous effort to avoid talking of his English years, he always put much heavier emphasis on a different period altogether, one which had occurred long before there was any thought of England. This was the critically formative time he had spent with his family on his New Hampshire poultry farm—a matter of nine years, of which the first five were crucial—always in any case closer to his heart. Where the living poet seemed by his silences to deny any great significance to the English stay, others were not usually in a position to disagree.

Neglect of the Beaconsfield period appears even more curious when it is realized that a principal reminder of that time still exists. The house—cottage, rather—in which the Frosts lived during those eighteen months is still there, standing on its original property, still virtually the same inside and out. As with so much in England, the passing of seventy-five years has left almost untouched not only the house, but the street and the neighborhood as well. This unplanned preservation of Frost's old residence—the Bungalow, as it was called, situated on Reynolds Road—is no more than fitting. For of all the many houses Frost lived in during his life, this plain old structure, though on foreign soil, is most entitled to a place in America's literary history, alongside the houses of Hawthorn, Whitman, Poe, Longfellow, Dickinson, and a few others. The only Frost home that could contest for the honors with the Bungalow would be the farmhouse in Derry, New Hampshire, and that building, with its original property, has already been made into a state-run museum.

It is true that for a good many years after the Frosts left it, the precise location of the Bungalow was lost, so that those Frost admirers who went in search of it usually came away disappointed. This was to be expected, however, since Frost was gone from Beaconsfield before any of his near neighbors or the town at large had a compelling reason to be aware of the link. But Frost did not forget. Twice he went back to England, both times visiting his old home. In 1928, with his wife, he made an avowedly sentimental return, seeing old friends and calling at remembered haunts, including a brief stop at Beaconsfield. Of this visit, however, no detailed record is available. It is not even known if he actually entered the old cottage, then still a private residence (as it remains today).

Much more intriguing was the return to Beaconsfield he made in 1957. On that occasion, after a good deal of walking back and forth along Reynolds Road, he finally confessed to his companions that he was unable to pick out the house that had been his. This curious failure, in all probability, was deliberate, so the fleeting incident is worth pursuing, if for no other reason than that it shows the poet to have been more vulnerable than some of his critics like to admit.

In England to receive honorary degrees from both Oxford and Cambridge, Frost took time between the various ceremonies at the two colleges to visit a number of the old sites. With him on these side trips were several friends, including his biographer Lawrance Thompson. It was mid-June before he was able to get down to Beaconsfield, with results as succinctly described by Thompson in his notes: "Discovering that Reynolds Road made a semi-circular loop, RF said that when he and his family occupied 'The Bungalow' in 1912–1914, only the right-hand half of the loop had been a road, that 'The Bungalow' was at that time the last house on the right-hand side of Reynolds Road. Confused by the semi-circular continuation of houses in 1957, RF was unable to identify the house in which he had lived."

Of course it is possible that Frost really was unable to identify the house. He was eighty-three years old (though a vigorous eighty-three), and could well have lost his bearings after so much hurrying about for the prestigious awards, often trailed by an insistent press of reporters. Yet there are additional facts which make that conclusion, for one observer at least, more than unlikely.

As old ordinance survey maps of the area show, Frost was only partially correct in his description of the changes he saw in 1957 along Reynolds Road. What Thompson calls "the semi-circular continuation"—that is, the short loop linking the two streets—was very much in existence in Frost's time, though it was ungraded. It even had a name, Baring Crescent, which it still carries. While it is true that in 1912–1914 the Bungalow had stood as the last house on the right—just before the start of Baring Crescent—the three houses afterward erected beyond it, which still stand, are of a totally different character. Where the Bungalow is small and of stucco, these newer structures are larger and are built of red brick.

Several other features of the immediate vicinity have a bearing on Frost's supposed confusion that day. The front yard of the Bungalow, for instance, was and is by far the deepest frontage of any of the fourteen dwellings on the street. It is large enough to have prompted Mrs. Frost to write that it might serve as a tennis court, though it is not quite so big as that implies. There is also a landmark, present then as now, which would have been hard for Frost to overlook. Opposite the Bungalow, directly across the forty-foot width of Reynolds Road, there stands a two-story house of distinctive build, appearing somewhat awkward or lopsided, looking quite unlike any of the other houses in the area. Its light tan walls are made of a rough, pebbly grout, and it is the tallest building in the street. After staring across at this house daily for a year and a half, as the Frosts must have done, it would not be easy to forget, no matter how many years had fled by (I make this assertion with some confidence, based as it is on my own two-month residence in the Frost cottage while researching this book in the summer of 1985).

But why should the poet have pretended confusion in so innocuous a matter? The most probable answer is that he did it for a reason not rare among sensitive souls, whether poets or not, who are given overmuch to brooding about the past. An aged man, of highly emotional nature, sensitive in the extreme, Frost may well have found at the last moment as he walked down Reynolds Road that he could not bring himself to stir up old memories. The painful contrast between his lonely present, though filled with honors, and those far-off days when he had lived in obscurity on this quiet street with a happy, growing family may well have been too stark for him to face. By 1957, of the five who had shared the Bungalow with him, three were long dead—his wife from a heart attack, his daughter Marjorie in childbirth, and his son Carol by suicide—and a fourth, his daughter Irma, was confined in a mental institution. It would have taken a hardier, more calloused spirit than Frost's to have lifted the knocker on the door of the Bungalow that day.

It may be, also, that some vague feeling of personal guilt stayed his hand, a nagging doubt that in some unintended way he had allowed his own artistic ambitions to crowd too heavily on his family. More than once in that empty, aimless time following his wife's death he was to sound this mournful idea, which has been unthinkingly repeated ever since, even amplified, by certain of his critics. What may have been his first open reference to it outside the family has been preserved in the diary of the friend to whom, some four months after his wife's death in 1938, he directed the outburst. "Frost told me," wrote Charles Foster, "that he was a God-damned son-of-a-bitch, a selfish person who had dragged people roughshod over life. People didn't understand who wanted to make him good. His rebellion looked so good, he said, but he was always a person who had his way, a God-damned son-of-a-bitch, Charlie, and don't let anyone tell you different."

Against that self-lacerating admission may be placed a remark to the opposite effect, to be found in a letter written in December 1914, when he was experiencing his first heady rush of poetic success. To a young friend just beginning to face life's challenges he bravely insists, "What a man will put into effect at any cost of time money life or lives is sacred and what counts. As I get older I don't want to hear about much else."

Of course, in neither case was he voicing, consciously and exactly, what lay in his heart at those moments. Whenever he was strongly moved, his form of expression always sought the added force of hyperbole. Frequently, not always deliberately, he far overstated his meaning, particularly true when he was engaged in talking (and Frost, it need hardly be said again, was one of the great talkers, in power of fascination the equal of Coleridge). Much nearer his real mood on such occasions, agreeing with what is sooner or later learned about life by the tenderhearted, was the earnest puzzlement he expressed in an arresting notebook jotting made in England. It refers, evidently, to no specific incident but was perhaps prompted by some passing family quarrel: "Evil clings so in all our acts that even when we not only mean but achieve our prettiest, bravest, noblest, best, we are often a scourge even to those we do not hate. Our sincerest prayers are no more than groans that this should be so."

But here we verge on the question that, since the work of Lawrance Thompson, has become most insistent of all in connection with Frost's life: to what extent does the flesh-and-blood man resemble the surprisingly flawed creature—unrelievedly petty, arrogant, jealous, vain, vindictive, selfish, spiteful, in short a "monster"—portrayed by Thompson in the three-volume biography whose publication began soon after the poet's death? Some answer to that question has recently been attempted, notably by two writers, the critic William Pritchard in 1984, and one of Frost's former editors, the writer Stanley Burnshaw, in 1986. These two between them, Burnshaw in particular, have effectively unmasked the rather fierce personal bias that came to dominate and distort Thompson's view of Frost, startling in an official biographer, to say the least. The resulting discussion, however, has continued as it began, on a fairly generalized plane, so that Thompson's presentation of his subject in a myriad of specific instances has still to be tested. In these pages, where necessary, such specific testing will be carried out, but in each case demonstrable fact will be called on, and not, as too often with Thompson himself, the piling up of mere assertion based on unverifiable anecdote. This is a procedure or technique of Thompson's narrative that has inevitably had its pernicious effect, well illustrated by a review of the Thompson biography which appeared in the *New York Times* in 1970. Written by the otherwise very able Thomas Lask, the review declares Frost's mind and character to have been "unattractive, nay repellant," a conclusion that struck Lask as irresistible because "Mr. Thompson's dossier is so full and cumulative that it overwhelms all one's reluctance to sit in judgment." How neatly those words capture the lax attitude that, all these years later, still holds sway, even to an extent in scholarly circles!

Here, at the start, only one crucial fact need be stated in this regard, a fact which, for some reason not clear, has escaped the notice of all those who have chosen to write about this deceptively complex man. The well-rehearsed defects, or supposed defects, in the Frost character and personality can almost all be referred to the last third of his life, beginning with the loss of his daughter Marjorie in 1934, the poet among his children. With the deaths of Elinor in 1938, of Carol in 1940, and culminating with Irma's final breakdown in 1947, the virtual wreck of his inner serenity was complete—"I have nothing left but work and ambition," he said ominously a few months after Elinor's death. Whatever may be the exact truth about Frost's personal shortcomings (and if the wrong done long ago to Wordsworth is any guide, it will be many years before anything like a full and fair verdict is at hand), it can be said with conviction that the traits now so loudly deplored were in those earlier years far less pronounced, where present at all.

Only after successive loss, disappointment, and tragedy had taken their toll of an essentially brave and generous heart did Frost's view of life, his attitude toward people and events, start to unravel (and with what detriment to his poetry!). In all the many hundreds of letters he wrote in his lifetime, and no less in his verse, there is evidence enough, to a sympathetic eye, of the affecting way he forced himself to bear misfortune, and often enmity, in silence. Is there in all of literature a more quietly revealing statement in brief of the special burdens mere existence can sometimes impose than the closing lines of his "The Wind and The Rain"?

> *I have been one no dwelling could contain*
> *When there was rain;*
> *But I must forth at dusk, my time of day,*
> *To see to the unburdening of skies.*
> *Rain was the tears adopted by my eyes*
> *That have none left to stay.*

Beginning with the work of Lawrance Thompson, who did not really start to know his subject until after 1939, when he became Frost's official biographer, everything said about the poet's early years has been darkly colored and obscured by the relentless, at times merciless, scrutiny given him later, during the days of his fame. This sort of retrospective bias, largely unconscious no doubt, and though arising from the purest of scholarly motives, can be especially damaging in that it is by no means easy to disentangle. In Thompson's work, as analysis reveals, such bias is pervasive, even determining his choice of adjectives, relentlessly negative where Frost is concerned. In this matter, at least, the more restricted focus of the present narrative becomes a decided advantage. Even relatively minor incidents, or what have been considered minor, are brought into prominence, permitting a fresh and much closer look at episodes that have become stale in the telling.

Frost biography, despite all that has been written about him, is still in its primitive stages, a simple fact, but one not sufficiently recognized. When a writer has enjoyed a life as long and influential as Frost's, piecing together the fullness of that life while probing for its artistic sources often seems to require an effort equal in length to the amount of time he spent on earth. By that measure the Frost saga has a goodly distance still to go, and the task has not been made any easier by Frost himself. With his evasions, his casual handling of facts and dates, and his active dislike at times of the intrusions of biographical probing, he has set up some formidable barriers, especially with regard to his English years. As he grew older, however, and became freer in talking of his early struggles, he would now and again briefly confess how much England had really meant to him. "I had nearly a perfect life over there," he once remarked to a friend in sudden candor as he was entering his sixties, "a romance such as happens to few." It is the day-to-day reality of that romance, in both its Beaconsfield and its Dymock phases, and in as great detail as may be, that I have tried to recapture in these pages, along with something of what happened before and after.

Considering what has been allowed to pass more or less unchallenged in too much of Frost biography up to now, I should like to add a word here about my sources and the use made of them in this narrative. Without exception, and despite what may now and then appear, I give the reader assurance that every slightest detail in my text rests squarely on demonstrable evidence. Complete sources for all of this careful underpinning— documentary, for the most part, but in a good few instances physical— will be found extensively laid out in the notes at the rear of the book.

I should add that mixed in with these notes will be found much additional discussion treating more random matters that I believe to be of some value or at least interest in Frost studies, but which would have needlessly encumbered the main narrative. These are peripheral questions, it is true, but I make no excuse for including them. Most readers who join me in these pages, I feel, will possess some of the same curiosity, not to say fascination, that I do concerning every facet of the life of so unique and compelling an artist and personality.

I'VE OFTEN SAID IN TEACHING THAT THE BEST KIND OF
CRITICISM I KNOW IS NOT IN ABSTRACTIONS . . . IT'S
IN NARRATIVE.

> —*Robert Frost*
> *Bread Loaf School*
> *10 May 1950*

O N E

BEACONSFIELD

The Bungalow

PULLING noisily into the evening rush at busy Euston Station in central London, the boat train from Glasgow glided ponderously to a stop amid hissing clouds of steam, on schedule after its regular eight-hour journey. Promptly from its many-doored side a bustling crowd of passengers spilled out along the wide platform, among them the thirty-eight-year-old Robert Frost, his wife Elinor, and their four excited if tired young children. That same morning the steamship on which the Frost family had sailed from Boston, a small cargo liner named the *Parisian*, had docked in Glasgow. The voyage had been a rough one, and Frost, his wife, and their eldest daughter, Lesley, had frequently been miserable with sea sickness. Once ashore, the three sufferers had soon recovered their spirits. Then all had settled down, "the six of us by ourselves, in the snug compartment of the toy train," as Frost wrote afterward, for the long rail journey to London. The date was Monday, September 2, 1912.

At the station Frost arranged to leave in storage several small crates of household items, then he telephoned for rooms to the nearby Premier Hotel. The decision to come to England had been made rather suddenly, barely two weeks before departure, so that there had been no time to confirm reservations by mail. Now he was relieved to hear that the Premier had rooms available. Bundling family and luggage into a motor-cab (horse-drawn four-wheelers and hansom cabs still crowded the streets of London, along with automobiles, and people had learned to add

15

the word "motor" to make the distinction), Frost took them on the short ride to the hotel. Located just one block behind the British Museum, overshadowed by the huge, Victorian sprawl of the ornate Russell Hotel, the Premier was one of the smaller, cheaper establishments ringing broad, tree-crowded Russell Square.

Tired from their journey, but awed at finding themselves, in Elinor's words, "all alone, without a single friend in the biggest city in the world," Frost and his wife were not ready to end their long day. After putting their three younger children to bed, and leaving thirteen-year-old Lesley in charge, they went out for an evening at the theater. The *Times* that day had carried an advertisement that George Bernard Shaw's long-running, maliciously witty attack on middle-class values, *Fanny's First Play*, was to give its 575th performance that same evening. The theater, the Kingsway on Great Queen Street, was close to the hotel, hardly a ten-minute walk. Soon the two Frosts were sitting in the audience, no doubt feeling a bit dazed amid all the laughter at the thought of how far they had come in just nine days from the secluded town of Plymouth in the New Hampshire hills.

During the next few days, while Frost busied himself hunting for a house to rent in the suburbs, Elinor kept the children occupied with seeing the sights, including tours of the city by bus ("the streets are full of motor-buses," she wrote home, "which glide along hooting and tooting, and which find their way miraculously through the crowded streets. They are two storied affairs, and it is fun to sit on the upper story, out in the open"). Handicapped by his lack of preparation, Frost was uncertain even as to which of the many towns and villages round the city's perimeter would best fit his own and his family's needs, as well as his severely limited finances. Remaining close to London was his first hope, but a day or two of fruitless searching convinced him that rents in the nearer suburbs were far out of reach. It was a sobering experience, finding at first hand that all the talk back home about everything being cheaper in England simply wasn't true.

Increasingly worried by the financial drain of hotel living, by September 5 or 6 he had decided to seek some competent help, and, typically, he managed to find an unusual way of doing it. In the process he created the first of those nagging little puzzles to be found strewn through his English years, and indeed through his life generally. In this particular case, something more is involved than just the finding of a suitable place to live through the guidance of a kindly stranger. That same stranger not long afterward was also to play a part in one of the true turning points of Frost's life, the acceptance of his first book by a London publisher.

When Frost sought help in finding an English residence, it seems that he did not take the sensible step of applying to a real estate agent. Instead, wrote Gorham Munson, Frost's earliest biographer, "he repaired to *T. P.'s Weekly* which conducted a department of country walks and inquired for quiet places in the countryside where he wished to live. The conductor of this department was an ex-policeman (and therefore as becomes a London 'bobbie,' intelligent in giving directions), and Frost took a fancy to him. On his advice he settled in the little suburban town of Beaconsfield." The same obliging if nameless ex-bobby appears in a half-dozen subsequent accounts of Frost's house-hunting, all of them equally vague. In the Thompson biography, some new facts are added, though curiously the columnist is still unidentified. Frost, Thompson explains, "had read in the English newspaper, *T. P.'s Weekly*, a 'highways and byways' column, which clearly implied that the author of it was well informed concerning rural areas in the vicinity of London." Frost called at the paper's office, says Thompson, and found that the writer was "a genial, ruddy-faced, pipe-smoking ex-policeman eager to have someone draw on his knowledge. Appointing himself as guide, the ex-policeman showed Frost a few unsatisfactory houses, and finally took him twenty-one miles north of London on the Great Western Railway to Beaconsfield."

Thompson's access to his subject was close and long, so it is a pity that he did not make an effort to fill in the blanks in this incident. A few pertinent sources are still at hand, though, and they permit a slight rounding out of the picture. They also show that Frost's memory, often dismissed as wildly imprecise, was in a general way quite reliable.

T. P.'s Weekly was a popular literary journal of thirty-two pages issued at London every Friday. Its offices were located at 29 Henrietta Street, in the heart of the West End, less than a mile—say a dozen blocks—from the Frosts' hotel in Russell Square. One of the paper's regular features was a column called "Travel Talk," which ran each week for five months of the year, May to September. Dealing not just with country walks, or highways and byways, it gave advice on holidays and touring all over the British Isles, and on the continent as well. Linked with the column was a service in which readers' questions were answered, in print or for a small fee by mail. Unfortunately, the column carried no regular byline, and only a few times during that summer was it signed, not always with the same name. Frost had been familiar with the journal even before leaving America, copies having been sent to him from Vancouver by his friend and former pupil John Bartlett, so it is not improbable that he may have had it in mind from the start to approach the column's author.

The day Frost reached London he would have found on the stands the issue for August 30, in which "Travel Talk" was concerned mainly with France, offering only a few snippets on Britain. The next issue, that for Friday, September 6, also dealt mostly with the continent. Interestingly, however, the issue of the weekly for September 13—which would have been in preparation on the day Frost showed up at the office to ask advice—concerned itself with "A Literary Jaunt Round Hampstead" (a section of London then still considered a suburb). In this edition of the column all the great literary names of the past with links to Hampstead are paraded, including Samuel Johnson, Wordsworth, and Keats. Urging Hampstead's attractions for sight-seeing excursions, the column's author ends with a generous offer: "If any parties feel inclined to visit these delightful heights, and know no guide, the writer would be only too glad to lead the sentimentalists." There is no way now to be sure, but this sounds much like Frost's genial ex-bobby. Further, the subject of that day's column fits well with Frost's general recollection of it as dealing with "some place or another near London where people could go on picnics and sight-seeing trips." The name signed to the column that day was Percy Merriman, an individual otherwise unknown (except as the probable author of a handbook for soldiers in Britain's territorial forces).

In their search for a house, Frost and his guide may well have gone elsewhere to start with, but within a few days, certainly at the latest by Monday, September 10, the two had reached Beaconsfield. About forty minutes by train from London's Marylebone Station (or from Paddington, which Frost seems also to have used), Beaconsfield was officially a town but in reality was little more than a large village. Densely populated, more agricultural than industrial, it was just beginning to interest commuting Londoners as a pleasant place of residence. As Frost and his friend alighted from the train and walked up the long rise beside the tracks to the main street, called Station Road, Frost must have smiled at what he saw greeting him. Spelled out in huge letters high in the air was his own name, displayed on the cutout billboard of a real estate broker, A. C. Frost, whose offices stood just underneath the sign.

Coming up to Station Road, the two found that they were not in Beaconsfield proper, but in a much newer part of town. Out of sight a mile to the southeast lay Beaconsfield Old Town, with its picturesque

vide sweep around a broad built-up
ant London-Oxford route, the Old
ng like eight or nine hundred years.
et been in existence a decade.
is namesake's services, or how many
Beaconsfield, New or Old, are matters
tate office still stands, on the same site,
lost). In any case, at some point that day
is guide were somehow directed down
shown a small cottage fronting on the
een built in 1909, it was available imme-
nable rent of $20 per month on a year's
traggle of dark green vines clinging to the
eeply sloping roof of shingles, the cottage
y reminiscent of the neat, white dwellings
New Hampshire.
aved road, the cottage stood on a rectangular
in a quarter-acre. Behind the cottage was a
wide, deep, grassy g... or yard, complete with trees, flowers, and
shrubbery. Fairly close on one side there was a neighboring cottage of
somewhat similar build, but on the other side, where the curve of Baring
Crescent began, there was only an extensive open plot. Round most of the
property there grew tall, thick hedges, some of dogwood, but mostly of
thick, gnarled, broad-leaved laurel, no less than twelve or fifteen feet high.
The rear of the property was also nicely walled off from disturbance, for
past the wooden fence that bound it at the back there stretched the
extensive cherry orchards of Seeley's farm, one of several such orchards in
the area. All the other houses along Reynolds Road, on both sides, were
also enclosed by high hedges, so that the long, straight stretch of some
hundred yards was pervaded by a comforting sense of quiet and privacy.

Inside the cottage, Frost found that the small interior had been cleverly
designed, combining the largest possible number of rooms with the
demands of privacy, each room having its own door. From the entrance,
an unusually narrow hallway ran back to form a capital T. Off this
hallway at various points there opened a small, squarish living room, a
dining room that could only be described as tiny, two bedrooms, one of
which was also very tiny, a cramped bathroom, and a serviceable kitchen
with a coal-burning stove. No built-in closets were to be seen, but there
was a low attic for storage space, reachable by ladder. Four of the rooms
had fireplaces, low and shallow, for heating purposes.

The place would be a tight squeeze for a family of six, Frost saw, even using the little dining room as a bedroom, which would be necessary. Still, everything considered, particularly the rent, which was well under the usual minimum for the area, and with several shops and the post office nearby, and the railway station only a five-minute walk back along Reynolds Road, it must have seemed just right. Eager to have things settled, not wanting to lose the chance, before leaving Beaconsfield that day Frost made arrangements to take the place, on the stipulated year's lease. House numbers had not yet been assigned on Reynolds Road, so each house was identified by a name. Frost found that his new home was registered as the Bungalow, a prosaic designation that lacked the ring of some of its slightly larger neighbors: Kingsboro (the tan, lopsided house directly opposite), Clevedon (the house on the right), Denmill, Oakdene, Danesbury, Little Seeley's, and so on.

With arrangements made for delivery of the crates from Euston Station in London, the Frosts proceeded to buy some new and some secondhand furniture, probably in High Wycombe, a large town four miles west of Beaconsfield. For six beds, a kitchen table and chairs, some small occasional tables, and several large wicker chairs for the living room, "that bend when you sit in them," as Frost said, they paid the fairly large sum of $125 (another reminder that the English economy would be no kinder to his limited income than had New Hampshire). The crates from the station yielded further comforts in the shape of two rugs, one of which covered the wide boards of the living-room floor, as well as bedclothes, pictures, books, tableware, and a typewriter. There were also two items that Frost had to reassemble, a favorite rocking chair for Elinor, and his own long-cherished Morris chair with its stout wooden frame and adjustable back, just right for sitting and writing when a board was laid across the broad arms.

Well before the middle of September the Frosts arrived in Beaconsfield in force, coming by train from London, and proceeded to take possession of their new home. As it happens, there still exists a good, brief description of the arrival that day, written soon afterward as a school essay by nine-year-old Irma, its straightforward, child's-eye description seeming rather like a clip from an old movie. Titling her composition "Our New House," she is careful to start with the walk up from the station:

We got out of the train in Beaconsfield station. It was all new to us, and we walked up the road, and through many roads. There weren't many people in the streets. "I must go into the grocers," said Papa, "and tell him to come in the morning." Papa went in and we waited at the door. The grocer said a lot of things, and Papa said, "You come in the morning," and he said, "Yes," and we went on our way and Papa went up to the bakers. We went up to our house. The rest got a way ahead of Carol and I. Pretty soon Papa came up behind us. I ran back to meet him but Carol went with the rest. Papa pointed to our house and I saw people putting "fernercher" in our house.

Her reference to the family straggling through many roads is a child's exaggeration, for no more than three roads were involved: from Station Road a right turn over the tracks into Penn Road, a left at the Railway Hotel to cross Penn Road, then a bearing right into Reynolds Road. At the cottage, instead of going in at the front, Frost and his daughter went around to the right side and unlocked the French doors into the small dining room, soon to be the third bedroom. Irma's telling of her first hurried tour through her new home reflects the layout of the rooms quite accurately. What she saw in the kitchen indicates that the Bungalow must have for some time been standing untenanted:

> The others had gone in already. Papa unlocked the side door, and he put the key on a nail. We went through that room into the hall. Then we went into a big bedroom, and then into a small one, and then into the sitting room where the furniture was. Then we went out through the hall into the kitchen. There were some men washing the room. It was awfully dirty. Mama and the children had gone out in the garden, so we went out too. There was a hothouse, a summer house, and some dead flowers. We looked around and then we went in and placed some of the furniture around.

The sizes of the available bedrooms pretty well dictated how they would be apportioned. Beds for the three girls were probably set up in the bigger bedroom, which would have just accommodated them. Carol would have been put in the tiny bedroom all by himself, while Frost and his wife would have taken what had been the diminutive dining room. A corner of the living room was requisitioned as a dining area, and there the kitchen table was placed, disguised under an elegant table cloth. Taking meals in the living room, necessary since the kitchen was too narrow for even a small table, must have proved one of the family's chief sources of discomfort. All the food, plates, and utensils for each meal had to be carried in from the kitchen, the server maneuvering around three separate corners while elbows brushed the walls along the three-foot-wide hallway.

But such drawbacks were in the future. With beds made up, pictures hung, books stored on shelves, and the two favorite chairs placed on either side of the red-tiled living-room fireplace, the little house soon took on a more homey air. To a friend back in the States Frost wrote, "You . . . ought to see how few pieces of furniture we keep house with. It is cosy enough, but it would be a lesson to you in plain living." (Thinking back in later years, when he no longer had Elinor at his side, and the glow of his English adventure had worn off a little, he changed his mind about how cosy it had been. Ruefully, he said that during those eighteen months in the Bungalow, "we just camped").

Elinor, genuinely charmed with the house and its setting, was not unduly bothered by the plain living. Uncluttered rooms, she noted, made for easier housekeeping, which pleased her, for housework was a chore she had never relished, often ignoring it, as her husband said, "until it has piled on top of her." With good stores near at hand, especially bakeries where "one can buy a great variety of well-baked, wholesome bread and cake," she expressed herself as quite content on Reynolds Road, several times in letters referring to her "dear little cottage." Nor did the children feel deprived. To them, as Lesley said later, the cottage never seemed at all cramped, and they also had the deep, grassy backyard which, thickly hedged round as it was, served them in good weather almost as another room. They also had the greenhouse, which did nicely on wet days. Adding to the sense of comfort and helping to lessen any feeling of being crowded, was the family's own natural closeness. "My mother never worked alone in the kitchen," Lesley said in recalling her life in Beaconsfield. "We all congregated around the stove or the ironing board or the sewing basket and *talked*."

After they had spent a few mild September afternoons strolling in the nearby woods and lanes, including "some stretches of fine old beech trees" that lay on the far side of the Old Town in the village of Burnham Beeches, Elinor and the children at last began to feel at home. Struck by the neat contrast with the wilder aspect of her own New Hampshire countryside, Elinor noted with approval that around Beaconsfield "there is no waste land; the fields are all smooth, the pastures are a vivid green, and the woods all cleared of underbrush centuries ago." She was also quick to spot another mark of the area, the absence of wooden houses. Almost every structure in Beaconsfield, she remarked, was built of stone, brick, or stucco, "creating a very different and picturesque effect."

The town itself, even the newer portion, also had its attractions. A bit too near London and a bit too up-to-date to be taken as really quaint, it still had in the weathered, tumbled aspect of its squat old buildings and in its ancient customs some quaint touches. Every evening an official lamp-lighter made his rounds to the town's dozen or so gaslights, two of which lit streets near Reynolds Road. Colorful itinerant peddlers were a fixture of the area, and these must have come knocking sometimes at the Frosts' front door. There was the Muffin Man, who strolled along balancing a large wooden tray on his head while loudly clanging a hand-bell. There was the hardware merchant with his little donkey-drawn covered wagon hung with jangling pots and pans, and the bowler-hatted knife grinder with his pony and cart (Old Goff, they called him). In summer there was the Catch-'em-Alive man, seller of treacly flypaper who advertised his wares by pasting samples to the crown of his battered old beaver hat.

Town activities—there is no memory of the Frosts attending any of these, though their attendance at some is more than likely—included bazaars, flower shows, concerts, dances, some Shakespeare, some Gilbert and Sullivan, an annual Wild Beast Show, and a town band. The glittering event of the year, attended by the area's blue bloods, was the annual Drag Hunt. Once while the Frosts were there King George V himself came to town—on December 20, 1912—to pay a call on Lord Burnham and be welcomed on the ancient common by a festive crowd of villagers and school children. For this event all six of the Frosts came down from Reynolds Road to be on hand. (Curiously, there is only an oblique echo of the occasion in a letter Frost wrote five days later. Commenting on a different matter altogether, he says breezily, "By we, I mean me and the King and Lord Burnham and the rest of the English," and he drops it there.)

With England's school year already two weeks old when the Frosts moved into the Bungalow, the matter of the children's schooling soon became urgent. Both Frost and his wife were experienced teachers and, before they put their children under the care of a school system about which neither knew anything, they wanted to learn something of its methods and standards. With this in mind, Frost paid a visit to the Beaconsfield grammar school, and what he encountered left him with the conviction that it would not do for his children.

The school building, a low, rambling structure capped by a pointed bell tower, stood near the center of the Old Town, just behind the large and impressive parish church and only a few feet from the ancient, half-timbered rectory. Cordially welcomed by the principal, a man named Arthur Baker, Frost was introduced to several of the teachers, most of them women, and then taken to the main classroom. In some surprise, he saw that the room, a large one, had been divided into two makeshift areas by the simple expedient of hanging a wide green baize cloth from the ceiling. Rising from both sides of the cloth, the voices of teachers and pupils, even kept low as they were, mingled annoyingly in the air. It was a temporary arrangement caused by insufficient space, but it made a bad impression on Frost. For presentation to the American visitor, the younger boys, all wearing their customary stiff white collars, were made to stand on their benches and sing a song to the accompaniment of an old upright piano.

Afterward, as the two walked back to the office, the principal stopped to point out the school library, a simple bookcase holding about two hundred books. Glancing over the titles, Frost decided that none of the books seemed well suited to a student's needs or interests, a fact he silently judged to be unfortunate since, as he understood, the town itself had no library (it had one of sorts, a small reading room in the Old Town with a paying membership). The principal, a tall, quiet, craggy man, Frost found to be quite friendly and likable, as he did the other teachers. Before the visit ended, however, he was disappointed to hear Baker admit ignorance of the Montessori Method, then in the first flush of its acceptance in the United States. A while later Baker also expressed some personal doubts about the value for educators of any sort of formal psychology studies. This was an attitude not uncommon then, but it was an unfortunate confession to make to a man who shortly before had been teaching the subject in a New Hampshire teachers' college.

It was contact with the students themselves—there were 112 boys and girls on the rolls—that seems to have finally decided Frost against enrolling his own children. In a letter written soon afterward he comments frankly, "One would have to go to the slums of the city for their like in face and form in America. I did not see the sprinkling of bright eyes I should look for in the New England villages you and I grew up in. They were clean enough—the school sees to that. But some of them were pitiful little kids. Mr. Baker stood them on their seats for me to inspect like slaves in the market—cases of malformation and malnutrition. Too many of these in proportion, I thought." In this, Frost was only encountering a situation all too familiar to the British educational authority of the time (and borne out with regard to Beaconsfield by a perusal of the school's log book for 1912–1913). Soon he found what was the truth, that "no one here sends his children to the government schools if he can possibly send them elsewhere."

But if he was not to take advantage of Beaconsfield's free public schools, neither could he afford the expense of enrolling all of his children in a private school. In the end, hard as it was to prove on their precarious budget, the Frosts sent two of the four, the oldest girls, Lesley and Irma, to a nearby dames' school (probably one conducted in The Manse on Lakes Lane by the daughters of the local Congregationalist minister). Seven-year-old Marjorie and ten-year-old Carol were to be taught at home in regular daily classes by their mother. This imposed an extra burden on Elinor, which was lightened when Frost took on some of the family's cooking chores.

Weary from the month-long effort to transplant his family, relieved to be settled in such pleasant circumstances, during late September Frost took time out to explore his new surroundings. Going off on long walks by himself, he tramped round much of the environs of Beaconsfield, at least once contriving to pass the house of G. K. Chesterton in Grove Road— four streets over from the Bungalow—noting, as he wrote later, that it was "a big house all windows, nearly all." Not a year before, in Plymouth, Frost had read with delight Chesterton's popular book *Heretics* and had given it as a gift to a friend. He was conversant with many of Chesterton's works, and in time would reveal a strain of paradox much like that of the Englishman, and used for the same purpose, to shock. Yet, though Chesterton's huge, caped figure was much in evidence about the town as he walked to stores, to the bank, to church, the two never met, nor did Frost ever lay eyes on him. Here, if ever, fate stumbled, for a friendship between these two, fabulous wits and talkers both, ripe and staunch in opinion, could have been memorable.

Frost also soon became aware of the town's other literary notables of the past, the great Edmund Burke, and at a more distant remove in time, Edmund Waller, leading poet of the seventeenth century. There was also Thomas Grey, whose grave in Stoke Poges was only two miles from Reynolds Road. Most intriguing of all was the small cottage, so like his own in size and cramped conditions, where John Milton, escaping a London plague, had lived for eighteen months with his wife and three daughters while he finished writing *Paradise Lost*. Well preserved, the little red-brick structure stood at the roadside in the village of Chalfont St. Giles, four miles off. Though Frost's walks often took him in that direction, it is not known that he ever visited the cottage.

These heady days of wandering free over the countryside also produced the first poem he wrote on English soil, "In England." The casual result of an idle moment, it was a brief lyric in which he tried to capture his delight over finding himself living in the land he had often thought of as "the cradle of lyric poetry." He must have been in an unusually giddy

mood when he wrote the poem, however, for beneath its smooth rhythms
it is curiously flawed:

> *Alone in rain I sat today*
> *On top of a gate beside the way,*
> *And a bird came near with muted bill,*
> *And a watery breeze kept blowing chill*
> *from over the hill behind me.*
>
> *I could not tell what in me stirred*
> *To hill and gate and rain and bird,*
> *Till lifting hair and bathing brow*
> *The watery breeze came fresher now*
> *from over the hill to remind me.*
>
> *The bird was the kind that follows a ship,*
> *The rain was salt upon my lip,*
> *The hill was an undergoing wave,*
> *And the gate on which I balanced brave*
> *Was a great ship's iron railing.*
>
> *For the breeze was a watery English breeze*
> *Always fresh from one of the seas,*
> *And the country life the English lead*
> *In beechen wood and clover mead*
> *Is never far from sailing.*

Picturing England as a ship is effective if unoriginal, but the focus of
the thought in the verse is otherwise strangely awry. A speaker, moved by
various small natural happenings, is suddenly reminded that he is in
England. Yet the poem gives no reason why he should have been unaware
of his location in the first place, that he is in fact a foreigner lately come to
these shores, necessary knowledge if the poem is to be anything but a
puzzle. There is also the lesser question of how Frost, or anyone, would
be able to distinguish between the feel of a watery breeze and the feel of
rain, salty or not, hitting him simultaneously. (And why, a stickler might
ask, was he sitting on a gate in the open in such foul weather to begin
with!) Frost himself soon recognized the false note he had struck, for he
never published the poem and soon forgot all about it. Still, the lines do
afford a modicum of critical interest, even apart from their being perhaps

the final example of his early romantic manner. One of them—"The hill was an undergoing wave"—would surface again a year later, subtly altered, to take its place as the pivot of one of his best-known poems, "Mending Wall."

When he was not exploring the countryside or visiting such nearby towns as High Wycombe, Jordans, or Gerrard's Cross, he took the train to London. There, like any tourist, he would spend the day trudging around the streets of Bloomsbury, Soho, and the West End, and along the Strand. While he made a number of these solitary excursions, only one of them managed to find any echo in his letters or talk, and that occurred when he attended a suffragette meeting expressly to hear a speech by George Bernard Shaw. Held at Caxton Hall, near Buckingham Palace, on Thursday, September 26, the meeting had been called by the Women's Tax Resistance League, "to protest against the imprisonment of Mr. Mark Wilks for his inability to pay the taxes on his wife's earned income." Later Frost described how Shaw in his talk had teased the audience, mostly women, "Till they didn't know whether he had come to help (as advertised) or hinder them." As the news reports show, that is a fair enough description of what took place. Shaw, telling his audience that he "never spoke at Suffrage gatherings," got his first laugh by saying that he refused to join those "superfluous males who gave assistance which was altogether unnecessary to ladies who could well look after themselves." In somewhat muddled fashion, in his talk he touched on various matters of family finance, frequently making playful references to his own wife, and prompting much laughter.

Not important in itself, Frost's presence at this meeting is worth noting because it marks his second deliberate encounter with Shaw during his first month in England (and a cryptic jotting in a Frost notebook of about this time reads tantalizingly, "Pursuit of GBS."). Exactly what may have been his reasons for this active interest in the Irishman remains uncertain, but it does serve to emphasize a fact now frequently overlooked, that for some considerable length of time Frost thought quite seriously about becoming a playwright himself (and wrote several one-acters, only one of which has been published). It was an ambition he did not relinquish easily, and which must have played some crucial part in helping him to develop the dramatic qualities that underlie the great narrative poems he was shortly to write.

The British Museum Reading Room, for which he was readily granted a reader's ticket, became one of his haunts while in London, and he was also drawn to the famous row of bookstores, mostly secondhand, along

Tottenham Court and Charing Cross Roads. In one of these stores, one day in early October, he picked up a small volume of poems by W. E. Henley and noted in passing that it had been published by the firm of David Nutt. Though unknown to him then, it was a name destined before very long to loom large, not entirely to his benefit, in his own career.

Proximity to London was clearly important to the Frosts, at least during the first part of their English residence. Both had had enough, for a while, of small-town living, and in fact for years they had dreamed of living near New York. Despite finding London to be "a foggy, smoky place," both now wanted to be close enough to feel the stimulus of the city. As Elinor admitted, if it hadn't been for the children they would have "taken lodgings in the city itself instead of a house so far out, as the life there would have been more exciting," though she didn't say how they would have afforded anything decent.

In any case, the family was now settled in a pleasant suburb, with a year's lease at a low rent, and it wasn't long before Frost began to find that the twenty miles separating him from the metropolis posed no real hardship. Fast and frequent trains were to be had almost at his door, connecting at Paddington or Marylebone Stations with the comfortable, speedy underground, which reached to every corner of the sprawling city. This growing feeling of closeness may well have been the source for a strange idea he conceived not many days after occupying the Bungalow, strange at least for so able an observer as Frost.

Sitting up late at night to finish a letter to a friend back home, he remarked offhandedly, "When I leave writing this and go into the front yard for a last look at earth and sky before I go to sleep, I shall be able to see the not very distinct lights of London flaring like a dreary dawn." Perhaps in trying to impress his friend with the thrill he felt at being where he was, he simply overstated matters, perhaps he wasn't being quite serious. But the truth is that the glow of lights arising from nighttime London, distinct or otherwise, was and still is wholly out of the sight of anyone in Beaconsfield. The situation of the town, and the terrain of the intervening twenty miles prohibit all possibility of seeing anything of the dimly flaring illumination. From the grassy, hedged-in front yard of the Bungalow on clear fall nights, as still may be judged today by anyone standing there, all that can be glimpsed in the night sky toward London are a few late-lingering shreds of daylight palely tinting the darkness.

HAVING IT OUT WITH MYSELF

TO THEIR neighbors along Reynolds Road, curious about the new-
comers, it was not quite clear what had brought the American family
into their midst. On the surface it even seemed that there might be some
dark secret behind it all, something wrong back home. They appeared to
be on the poor side to have traveled so far, and they kept pretty much to
themselves, sending only two of their four children to school. Frost
himself had no obvious trade or profession, apparently nothing to keep
him busy. Yet only now and then did he leave the house for a whole day,
when he took the train to London or went for long walks with his
children. His nondescript habits of dress also drew attention, one neighbor later recalling how he usually looked "as if he had been working in the
fields yet never had been."

The natural curiosity felt by Frost's Beaconsfield neighbors has in a
way been echoed ever since by critics, biographers, and those drawn to
his story. Why did this died-in-the-wool Yankee, his heart belonging to
the simple life to be found in the northeast corner of his own country,
decide to take himself and his young family into such distant, unfamiliar,
and apparently uncongenial surroundings? There is no need to puzzle at
length over the question, however. Frost quit his job as teacher, left
America, and went to England for reasons that were at the same time
quite uncomplicated, rather brave, and certainly, in any practical view,
foolhardy. He did not go there with any expectation or hope—perhaps it
might be truer to say any conscious hope—of finding a publisher for

poetry already in existence. Despite his age, and despite having a growing family to support, he was taking one last gamble, allowing himself the freedom and the isolation he coveted to do nothing but write. England was simply the place in which he chose to do it.

In reality, on resigning from the Plymouth Normal School his first thought as to a destination was for something much closer to home, a return to the farm life he had known earlier. In the summer of 1912, before making the decision on England, he went so far as to rent a small farm in the Franconia region just north of Plymouth, intending to buy it if financing could be arranged. For whatever reason, this idea was eventually rejected in favor of a complete departure from familiar ground.

The actual choice of England was the result of a coin toss, or so Frost himself and others of his family often claimed (though it is easy to believe that had he not liked the result he would have ignored it). The clearest statement concerning the moment of decision was provided some years later by Lesley, who would have been old enough at the time to recite the circumstances from memory. Toward the end of the Plymouth school year, she explained, "it became increasingly clear that my parents wanted a dramatic change of scene, together with time away from the burdens of teaching, for getting more poetry written"—and here, it should be noted, her mother is given an equal share of responsibility for the drastic move, a fact amply borne out by other evidence. Just where the dramatic change was to be found, once a return to farming had been abandoned, became a topic for excited family discussion during the late summer of 1912. Possibilities ranged widely round the world, all the way from Canada to Mexico to Australia. By August the choice had narrowed to two localities, Vancouver, in British Columbia, where Frost's friend John Bartlett was living, and England. It was Elinor, apparently, who favored England, and it may even have been she who first suggested it. Frost's earliest preference, it seems, was for crossing not the ocean but the continent:

My father leaned strongly to the wild, natural beauty of Vancouver: mountains to climb, great beaches to tread. My mother longed for England with all her heart, to live, as she put it, "in a thatched cottage" as near Stratford as possible. And so it came about that on one day of destiny the question was settled by the turn of a coin. We were standing around my mother who was ironing in the kitchen when my father said, "Well, let's toss for it," and he took a nickel from his pocket. "Heads England, tails Vancouver." Heads it was! All that had been contemplated was fresh scenery, peace to write, the excitement of change.

Frost's own stray recollections deepen the reality of his daughter's account, particularly concerning the part played in the decision by certain family pressures. The listless, even indulgent course his life had taken since his high school days, including twice turning his back on a promising college career, had caused much sad disappointment among his well-meaning Massachusetts relatives, who were not slow to lament his failure. Aside from that familiar theme, the main idea he sounds in the following passage was not, of course, peculiar to him. It is the perpetual cry of all earth's dreamers yearning for the time and the opportunity, the bare chance, to achieve what they see as their destiny. As the school year in Plymouth came to a close, he recalled,

> my mind was made up. I would stop teaching. It was not for me. Why keep on working when you get nowhere for the effort? Why have only your labor for your pains? I said to my wife, "It'll never do to go on like this. I'll just turn into a machine, and what will happen to my poetry? We must get away somewhere, anywhere, only away." I wanted to be as far away from the nosey relatives down Lawrence way as I could get, clear off. For by this time word had percolated down there that I was becoming a man of respectability, quite a change, perhaps I might even one day head up a big institution of learning . . . They were good people who honestly were trying to save me from myself. I had no choice but to run away somewhere and hide.

Those words were taken down in the 1930s, but he had earlier offered much the same admission about his sensitive response to the clucking of relatives, including those of Elinor, many of whom also lived in the area. "I went to England to write and be poor," was the way he put it in a letter of 1915, "without further scandal in the family." On a later occasion he added that "England seemed far enough away from everyone who knew me . . . I expected to be lost among strangers there." This personal element is always overlooked in discussions of why he took himself so far from home, yet it wonderfully sharpens the perception of Frost, as man and poet, to glimpse him as not exempt from such ordinary human embroilments.

Perhaps equally important, especially in the timing of the move, was a growing awareness of his advancing age. As his fortieth birthday loomed—it would arrive on March 26, 1914—like many an ambitious soul before him he saw it as some sort of boundary or limit beyond which he would find either lifelong fulfillment or permanent regret. "But really," he insists ringingly in a letter written during his first spring at the

Bungalow, "I am going to be justified of my poetry before the end. I have hung off long enough. I wasn't going to pass forty without having it out with myself on this score." In that brief remark—really a cry weighted with frustration, with smoldering desire, and with a still-churning apprehension—is all the consciousness of the twenty anxious years he had passed since the unforgettable day when he saw his first published poem, "My Butterfly," glowing on the front page of the New York *Independent*.

As it happens, all these thoughts and feelings regarding his purpose in leaving both his job and his country can be found pointedly expressed in what was probably the first letter he wrote from the Bungalow. Dated no more than two or three days after moving in, it is addressed to the one person who through all those twenty years—and, it must be said, on very little evidence—had retained some faith in his ultimate success as a poet. This was sixty-seven-year-old Susan Ward, former subeditor of the *Independent*, the woman who had accepted and published that first poem. Out of touch with his friend during the whole of the previous six months, he now felt some need to inform her of the drastic change that had come over his life. Interestingly, his words tumble out with the breathless rush of a schoolboy explaining some doubtful action to an indulgent mother or teacher. Starkly present in the letter, also, is more than a touch of the bitterness he would later claim never to have felt:

Perhaps I ought not to conceal from you, as one of the very few mortals I feel in any sense answerable to, that I am in the mood called aberrant. Psychology holds me no longer. What have I taught for, anyway, but to confute my well-wishers who believed I was not enough of the earth earthy to be above a fool? And now that I have proved myself as a teacher in two departments of learning without benefit of college, my soul inclines to go apart by itself again and devise poetry. Heaven send that I go not too late in life for the emotions I expect to work in. But in any case I should not stay, if only for scorn of scorn—scorn of the scorn that leaves me still unnoticed among the least of the versifiers that stop a gap in the magazines . . . I may be too old to write the song that once I dreamed about ("The tender, touching thing")—at least I can achieve something solid enough to sandbag editors with.

His exact plan for this writing campaign, faced in a mood of grim confidence that he revealed only to Miss Ward and to her only in this one flash of confession, was still somewhat vague. In general, it allowed for a period of two full years, devoted mostly to poetry but leaving time for some prose writing as well, by which he hoped to bolster his finances. The first year was to be spent in England, with side trips to the continent. For the second year he would take his family over to France. That way, if success eluded him and he had to retreat once more to teaching in some New Hampshire school, the children at least would have seen something of the world.

*   *   *

AS the family settled into its new routine at the Bungalow there came the inevitable letdown following so much excitement. Frost himself, taking a sober second look at his brave gamble, especially his slender finances, became acutely conscious of his "isolation so far from home and help." With only some hundreds in savings, far less than a thousand, and an $800 annuity from his grandfather's estate, due each July, but lacking all prospect of further income, he suddenly felt "scared." The mood of self-doubt shook him considerably, but it didn't last long, and it provided, as he said, just the stimulus he needed. With renewed energy he turned first to the writing of a novel, rather naively hoping it would bring him a fairly rapid financial return.

Several times Frost had considered writing fiction, as well as plays, mostly as a means of escaping from the drudgery of teaching, or simply as a way of providing better for his family. The novel he had in mind now, perhaps begun even before he left Plymouth, was to be heavily auto-biographical. It would draw on his own farming experience, first his younger days as a helper in summer vacations, then the nine years he operated his own poultry farm in Derry, New Hampshire. The plot would play off the conflicting attitudes of an old hired man of long experience and a part-time hand fresh from college. Apparently he made a good start on the tale, drafting at least part of the first chapter, but then his resolve began to flag. "I was always that way," he later explained, "two or three days on end I would write prose, first having resolved it was the thing for a man with a family to do. But just when I thought I bade fair to produce a novel, right in the middle of chapter three or four I would bring up in another inconsequential poem." This time it was not the writing of new poems that defeated his good intentions, but a bold and impulsive decision to seek book publication for old ones.

Several versions exist of how and when Frost conceived the idea for his first volume of poetry, and put the manuscript together. Differing in details, all still make it appear that the book—including its overall theme, arrangement, and selection of poems, and its evocative title, *A Boy's*

Will—was wholly the result of a sudden inspiration one night in the Bungalow after the others had gone to bed. Alone in the living room, Frost took what he called his "stack" or "pile" of loose manuscript and seated himself on the floor in front of the fireplace. With the separate sheets laid out around him (by all evidence, the number of completed poems he had at the time was well over a hundred), he began his customary task of "weeding out" those poems, partial or complete, which had ceased to interest him. What happened next is most conveniently told in the words of Lawrance Thompson's official version, now generally accepted.

That night, Thompson explains, Frost "could not resist the impulse to see if he had enough to make up a small volume. Never before had he found the courage to begin preparing a manuscript for submission to a publisher, and even now he was not sure he was doing more than playing a game. He spread the pages out across the floor in the lamplight, occasionally crumpling up a sheet of paper containing a false start and tossing it into the fireplace." Unable at first to find a unifying pattern, Frost gradually came to see that he could "shape a selected group into a spiral of moods, upward through disappointment and withdrawal to aspiration and affirmation . . . a motion out of self-love and into his love for others." Gathering the selection, amounting to some thirty poems, into a three-part arrangement, he then had the idea of achieving some continuity "by giving a brief gloss or note under each title as it appeared in the table of contents."

Something resembling this account no doubt did happen one lonely night before the fire in the Bungalow, but it was not the impulsive action Thompson depicts. Far from being the result of one night's inspiration, the idea for *A Boy's Will*, and the manuscript as well, had begun to take shape even before Frost arrived in England, and over a period of months if not years. In a letter written from the Bungalow in November 1912, no more than six weeks after the fact, he alludes to the manuscript of *A Boy's Will* and says, "I brought it to England in the bottom of my trunk, more afraid of it, probably, than the Macnamara of what he carried in his." In a later offhand remark about *A Boy's Will* he explained that "the little pile of lyrics which went into my first book had stayed all the time around thirty, what with burning one and writing another." Though bare of specifics, those words can hardly refer to a matter of a few days or nights, especially when it is recalled how very slowly Frost composed, how he was inclined to put an intractable poem aside and, as he said, "leave it to cure."

What Frost actually did that night sitting before the fire on Reynolds

Road is not hard to reconstruct. He simply brought to completion whatever parts of the existing manuscript were still unfinished, perhaps making a final choice among the poems, and deciding on the three-part design. One thing which he definitely did was to make a basic change in the glosses he had already provided for each poem, what he called his "marginal notes." These he rewrote, as he said later, "taking the capital 'I' out, and stressing the third person, transfering them thus over to an imaginary individual," which would certainly have improved the presentation. That the glosses had already been written, and in the first person, affords still another sign that the manuscript was in existence well before that critical night.

The book's strong thematic design, though uneven, was a good one. But this is so not because it added any artistic depth or dimension, a doubtful claim which has only recently found a voice, but because it strengthened the volume's appeal for publishers, certainly Frost's reason for doing it in the first place. The unifying theme he chose, however, the emotional education of a growing boy, from one point of view was peculiar: while the description suits well with the poems themselves, it requires some stretching of the imagination to make it fit the reality of the volume's background. The truth is that the poems in Frost's first volume arrestingly document one of the more intriguing examples of a late-maturing personality, both artistically and humanly, to be found in English literature.

For some reason it has not yet been realized what a gap in age there exists between the youth seen in the poems of A Boy's Will, and the age of their author at the time of writing. Most were not written by or about an adolescent at all, nor were they meant to be reminiscent of boyish concerns. They were the earnest products of Frost's thirties, recording the changing moods of a full-grown man. Of the thirty-two poems in the book, only a single one can be referred to his late teens ("My Butterfly," which certainly has the weakest claim of all for inclusion). Perhaps another three can be assigned to his mid-twenties. But much more than half the entire total was written as he approached and passed the age of thirty-five. Frost himself inadvertently makes all this clear when, in another connection, he tells a correspondent that A Boy's Will "comes pretty near being the story of five years of my life," explaining that the book was mostly written "on the farm in Derry." He was twenty-six when with his wife and first child he moved from the town of Lawrence to the small poultry farm in Derry, New Hampshire. He lived on the farm, slowly learning about himself, about the life of the country, and about his art, for nine years (and remained in farming country for another three years as a teacher). He lived the crucial country phase of his life, in other words, while he was still as emotionally pliant as any youth in his teens, yet was far advanced intellectually. A mood and an outlook more receptive to deep and lasting influence can scarcely be imagined.

Though he must have put considerable effort into completing the manuscript for *A Boy's Will*, he did so without having any real intention of submitting it to a publisher, or so he said later. Not until a few mornings afterward, following a brief, bantering exchange with Elinor, did he begin to see publication as a real possibility. "I think I shall run up to London tomorrow and find a publisher," he ventured jauntily. Rather than joining in the joke, Elinor became serious about the proposal and quickly offered enthusiastic encouragement. At that moment, as Frost recalled it, book publication in England began to seem worth pursuing: "I was up bright and early the next morning waiting for the London express on the Great Western."

While the timing of all this is not easy to clarify, it is certain that Frost did not, after that exchange with his wife, go promptly to London. There was a necessary delay during which Lesley, at her father's request, made a typed copy of the manuscript, a formidable after-school chore for the young girl. The task occupied at least a week, perhaps a good deal longer since she was using the family's cumbersome old Blickensderfer machine, brought from home. Judging from all the circumstances, it would have been the middle of October when Frost took his manuscript on that fateful trip to town.

Aside from a few incidental references in his letters, the earliest direct record of what happened next is to be found in a 1921 newspaper interview. It puts further emphasis on the haphazard nature of the event, hardly a surprise, even making Frost himself appear rather inept. As Frost recalled it, he began his search by calling on his ex-bobby friend at *T. P.'s Weekly*, and again his backdoor approach paid off:

> I went down to London to see a man whom I hardly knew, the man who had told me where I could get my little cottage . . . I asked him if he knew of some small respectable publisher who might buy my poems and not kick me out of the door. He said that no one published poems and that I would myself have to pay to have them printed. I never wanted to do that. Somehow I never liked the idea. In conversation this man named David Nutt. Then and there I went over to Nutt's establishment, left the poems,

and in two days he wrote me to come in and sign a contract. So you see it was a very accidental beginning.

Left out of that account, either by Frost or by his interviewer, are several details that add a touch of reality to the picture. Initially, it appears, the columnist at the weekly was a good deal less than encouraging, and didn't try to hide his opinion. "When I told him," said Frost, "that I had come up to London to get myself a publisher for my book of poems, he laughed uproariously . . . a stranger from a faraway land, coming to a country of great poets and hoping to find a publisher for his unknown wares! The idea *was* fantastic. Nobody knew it better than I."

Ignoring the laughter, Frost asked for suggestions. At the mention of some well-known and highly regarded firms, he interrupted to say that he was hoping for "somebody less pretentious." The columnist then listed, among others, the name of David Nutt, and Frost promptly remembered seeing the Nutt imprint on a volume of Henley's poems in a bookstore the month before. It was mainly the joining of these two facts, the conjuncture of a small, approachable publisher with the name of an established poet, which decided Frost to go to Nutt.

That Frost should have sought advice from a former policeman and travel writer may seem a strange thing to have done. Certainly it enforces the picture of him as woefully amateurish and groping in such matters. Still, it must be remembered that he was alone in the huge city, without the slightest contact, literary or otherwise. An obliging acquaintance on the staff of a leading literary periodical, one to whom he had taken a real liking at their first meeting a month before, was a sensible first step. At that very moment, in fact, *T. P.'s Weekly* was running a feature called "The Great Publishing Houses," and Frost may well have been attracted by it, perhaps hoping for some inside information (Nutt was not mentioned in the series). In making his suggestions, the columnist seems to have assumed that Frost, like other ambitious unknowns of the day, would readily accept the need to subsidize his book. At any rate, he is supposed to have added, "little books like that cost the author about fifteen pounds," a remark which makes it probable that the man did indeed have some knowledge of the book business.

That Frost went direct from the weekly to the Nutt office that same day is not unlikely. The two sites were only a few blocks apart, requiring a walk of five or six minutes from Henrietta Street, either straight up St. Martin's Lane, or a slightly shorter route through several side streets.

Nutt's offices were listed in the London directory at 17 Grape Street, which was an old building tucked into a short, very narrow thoroughfare just off New Oxford Street, and it was to that address that Frost recalled going first. Once there, he would have found that Nutt's editorial office was no longer in Grape Street. It had been moved a block away, joining several other tenants in a large building at No. 6 on busy Bloomsbury Street, just around the corner from the British Museum. Disappointed in his hopes for an interview that day, he was given an appointment for later in the week. For some reason he failed to leave his manuscript with the publisher for reading, which in the circumstances seems peculiar. Probably, as will be seen, he did offer to leave it but was asked to return with it in person.

While relatively small, the firm of David Nutt was among the oldest and most respected in London, facts which Frost may have taken the trouble to verify with a quick trip to the British Museum Reading Room. Years later, citing Nutt's "dignity" as one of his reasons for signing with the firm, he explained that Nutt "specialized in certain kinds of books, good books, with a few but select authors in their stable," which sounds as if he had done some checking. In any case, when he returned to Bloomsbury Street a few days later he was taken into an office where he expected to meet David Nutt himself. Instead, he found himself facing an attractive, middle-aged woman dressed all in black, and speaking with a decided French accent. Obviously in mourning, she exhibited a rather nervous manner, striking the surprised Frost, in his own words, as "the most erratic, erotic, exotic type imaginable" (admittedly, this array of qualities may not have all been on display at this first visit). Not bothering to introduce herself, the woman said that she would speak for David Nutt, and that she understood Frost had a manuscript to show.

The woman Frost met that day was Mrs. M. L. Nutt, widow of Alfred Nutt, son of the firm's deceased founder. With the aid of a son, she was then running the business herself, her husband having died two years before. Since she was destined to fill one of the central roles in Frost's early success, a closer look at her, to the extent allowed by the few available sources, is of some interest. Originally she had served her husband, before marriage, as the firm's secretary. When he died in an accident in France, she took over direction of the firm, but had quickly run into difficulties. About the time of Frost's visit, or soon after, she began searching for expert help, on business procedures and financial matters. As it happens, the man she turned to first, later to become well known in

London's publishing circles, has left a record of what, apparently, fast
became an unpleasant encounter. Sir Stanley Unwin in his autobiography tells how Mrs. Nutt invited him to join her faltering firm as publishing manager: "I don't think that I have ever encountered anyone so
suspicious. The negotiations were interminable but led nowhere. As soon
as I looked like coming to terms with her solicitor she threw me overboard
on the ground apparently that I was in some mysterious way in league
with him. I would then start afresh, but as she could never finally make
up her mind what she wanted, nothing ever came of the negotiations."

Unwin's frank portrait of Mrs. Nutt as a businesswoman, in light of
Frost's own later and mostly unhappy relations with her, rings true. Some
further small insight into what must have been a bristly personality can
be gleaned from a novel she wrote, which was published a few months
before Frost first met her (published by herself, thereby offending a long-
standing tradition against publishers bringing out their own works). If
the book, a lame performance, faithfully reflects her own outlook, then
she is revealed as an early feminist, though a quirky one (how her wearing
widow's weeds more than two years after her husband's death fits into this
picture is hard to say). Condemning men as hardly more than purveyors of
evil, she exalts the role of women as mothers, homemakers, and purifiers
of society in general. Women, she suggests, by following certain rules in
the selection of their husbands, and by careful nurturing of their children, can bring about a superior race. She had raised two sons herself,
one of whom was an invalid. It was in a successful effort to save this
invalid son from drowning that her husband had died.

Nothing else is known of the woman, and even her given name is
nowhere to be found on record, only the initials. Within a few years of
publishing Frost's books, the Nutt firm began to founder, perhaps
because of bad management, perhaps because of the times, and at the
close of World War I it went into bankruptcy. Soon after that, Mrs. Nutt
disappeared from London, leaving no trace. One report has her dying in
poverty in France during the Second World War.

The initial meeting between Frost and Mrs. Nutt would have taken
place by Friday, October 19, at the latest. It was a brief meeting, and it
appears certain that when Frost left the Nutt office that day he was not in
the best of spirits. Aside from discomfort with the woman's "erratic"
manner, whatever that may indicate exactly, there was his annoyed surprise at the unexpected way she skirted the whole notion of vanity
publishing, actually raising the question of a subsidy for his proposed

book. This is not conjecture, for Frost's own description of the meeting still survives. It makes his annoyance clear, and also shows that the lady was no novice when it came to pressuring naive poets:

> I must admit that she eyed me suspiciously when I mentioned that I wanted a book of poetry published; she had a right to. And she was formidably enough dressed in her black outfit to have scared most anybody, almost scared me. No market for poetry! Nobody would read it even if they bought it! After all, the day of poetry was past, and all that. Then, having as she thought, disarmed me, she said she might, she just barely *might* publish it if I would pay part of the costs. I told her emphatically *no*. I would never do it. So I started to gather up my manuscript, which till then she had scarcely even glanced at, very firmly telling her I had never stooped to paying to have my poems published, and I would never do it. Seeing I was firm she softened a bit and told me to leave the manuscript and let her have a look at the poems. "If they're good I'll take a chance," she said, adding, "but you'll change your mind and help bear expenses." Again I said no, I wouldn't, and after receiving her assurance that she would make her decision soon and notify me down at Beaconsfield, I took the train back home very doubtful of the outcome.

Here Mrs. Nutt may be seen employing her no doubt standard approach for prospective vanity authors. Even before touching Frost's manuscript, she declares she will consider publishing the book if Frost is willing to advance some cash, agrees to "help bear expenses." Equally evident is Frost's innocent attitude as he roundly insists that he will never pay to have his poems published. But that is just what he eventually did. Ignorant of the business side of book publishing, caught firmly in the net of his own fast rising hopes, he would fall a ready victim to Mrs. Nutt's contractual strategy. In the end, as the records show, he was to pay rather more than the fifteen pounds predicted by his columnist friend.

*   *   *

BACK in Beaconsfield, his good intentions regarding his novel now forgotten, Frost gave himself with increasing fervor to the writing of poetry. Very soon, almost without warning, as he told a correspondent in some wonderment, he found himself caught up in a breathless surge of composition—filling most of every day, it also kept him up writing and revising each night into the small hours. It was an exhilarating situation, rare in his personal experience as a writer, and it made him feel, he said, like "a pawing horse let go." Later he would alter the figure and would go so far as to describe what happened as nothing less than a "great harvest." The phrase was no exaggeration.

In the fall of 1912, in a magnificent burst of creative power, Robert Frost embarked on a period of sustained writing for which there can be few parallels in English or American literature. Composing steadily day after day, by late spring he had produced at least a dozen finished poems, perhaps as many as fifteen. All were quite lengthy, all were written in a markedly original strain, and nearly all have long since taken an honored place in American and world literature. Powerfully evoking the life of the New England countryside, an area into which he had not previously strayed in search of subjects, they explore the interior lives of ordinary individuals and bring to his work for the first time what one critic has well described as a "humane realism." Couched in a style arrestingly new to the language, these poems gave off the authentic tones of the everyday Yankee voice, all blended intimately with the traditional air and vigor of formal blank verse.

Equally striking was the fact that these new poems were a radical departure from those in the manuscript he had just left with Mrs. Nutt— that is, all but one. Of the thirty-two poems in *A Boy's Will*, only the sonnet "Mowing" had any real affinity with Frost's new technique and subject. But "Mowing," too, was almost certainly a Beaconsfield product, finished just in time to make a last addition to the book (though it may have been begun in Plymouth). This was a profoundly fitting development, for it is not too much to say that the fourteen lines of "Mowing," identifying as they do "the fact" as the inspiring basis of all imaginative construction, form a sort of manifesto for the poetry Frost was to write not only in England but during the ensuing fifty years of his career:

> *There was never a sound beside the wood but one,*
> *And that was my long scythe whispering to the ground.*
> *What was it it whispered? I knew not well myself;*
> *Perhaps it was something about the heat of the sun,*
> *Something, perhaps, about the lack of sound—*
> *And that was why it whispered and did not speak.*
> *It was no dream of the gift of idle hours,*
> *Or easy gold at the hand of fay or elf:*
> *Anything more than the truth would have seemed too weak*
> *To the earnest love that laid the swale in rows,*
> *Not without feeble-pointed spikes of flowers*

(Pale orchises), and scared a bright green snake.
The fact is the sweetest dream that labor knows.
My long scythe whispered and left the hay to make.

The steady back-and-forth swaying of the scythe cutting through the resisting grass induces a reverie in an unidentified but thoughtful mower (who else but the young part-time hand in the discarded autobiographical novel?). Out of that reverie, deeply probing, is born the artist's realization that "more than the truth" was superfluous to the kind of poetry Frost now wished to write. The piercing nature of reality itself, everyday life, observed keenly and with the heart, was more than ample. "A poet must lean hard on facts, so hard, sometimes, that they hurt," is only the earliest of many Frost comments on the revelation he experienced, a revelation now fixed permanently and wonderfully in the lines of "Mowing." And then, in the very last word of his sonnet, a position which invited the full weight of a reader's attention, he cleverly demonstrated his meaning—and signaled the nature of all his poetry to come—by deliberately inserting an expression till then used and understood only by farmers.

Here, finally, in its simplest form, is the most tantalizing unsolved puzzle of Robert Frost's career. It is a puzzle founded on a curious contradiction, one which any attempt to tell the story of his life in England must confront: How is this remarkable upwelling of creative power, so finely original, so radical a departure from all he had written before, to be explained? This poet of sentimental moods and relentless superficial brooding, this mature husband and father who wrote as if he were still a melancholy youth, how did he so swiftly become capable of such high artistry? Did he find his voice and subject, as some say, only after coming directly under British influence, following the lead of specific British models in the literary ferment of pre World War I London? "The change was sudden," one respected writer affirms, stressing the change of scene. "It occurred when his imagination grasped the possibilities of the region he knew so well, when, by leaving home for a brief sojourn in old England, he came to see in the life of rural New England a remote, ideal world." In one form or another this verdict is now general, or almost so, to the point where serious critics feel able to state flatly that the alteration was wholly indebted to English writers: "It was his trip to England and his exposure to cosmopolitan literary trends that enabled him to discover the value of his experience in New Hampshire."

Or is the truth, as others believe and as Frost himself claimed, just the reverse? Had he in some measure already found himself long before leaving America, and had it happened while he was serving a lonely apprenticeship on his secluded New Hampshire farm? Had he actually completed some of these new poems—including, for example, "The Death of the Hired Man"—so early as the year 1905, only to be thwarted by a succession of obtuse American editors? Such questions bring to the surface still other and more pressing considerations, among them what surely must be the strangest circumstance of all. If Frost had indeed begun to write in his new style so early as 1905, or thereabouts, then it must be accepted that at the very time he was forging a new world of poetic art, he also continued to write in his youthful, weakly self-centered style—a great poet and a very minor one simultaneously inhabiting the same mind.

There is also the question, of equal interest but seldom addressed, as to possible sources for this fascinating new voice—the voice itself, as distinct from the subject matter—now so unforgettably a part of American poetry. Was this compelling sound derived from a merely generalized attention that Frost may have paid to the rustic life he met around him in his farming days? Or is it possible to trace for it a more precise, more individual lineage?

Fortunately, though they do not yield themselves up easily, calling for a separate journey of exploration back into Frost's obscurer years, answers to all these questions are not past finding out.

THREE

NEVER KNEW
A MAN I LIKED BETTER

O UT of the dismaying jumble of fact, near fact, and loose conjecture which at present makes up the bulk of Frost biography, there emerges a small cluster of documents bearing directly on his sudden poetic flowering in England. By themselves, these documents provide the long-needed starting point for a more searching look at that intriguing development.

Almost a year before he left Plymouth for England, Frost wrote a letter to Susan Ward. At that time, December 1911, he had not been in touch with his friend for several years, so he apologized for being a "laggard," and enclosed an unusual Christmas gift, a handwritten booklet of some of his unpublished poetry. Consisting of twenty-two numbered pages, carefully folded and stitched together between stiff blue covers, the neat booklet held fully seventeen poems. They were meant as a "peace offering," Frost explained, but he adds frankly that he does not think highly of any of them. The booklet simply represents, he says, "not the long deferred forward movement you are living in wait for, but only the grim stand it was necessary for me to make until I gathered myself together. The forward movement is to begin next year." Joking mildly about being on the eve of accomplishment, he warns his correspondent that she mustn't laugh at his boast as she may have laughed at others because, "in my case you would find yourself mistaken. Elinor will tell you so."

The little booklet is still in existence and even a glance through its contents is sufficient to corroborate Frost's own low estimate. Flashes of grace and tenderness there are, and some evidence of prosodic skill, but none of the poems rises much above the ordinary (six of the total were to appear in A Boy's Will, most considerably improved by rewriting). More to the point, nowhere in the more than three hundred lines does there sound any presaging note of the distinctive verse that was to roll so readily from his pen only a year later in Beaconsfield. When Frost put this booklet together, whatever else he may have had in mind, or roughly in prospect, he had not yet actually written anything remotely resembling the kind of original poetry, the dramatic narratives, the "talk songs," of his great period.

A third document of the cluster is another letter, written ten weeks after the first, on March 4, 1912. Addressed to the small Maine publisher Thomas Mosher, it is an answer to an inquiry about his writing. He talks happily about the recent sale of two of his poems to magazines—"Reluctance" and "My November Guest"—and while rambling on he is led to make a veiled reference to still other poems which, for some unstated reason, he is not ready to show. Naming the two poems he has just sold, he comments teasingly, "I do not say that either of them heralds a new force in literature. Indeed I think I have others still under cover that more nearly represent what I'm going to be."

In the time that passed between those two letters, obviously something has happened to Frost as a poet, some development which appears to him as verging on the momentous. Indeed, if the comment to Mosher is read with care, it almost seems to claim that these new, unidentified poems he has kept "under cover" may well prove to be that "new force in literature" he mentions so breezily. What all this points to is a sudden, feverish period of composition, involving the production of verses so strong and original as to prompt in their author feelings close to jubilation. That he was in fact intensely caught up in the writing of poetry during some part of that ten-week interval is confirmed by a brief reference in another of his letters, written later from the Bungalow: "I always feel as if I was justified in writing poetry when the fit is on me—as it was last January." Furthermore, this sudden upsurge of composition, which began perhaps in the relaxed interval between school terms, has left some interesting traces of itself. They show that a pervading state of mental abstraction gripped him strongly at the time, and persisted for weeks afterward. The initial stimulus, or part of it, may have resulted from the novelty of his surroundings, for with his family he had arrived in Plymouth only some four months before, after having lived for eleven years in Derry.

Speaking to a class in the Normal School one day in late January, he suddenly became aware that he had drifted off his topic and was reciting poetry to his students: "I couldn't for the life of me say how afterward—I actually turned a recitation in the history of education into a recitation of irrelevant verse" (not just verse, but *irrelevant* verse). During those same days he found it hard to keep to schedules, usually arriving late for classes, coat buttons awry, hair disheveled, and tie askew, or no tie at all. "He would come hustling through the door," recalled one of his students years later, "breathless and muttering embarrassed apologies. We were given to understand that the clock had either gone on strike, or his wife had failed to hand him his hat at the proper time. We always grinned knowingly at each other, knowing that the reason for his tardiness was a book and the old arm chair." Several other women from that 1912 class also remembered their teacher as constantly preoccupied, all agreeing that "he always seemed to be wandering around in a fog, mentally."

Capping all was a peculiar incident that took place one evening in early February, just after a heavy snowfall, as he went for his customary walk on the outskirts of Plymouth, in an area he knew to be little frequented. Describing the incident some days afterward, he said he was proceeding slowly down one branch of a crossroad, when he looked up to see another walker,

> who to my own unfamiliar eyes in the dark looked for all the world like myself, coming down the other, his approach to the point where our paths must intersect being so timed that unless one of us pulled up we must inevitably collide. I felt as if I was going to meet my own image in a slanting mirror. Or say I felt as we slowly converged on the same point with the same noiseless yet laborious strides as if we were two images about to float together with the uncrossing of someone's eyes. I verily expected to take up or absorb this other self and feel the stronger by the addition for the three-mile journey home. But I didn't go forward to the touch. I stood still in wonderment and let him pass by

Abjuring the temptation to make psychological grist of this classic scene (confronting their own images at times of profound self-absorption is a not uncommon occurrence in the dreams and reveries of creative artists), it is apparent that Frost is here depicting himself, six months before he left Plymouth for England, wrapped in a mood of extreme mental abstraction. So stirred and even startled is he by a simple encounter with someone whose appearance, at a distance and against the stark white background, resembled his own, that he is brought to a standstill in the snow, wavering as to the reality of what he witnessed.

Read in the light of this creative ferment, occurring just prior to his leaving for England, several obscure references in Frost's letters from England begin to take on some meaning. In one, talking of the new blank verse narratives he was then writing, he makes a remark that appears to be perfectly straightforward but which inadvertently conceals some relevant information. "I had some character strokes I had to get in somewhere," he explains in a letter written from the Bungalow, "and I chose a sort of eclogue form for them. Rather I dropped into that form. And I dropped to an everyday level of diction that even Wordsworth kept above." In what exact state or form he "had" these character strokes before he recast them, is the pertinent question. Does he mean a series of generalized impressions carried loosely in his head, in other words raw material? The word "strokes" in itself seems to indicate more than that, calling for detail, specific features, individual coloring, pointing perhaps to the existence of actual manuscript.

Just how he "dropped" into the eclogue form it would be interesting to know, not to mention the related question of what he dropped *from*. But these are questions that up to now have refused to yield, even to speculation, and at this juncture it can only be suggested that the decision or development may have had something to do with his writing of "The Black Cottage." This deeply affecting and strangely evocative poem, which is only now beginning to gather serious critical attention, owes its entire setting and action, even its abrupt sunset ending, to Wordsworth's eclogue-like poem "The Excursion" (Book I, originally titled "The Ruined Cottage"). The story in Frost's poem is not essentially different from the Englishman's, though derived from the lonely life of one of Frost's Derry neighbors, a Civil War widow.

Further evidence to support the existence of actual, near-final manuscript brought from America to Beaconsfield occurs in a remark which, as too often, has been dismissed as one of the poet's exaggerations (even as labored humor!). In the same letter in which he tells of bringing the manuscript of *A Boy's Will* over in the bottom of his trunk, he goes on to state—and in full sincerity, judging by the context—that he has "three other books of verse somewhere near completion . . . And I wanted to be alone with them for a while." Titles for all three are given, and it is evident at a glance that two of them could easily accommodate the sort of poems he was to write in Beaconsfield: *Villagers* and *The Sense of Wrong*.

The third title, though it needs some explanation, is perhaps even more appropriate: *Melanism*, a word describing an abnormal condition in animals and men where there is an excess of dark pigmentation in skin, hair, and eyes. Several of the more somber poems in *North of Boston*—"A Servant to Servants," especially comes to mind—could fit perfectly well under such a symbolic heading.

These three manuscript books of verse are never heard of again after that one passing mention. But taken with all else said above, they help make it certain that when Frost sat down to write in the Bungalow in the fall of 1912, he did indeed have on hand early drafts of a large number of new poems, some of which no doubt were later abandoned. In light of such evidence, his downright assertion, made while he was still in Plymouth, that he had "under cover" some unpublished poems that "more nearly represent what I am going to be," takes on real substance. To dismiss those words as not referring to the poems completed in Beaconsfield, but to earlier efforts which never saw the light of day, places much too great a strain on what is probable. In addition, Frost's boast to Susan Ward in December 1911 about the imminence of his "forward movement" shows that even at so early a stage he had already begun to formulate his ideas of what this new poetry should be like.

But it is possible to go even one step further, identifying still another probable early source for these new poems—the plot of the discarded novel. As Frost described it to Lawrance Thompson, the novel was to be an exposition of the tension between two farm workers, one a youth who is virtually an outsider, and the other an old, experienced hired hand. A story along those lines might easily have held the seeds of such poems as "The Code," "The Housekeeper," "The Mountain," and "The Death of the Hired Man," to list obvious candidates. Many years afterward Frost did publish a poem, "From Plane to Plane," which he conceded had been taken directly from the abortive novel.

The conclusion to be drawn from all these various strands seems unavoidable: The marvelous burst of creativity that overtook Frost in the Bungalow was a continuation of work he had started while still engaged at the Normal School in Plymouth. Of all the dramatic narratives he wrote in Beaconsfield, in the several months following October 1912, very few could have been freshly conceived there. Most were based on preliminary work born out of the fit of writing that shook him at the start of the year back home. His writing had simply been interrupted, first by the demands of his teaching duties in the spring, and later by all the bustle and distraction of moving his family across the ocean. Perhaps it was the very existence of this body of preliminary verse, flawed as it may have been in its early dress, that finally decided him to quit the safety of his teaching position at Plymouth and take that one last gamble on his artistic future.

At Plymouth, then, starting about the time of his arrival there from Derry in the fall of 1911, Frost would have spent no small part of his time wrestling with matters of style and technique as he tried to bring alive the conversational tone he wanted. Happily, in two separate incidents, fleeting though they are, he can be overheard in his daily contacts practicing aloud the same sort of plain talk he was consciously building into his verse.

Memory of the first incident was inadvertently preserved by the young high school teacher whom Frost met on first reaching Plymouth, Sidney Cox. Just out of college at the time, Cox tended, as he admitted, to be somewhat stiff and superior in his approach to strangers, so that when he encountered Frost at a school dance one evening he was not favorably impressed. The middle-aged psychology teacher in the rumpled suit and gray workman's shirt, who slumped in his chair with legs crossed as he poked fun at other teachers, did not suit well with the youthful Cox's idea of an intellectual. The distaste was heightened as Frost talked on, Cox recalled, since in his speech and language, no less than his garb and attitude, he repeatedly betrayed "what seemed a lack of elegance." Cox couldn't have been aware of the fact, of course, but by his personal reactions to Frost's earthy talk—at that time a quite studied inelegance— he was in a manner aiding at the birth of great poetry.

The second incident is more fleeting but is perhaps even more to the point. It comes from a source who was closer in age and position to Frost, Ernest Silver, principal of the Normal School, with whom the Frosts shared lodgings. Describing the pleasure he says Frost often displayed in the salty exchanges picked up or overheard in rural areas, Silver remembered how his friend "would chuckle as he recalled and repeated expressions he had heard and cherished." As with Cox, the more experienced Silver was also called on to listen while Frost, not satisfied until he had rolled the sounds over his own tongue, tried out some new twist of phrase.

Rare glimpses like these into the process by which Frost gained his mastery over the spoken word are also valuable for what they imply about the sheer effort required, which by any estimate must have been considerable. Of no less value are the further indications about when and how he first became aware of the poetic potential of these regional speech patterns, and how his practical studies gathered strength (Frost himself never used the word *study* in this regard, always seeing the process as something much more casual and leisurely, even haphazard). But just here the trail veers off into the underbrush. Despite a diligent search through the whole decade preceding his stay at Plymouth—back through the years of his active employment as a teacher at Pinkerton Academy in Derry, back even further through the five leisurely years he spent in relative isolation earning his family's living as a farm-poultryman— nowhere can he be heard making use in his poetry of those distinctive sounds and attitudes. Here is a curious gap indeed, for the nature of the case puts it beyond doubt that it was sometime in the years of that decade, 1901–1911, when he mingled daily with his plainspoken neighbors in the southeastern corner of New Hampshire, that he began to conceive of their quietly evocative speech as the basis for poetry.

Regrettably, most of the detail of Frost's personal involvement in the life of the farming community around Derry has been lost or obscured. It is only in the frayed pages of some old school copybooks kept by Lesley that he can be glimpsed actually working on his farm or moving around the countryside. In one of these childish essays he is seen caught up in earnest conversation with his neighbors, nicely framing an important Frost habit, one that was to grow more pronounced with the years, his tendency to linger wherever good talk was to be heard. As youngsters, all the Frost children were expected to write a daily composition for review by their parents, and most often it became a record of some one of the day's slight incidents. On June 14, 1908, Lesley's essay concerned a trip she had made that day into town with her father. Proudly she tells how she guessed rightly that they would be late getting home (making surprisingly few errors for a child of eight):

> Saterday evening Papa and I were going to the village. We had to go to Derry Village first to see Mr. Mariam [Merriam] a minute and then go to West Derry. When we were eating supper I prophecied that Papa would at last find out that he had stayed too long at Mr. Mariam's and would have to hurry away, but then he would get to talking with somebody on the street and begin to walk slow so he wouldn't get home till about ten. Now what do you suppose happened. He did stay too long there, he stayed till nine o'clock when he ought to stay till half past seven and he did get to talking with somebody on the street who walked clear to Websters with us and walked so slow that we didn't get home till it was past ten. Now wasn't that a good prophecy.

Perhaps there is no need to belabor the fact that Frost's own still vividly remembered habits of casual conversation ("He talks all day and every day," commented one friend with only slight exaggeration), must have played a pivotal role in his ability to shape conversational verse.

Equally to the point, Frost was that rare thing, a great natural talker who was readily drawn to other talkers, prepared and even eager to listen. It was this tendency, so far as can be judged, that brought him, soon after the move from Lawrence to the Derry farm, into contact with a neighbor, of no literary pretensions whatever, who was fated to act as one of the kindling sparks of his dormant artistic life. This was his fellow poultry-man, John Hall, whom he first met in the fall of 1902 at one of the region's annual poultry shows. The two quickly struck up a friendship and Frost began paying fairly frequent visits to the other man's farm, drawn no doubt by the opportunity to learn more of the poultry business from an old hand, but also by the Hall personality.

Little is known about the fifty-seven-year-old Hall, except that he was the possessor of a salty wit that would have been at home, or so it seems, in the pages of Chaucer. Frost was afterward to use precise words in describing his friend's verbal abilities, saying Hall's talk was "homely, shrewd, and living," and that it had a "racy commonness." It was after listening to the unsophisticated Hall that it dawned on Frost one day that "real artistic speech was only to be copied from real life." Before that revelation, he said, his models had all been literary ones, other writers and poets, all in the Romantic mold.

A relatively poor man, Hall at heart was as much of a poet and artist, in his own distinctive way, as Frost himself, and every bit as fiercely dedicated. He operated a small poultry farm tucked into an out-of-the-way corner of Atkinson, the next town over from Derry. Living in bland disregard of money matters, he gave his attention to the only thing he really cared about, the breeding and grooming of fowl for show purposes. His stock included all manner of ducks and geese, but particularly hens, ranging over a large variety of breeds, some imported. Wanting to foster vigor in his birds, he provided them with little shelter, allowing the whole mixed flock to have the run of his few acres in all weathers, along with pigeons, doves, dogs, and several Angora cats. The multitude of show ribbons, blue, red, and yellow, that hung on the walls of his kitchen was sufficient testimony to the worth of his methods and to his mastery of the skills involved. Regularly each year his birds won or placed in several categories at the various shows, and at the time Frost met him at the 1902 show in Amesbury he had just been awarded the prestigious Sweepstakes Cup. Frost was a serious poultryman himself at the time, even harboring dreams of winning some ribbons, and he would have been mightily impressed by Hall's success, more so because of Hall's ability to talk captivatingly about what he was doing.

How often the two may have met after that initial meeting cannot be said. It must have been fairly frequent, however, for Frost was soon making literary use of his new acquaintance, capturing not only the salty talk and manner, but drawing extensively on Hall's knowledge of the poultry industry, especially the highly popular shows, "The Fancy," as such competition was called. This writing was done not as verse but in the form of articles for the poultry trade journals.

The last time Frost had attempted prose was for the Lawrence newspapers, some seven years before. The immediate impulse that moved him to try again came from the births of two children within thirteen months, his son Carol and daughter Irma, and the resulting increase in the family's financial needs. Even with the first payment of the grandfather's annuity, which had arrived in July 1902 (at first five hundred dollars, later increased to eight), his income from the farm, derived mainly from the sale of broilers and eggs, had never been really adequate. Unpaid bills at the doctor's office, at the grocers, the butchers, and the feed suppliers ate up a good portion of that first payment. A regular reader of one or another of the several poultry journals published in New England, Frost turned to these when more income was needed, writing a number of short fictional sketches about the poultry industry. Most of them, it is clear, were inspired by talks with Hall and based largely on information he supplied, for most are directly concerned with The Fancy.

Perhaps somewhat to his surprise, promptly on his first try Frost uncovered a ready market for these sketches. He was able to sell three of them immediately, at $10 apiece, and in the course of the next year or so he wrote and sold another half dozen. The first four of the group, while making a strong appeal to insiders, have little to interest the general reader. The fifth sketch, however, published in August 1903, reveals a conscious literary craftsman at work, able to lift his subject above mere poultry lore, reaching the level of true if minor art. Here, in the forgotten pages of *Farm Poultry* is the first tentative murmur of the voice that ten years later was to speak out boldly from *North of Boston*.

Entitled "Old Welch Goes to the Show," this fifth sketch tells of a dedicated breeder who in preparing his show birds does not hesitate, when occasion demands, to apply some unorthodox techniques, of a sort frowned on by show regulations. In his twangy talk, if perhaps not wholly in his methods, it need hardly be argued that Old Welch is closely modeled on John Hall himself:

Old Welch did not care about having his neighbors in when he was getting ready for a show, because, as he said, "The laity don't understand, and can't be expected to." Still, he did not admit that there was anything to conceal. He used to say, "I guess 'tis fair enough to groom and tame the birds a little before showing." He scorned the defense that if he was bad others were worse. Others might be worse, he was not bad. He was an honest man.

His saying about grooming and taming the birds obtained wide currency. He was asked, when caught in the act—which he called going over the birds for black feathers—grooming or taming? "Taming," he answered with the suggestion of a wink. Of course that made the uninitiated laugh. But so long as the gossip was confined to the neighborhood, Welch did not care . . .

One season disaster strikes and the old man's best birds are all lost in a sudden catastrophe, leaving him without even one prime fowl for showing. Some boys of the neighborhood, his friends, call in to see how the master is taking his defeat. One of them asks if he is going to do anything about it:

"Do? I ain't got nothing to do with." For an artist like Mr. Welch this was a confession indeed.

"Can't you show yearlings?"

"This strain ain't bred for yearlings, sonny." By which he was understood to mean that his strain did not hold up well—were good for one year only.

"But can't you doctor yearlings?"

"Doctor, doctor? Don't use that word to me, son."

The boy was too old to be easily cowed, so he only said, "Well, groom and tame them, then."

This appealed to the sport in the old man and he was mollified. "Let's see how many we have got of that first lot," he said. "All I ask is maturity. They must have maturity. I can't furnish that . . . I must get to the shows with something, or I shan't know 'tis winter except by the cold."

"What's the matter with that fellow?" said the youngster, with something of the real air.

"Haven't I learned you no better than that? Why there's pretty nearly everything the matter with him. His comb don't fit, his eyes ain't mates. He's yellow and his legs ain't. He's too high posted. He's whalebacked and hollow chested. But just to show you what I can do, I'm going to take that dog-shaped specimen and renovate him—renovate him."

"His eyes ain't mates, come to look at them. How will you fix that?"

"I've thought of a way. The hardest will be to make him throw a chest."

On the bedraggled cockerel Welch proceeds to apply his specialized skills. With a hot wire he sears the underside of the head feathers to bring the comb into line. Then he polishes the scraggly legs with butter to bring out the yellow, and inserts a colored lens in one eye to make it match the other. Delicately he rigs a tiny corset that pulls the bird's shoulders into conformity. At the last moment he pumps a little air under the skin of the chest, "a delicate operation almost requiring the services of a veterinary," which he supposedly copies from a similar practice with camels in Asia. The finished product Welch proudly displays to his admiring young friends, one of whom ventures, "I should think a good deal would depend on the judge when you showed a bird like that." To this tactful inquiry Welch in full assurance replies, "It does—it does. You have to be extra careful in choosing your judge. 'Tis with judges as with other folks, there ain't only now and then one that's suited to your purpose. Now I only know one judge this year that that bird'll do to show to."

The doctored entry takes a second place, which in the circumstances leaves Old Welch well satisfied. Afterward, when a prospective buyer approaches him about the prize-winning bird, he can't resist a last flourish. The cockerel, he explains, "owes just the leastest leetle mite to the way he was groomed. I shouldn't want to recommend him to you, because I ain't quite sure that he'd breed true."

A month after the appearance of Old Welch another sketch by Frost was published, this time telling of a breeder who buys a certain hen with the intention of entering The Fancy. From such frivolity he is permanently diverted, however, when he finds that he has on his hands a hen remarkable for her egg-laying abilities. Entitled "The Original and Only," the 1,700-word story is told almost entirely as a monologue. Some of its passages, in prose but feeling uncannily like blank verse, could almost have been lifted out of one of the later narrative poems in *North of Boston*. The tale's first-person narrator, unnamed but again certainly John Hall, explains first how the unfortunate bird's rare talents brought about her doom:

I can't say that she ever laid in the molt, and that's about the same thing as being plucked by nature. But I never asked her to lay in the molt. She laid

hard enough anyway to scare a man. I was always afraid she couldn't keep
the pace, or something would go wrong, and finally it did. She got to
making eggs faster than she could lay them. They came so fast that they
crowded each other and broke, and she died of a sort of internal custard, so
to speak. But I'm getting ahead.

In the purest Frostian strain of the later poems, the narrator goes on to
insist that before her death his good hen taught him some things, proper
evaluation of his other stock for one:

> I paid for her show points and got her eggs thrown in, but her eggs alone
> were worth the money . . . It was the contrast between her egg and that of
> the other hen, I suppose, that brought it home to me. The other hen laid
> about once a week, and when she did lay it was a dead-white, gritty, thin-
> shelled egg, just misshapen enough at the pick to be unhatchable. She was
> money thrown away, though she wasn't bad looking.

There was no actual need, insists the narrator, to brag about his prolific
new hen to other poultry folk, though of course he needn't lie about it
either: "There may be such a thing as a 300-egg hen, but I'm not going to
be the fellow to say so . . . I am satisfied to claim for her about 200. It was
more than that. But you don't catch me saying it was one more or a
hundred more." The narrator's dream of a new and profitable line of
special, bred-to-lay hens keeps him out of show business, and in the end
he is not at all sorry. "Fanciers are born not made," he concludes, "and I
wasn't sure that I was particularly born, and as the ministers say that's
the test, if you don't feel as if you are called, you aren't called."

The third of the three sketches in which can be heard a clear anticipation of the later Frost was a much briefer tale called "The Cockerel
Buying Habit," published in February 1904. In a way it is the most
interesting of all, since it foreshadows the structural device by which
many of the later poems create their peculiar power.

Presenting a discussion between a poultry breeder and his friend—
unmistakably Hall and Frost—the story takes place in a barnyard. It
treats the problem of a breeder who wants to start a strain of hens of his
own but fears the consequences of inbreeding. Nothing actually happens
in the story and it ends with the breeder still unable to make up his mind
on what course to take, leaving the reader with an unfinished feeling
(also a curious anticipation of Frost's method with some of his descriptive
pieces). The pertinent fact about it is the way the two voices are differentiated, the breeder talking country fashion while the friend's language is

more cultivated. Two short exchanges will give the flavor. The breeder speaks first:

> "You know how it's supposed to be when cousins marry. You can hear some awful stories against it."
>
> "You can hear just as many the other way, and more authentic."
>
> "Did I ever tell you how George Hill bred Cochins in till he got them that squat and fluffy and Cochiny they were a sight for sore eyes? But come to set their eggs one year there wasn't a single one fertile."
>
> "I believe you have told me, but I don't think he proved anything. So many considerations enter into a case of that kind."

It is near feeding time, so the two speakers, standing together in the yard, are gradually surrounded by the noisy, free-ranging hens. The visitor, who tells the story in the first person, looks around at the milling flock:

> "What's the matter with those? They're a nice looking lot," I protested.
>
> "If you don't see it I'm not going to tell you."
>
> All hens in a flock look pretty much alike at first glance, and it is hard to pick out individual characteristics. But I had to say something. "Perhaps you mean they vary somewhat in size. You have some very white birds."
>
> "I mean they're of all sorts and kinds. I've got some very white birds and I've got some not so white. I've got some big ones, and I've got some all fired runts. The fact is they come every which way. I haven't anything like a strain."
>
> As I looked I became convinced there was something to what he said.

While the friend does show sympathy for the breeder's dilemma, his language makes him appear detached, as if he stood apart from the everyday concerns of his neighbors. He is readily accepted by the breeder, who is seeking his advice in the matter, but still seems somehow as if he didn't quite belong. This ambivalence, resting on the two distinct modes of expression, is precisely the subtle mechanism that runs all through *North of Boston*, explicitly or as muted implication. It underlies in a fundamental way the volume's opening poem, "Mending Wall," which sets the tone for that whole book. It is also the mainspring for several even later poems generally accepted as major achievements, particularly "The Star-Splitter" and "The Axe-Helve."

Another fact of no little importance about these prose sketches is the way Frost handles the tones and expressions of regional speech. As in the later poems, he does so without any exaggeration in flawed vocabulary, twisted grammar, or bad spelling, thus avoiding all sense of parody. In view of so nicely controlled a touch, it is easy to believe his later claim that, while he wrote the poultry sketches primarily for money to help pay his family's mounting bills, it was done also "partly for the fun."

To be strictly accurate, however, the results he achieved in this matter of restraint must be attributed in some part to the limitations imposed on him by his market. He was writing stories that he knew would be read by the same kinds of people he was writing about, readers who would not have accepted anything like a caricature of themselves, least when it cut too close to the bone. If Frost by some chance had overlooked so relevant a point, the editors of the magazines for which he wrote would certainly have reminded him. As a matter of sensible policy they could not have opened their columns to the implied condescension usually present in the rawer kinds of dialect writing.

Frost's poultry sketches came to an abrupt end early in 1904, and interestingly enough the termination of the series also played its part in his developing artistry. Though he several times implied otherwise, it appears that it was not wholly his personal decision to end the tales. The action was forced on him because of a factual blunder he committed in one of the pieces, a blunder his editor failed to spot, causing the magazine some embarrassment. Ironically, the error arose from a misunderstanding over something told Frost by none other than John Hall.

In a factual piece of straight reporting he contrasts several different phases of the poultry industry. Hall he cites as an example of "A Typical Small Breeder," and in listing and commenting on Hall's methods, he remarks, "As for vigor, it is easier to get this right than not. What the stock need is a little judicious neglect. Mr. Hall's geese roost in the trees even in winter. Such a toughening process would be too drastic for hens, but these have to take it according to their strength."

On publication of the article a letter promptly arrived at the magazine's offices from a reader, more sarcastic than irate, who protested, "I am 45 years old and have been among geese all my lifetime, and I can never remember seeing a goose in a tree. I thought if I could get a breed of that kind I could dispense with coops." There may have been more than one such protesting response, but in any case this letter was published in full in the next issue, with the discomfitted editor adding lamely, "Letting Mr. Frost's statement pass is one 'on' us. The writer's attention was called to the evident error before the paper was mailed, but too late to make corrections. Then we thought we'd wait and see how many would notice it. Mr. Frost will have to explain."

Unwilling to confess his ignorance, Frost took the only other course open to him. Attempting to make light of his mistake, in his reply he remarked, "What more natural, in speaking of geese in close connection with hens, than to speak of them as if they *were* hens? 'Roost in the trees' has here simply suffered what the grammarians would call attraction from the subject with which it should be in agreement to the one uppermost in the mind." That bit of ponderous whimsy might have concluded the matter but Frost could not refrain from trying to recover himself a little further, and in so doing he stumbled again. "But the idea will have to stand," he went on, "viz., that Mr. Hall's geese winter out, and that is the essential thing."

Frost's answer ran verbatim in the next issue, but this time the editor himself took pains to correct his second slip, and in print. Baldly he comments: "Mr. Frost seems not to be aware of the fact that geese generally remain out of doors by choice practically all the time." For an editor to take this course, printing a writer's erroneous statement, then pointedly and publicly making a correction, rather than calling it to the writer's attention in private and beforehand, or himself making a correction on the spot, was unusual. To Frost it must have seemed that he was on the verge of losing an outlet for his prose, so to forestall that possibility he decided on one last stratagem, incidentally supplying a final example of the artistic use he was able to make of his friend.

In the issue of *Farm Poultry* for March 1, 1904, there appeared a fairly lengthy letter signed by one John Hall of the town of Atkinson. In it the breeder takes it on himself to set matters straight on the vexed question of the behavior of geese in winter:

> I noticed Mr. H. R. White's letter in your paper asking about the kind of geese I keep that sleep out in the winter. They are Toulouse, Embden and Buff. They don't roost in trees. I don't know how Mr. Frost made that mistake, for of course he knows better.
>
> We have often talked about the way they take to the water at night, a favorite place for them to hang up being on a stone just under water. A good many nights in winter, as well as in summer, I have no idea where they are; and I think they are better every way out of doors as long as there is any water not frozen over. But speaking of geese in trees, I don't suppose Mr. White has ever seen a duck in a tree. I have. And I once had a duck that laid her eggs in a tree high enough to be out of reach from the ground, and brought off twenty-two ducklings. These were Brazilians and I don't know what they won't do.
>
> It has always seemed strange to me how people succeed in keeping geese

shut up. If I shut mine up they begin to be restless right away, and go off in looks, especially plumage. Mr. White needn't think because I let my geese run wild I think any less of them than other folks. They are good ones—as they ought to be with the advantages I give them. They win, too, where they are shown.

The records in your paper ought to show what they did in Lawrence this year; but I notice they don't. So Mr. Frost was pretty near right about my geese; and if Mr. White wants some good ones that a little rather than not sleep out, I've got them.

The letter, written by Frost with Hall's concurrence, was a deft performance. In making Hall sound like the countryman he was, yet not too crudely, it shows a fine balance, further developing the sure touch displayed in the sketches. Sadly, however, the ploy failed to work, and having been exposed to his readers as something less than an expert in the matter of geese, Frost was quietly dropped from the magazine's columns. The last of his sketches, a slight insider joke on the subject of chicken feed, which had been accepted prior to the debacle over the geese, ran in the issue for April 1. Thereafter, almost two years passed before he was able to make another sale, but this last piece of fiction he was ever to write, also about The Fancy, is curiously devoid of atmosphere or impact.

Whether Frost would have continued to write prose had he not committed the one error unforgivable in the pages of a trade journal, cannot be known, though it seems likely. If so, then after 1906 he would have had to seek elsewhere for the expert help he needed, for in December of that year John Hall died. Nothing official has yet been uncovered as to the circumstances of his death, though Frost later attributed it to a combination of vexation and grief over the loss of his longtime "housekeeper," really his common-law wife. As Frost explained, after the woman quietly left the farm to marry someone else, the abandoned Hall "went down like a felled ox." Feelingly he adds, "I never knew a man I liked better. Damn the world anyway."

Through the years his friend's sad ending stayed with Frost, and some aspect of it eventually found expression in "The Housekeeper," one of the dramatic narratives in North of Boston. The poem's narrator (obviously Frost himself), one day visits the Hall farm in its owner's absence, and from the mother of the vanished common-law wife he gets the first news of what has happened. When he asks the old woman how she thinks Hall will manage to survive the blow, she says that it is more than likely he will just give up. In the woman's answer Frost offers a brief but affecting portrait of Hall's sensitive nature, somewhat out of tune with the tougher-skinned society of country life:

What I think he will do, is let things smash.
He'll sort of swear the time away. He's awful!
I never saw a man let family troubles
Make so much difference in his man's affairs.
He's just dropped everything. He's like a child.
I blame his being brought up by his mother.
He's got hay down that's been rained on three times.
He hoed a little yesterday for me:
I thought the growing things would do him good.
Something went wrong. I saw him throw the hoe
Sky-high with both hands. I can see it now—
Come here—I'll show you—in that apple tree.
That's no way for a man to do at his age.

The strength of Frost's tie to the untutored Hall, certainly an unusual friendship in many ways, is not difficult to understand. Apart from his interest in Hall's verbal abilities, there was the social contact, the visiting, and the common stake in the poultry business, all of which helped Frost to overcome his early feelings of isolation on his Derry farm, opening him up to the whole range of country impressions. For this service also, helping to bring Frost out of himself, Hall should be remembered. Yet, first and last, it was the talk that mattered.

Once, in explaining his methods of composition, Frost said that he always began a poem by imagining "the tone of someone speaking." Building directly on an extensive study of the poems themselves, critic John Lynen has ventured to describe Frost's imagined speaker. He sees him as "a many-sided and complex character, one who has a certain standard of values, and a particular way of thought. Most often this speaker is a rural New Englander, his attitudes, his word sense, and indeed his whole mentality dramatize the regional world and therefore function as a symbol to represent it. His personality is revealed by his manner of speaking, and since it is he who utters the poem, his manner of speaking is the poem's style." For Lynen, as for all Frost commentators, there was no thought of this inspired speaker being embodied in one actual man, and it may be that they are right. Certainly, the ideas and concepts of such admitted literary influences as Virgil, Shakespeare, Wordsworth, Thoreau, Emerson, and William James, even Turgeniev of *The Sportsman's Sketches*, are also deeply enmeshed in this idealized speaker. Yet surely, in view of all the testimony in the above pages, it must now be accepted that in the midst of this distinguished company there sits, very much at his ease, the figure of garrulous old John Hall himself.

The only direct quotation Frost ever made of Hall's talk (aside from the imagined dialogue in the poultry stories), occurs in a few lines at the close of "The Housekeeper." It is for that reason that the brief passage is worth quoting, though it affords only a faint murmuring reflection of the color and bite of the glib tongue that had so captivated Frost. In the poem, after the mother and her visitor have been talking for a while, the old woman looks through the window beside her and warns the visitor that Hall's rig is about to turn into the yard, and they shouldn't be caught talking about him:

> *John threw the door wide but he didn't enter.*
> *"How are you neighbor? Just the man I'm after.*
> *Isn't it Hell?" he said. "I want to know.*
> *Come out here if you want to hear me talk.—*
> *I'll talk to you, old woman, afterward.—*
> *I've got some news that maybe isn't news.*
> *What are they trying to do to me, these two?"*

Hall and his visitor step outside the door, and the poem comes to an abrupt close, the minor tragedy of the farmer's life having been made painfully clear in the prior exchange between visitor and mother. But there is one line from that closing passage which should be graven in oak and erected in a prominent position on the Derry farm, where it might stand in honor of the obscure poultry breeder who helped create one of the leading poets of the century. How much of the tantalizing secret of Frost's beginnings as a conscious artist, and his lifelong knack of vivid expression, are encompassed in the ten short words,

Come out here if you want to hear me talk.

FOUR

IDLING AWAY AN AGE

I T WAS early in 1906, after five full years of poultry farming in Derry, that Robert Frost at last faced the inevitable, "my first clash with realism," as he said, only half in jest. He was now the father of four children, all of them under six, with Marjorie the youngest at eight months. His family's support came from the $500 annuity received from his grandfather's estate, supplemented by a small and dwindling income from the poultry, a total no longer adequate. Even at that, his decision to seek a teaching position did not come readily, knowing as he did that its demands would work some profound changes in his previously unfettered existence. This was particularly true regarding the poetry, for any heavy involvement with outside occupation always tended to rob him of the energy he needed for writing. All his life he was to remain a constitutionally slow and deliberate performer, unhurried almost to the point of laziness. Whether actual laziness was involved, as has been charged, rather than an artist's need for broad gestational freedom, will remain an unsettled question. Frost himself in conversation danced around the topic, at times seeming to admit both thoughtlessness and laziness, but more often hinting at a species of egotism linked to an excess of the poetic temperament. "Poetry has been a self-indulgence with me," is how he expressed it once, "and there's no use trying to put a better face on it." (But when is true creation in art, or in science for that matter, not the result of self-indulgence?)

In such circumstances it is not surprising that his memory of the day on which he made his decision should have remained vivid. Going to bed the night before, not telling Elinor what he was thinking, he lay awake trying to convince himself that the "drudgery" of teaching would not entirely submerge his writing: "I let my wife sleep while I tossed and didn't bother her with the problem all night. I lay awake till morning, my heart thumping, dreading to have to go and see somebody about a job . . . Next morning, with rather red eyes, I brought up the subject to my wife, I convinced her that I was right, and she urged me to carry it out." Till then, Elinor had been as much in favor of their untrammeled existence as her husband, even after a dozen years of marriage firmly resisting his occasional and no doubt halfhearted offers to give up writing and take a full time job ("She seems to have the same sort of weakness I have for a life that goes rather poetically; only I should say she is worse than I").

With the personal backing of an influential friend in Lawrence, a Congregationalist minister, he succeeded in finding a position on the staff of nearby Pinkerton Academy, a Congregationalist institution, for the spring 1906 session. All too soon, as his teaching duties steadily enlarged, his fears about the waning of his creative drive were realized. During one rather lengthy stretch—roughly from early 1908 to mid 1910—it appears that he gave up writing altogether. While there is record of five poems having been published in this period, the record is deceiving. Two of the poems were negligible efforts that appeared in the Pinkerton students' newspaper, and two others, also slight, were certainly in existence by 1906. The only one of the five that might have been written in this period is the fine sonnet "Into My Own," published in May 1909. But that poem, revealingly, is a muted cry of anguish expressing a resolve or threat to run away from a life that was no longer "true."

Aside from his involvement with school matters, the years of 1908–1910 have always been the most obscure of Frost's adult life, their darkness unrelieved by documents or recollections of any sort, his own or others. He was then in his mid-thirties, an age when it would have been hardest for him, lacking all encouragement, to have clung to a belief in his poetic destiny. Increasingly resigned, he grew content to perform his duties as teacher and to care for his growing family, no longer a prey to the fierce hopes that had goaded him for so long. This decline of ambition, to the extent that it is now possible to retrace it, could only have been accelerated by a cluster of difficulties that assailed him in the spring and summer of 1907, including the death of a newborn daughter.

In March 1907, partly as a result of overwork, Frost came down with a heavy cold that soon turned to pneumonia. Contributing to his illness may have been a bad case of nerves, a fact Frost himself volunteered to an early biographer, Robert Newdick (who died prematurely, leaving much stray research unexplained). According to Newdick's scribbled note, during his first full year at Pinkerton Frost "suffered a nervous breakdown, prostration. Walked to Methuen, was given a lift to Lawrence, drank a beer, came home on the trolley, collapsed." Whether this otherwise unexplained occurrence can be connected with the onset of the pneumonia is uncertain, but in any event about this time Frost did take to his bed gravely ill. For some six weeks he was cared for at home by Elinor, who was then in her fifth month of pregnancy. It became an exceptionally trying time for both, for when Frost had recovered enough to be up and around, Elinor came down with some unspecified illness, at least partly sheer exhaustion. Frost, though still weak, had to take his turn at nursing.

Early in June, apparently recovered, Elinor went to stay at the home of a nurse-midwife in Derry village. There, on June 20, she gave birth to a girl, but there were immediate complications with the child's health, and only a day later the baby died. Worn down by the strain of the previous months, Elinor reacted to her loss by sinking into a deep depression, and in her grief she placed on her husband much of the blame for what happened. This information comes through an old school friend of Elinor's who visited her in Derry just after the baby's death. He found her, he reported, "in a very unhappy state of mind. She had given birth to a baby that had lived only a short time, and she was miserable because they would not let her have the child in bed with her and cuddle it and love it for the short time it lived. She complained bitterly of her husband, and said he was very heartless to her." In her unreasoning state of mind she probably said as much and more to the stricken Frost himself (none of this seems to have long survived that moment's dark unhappiness, at least no echo of it can be heard later).

In these trying circumstances, while Elinor was still being cared for in Derry, a separate incident occurred at the Frost farm involving Frost's only sister that pushed him further into a confused turmoil of anger and depression. Since the incident is one of those which has contributed greatly to the impairment of Frost's reputation as a man, and since it is reported only by Lawrance Thompson, it will not do to pass over it too swiftly. Further, as will be seen, it has obvious links to still another grave happening, a link which Thompson for some reason failed to spot, or simply ignored.

Frost and his sister Jeanie, though they never drifted entirely apart, had not been real friends since childhood. A year younger than her brother, unmarried, a teacher by profession, Jeanie's vaguely disturbing, often disruptive manner had caused trouble in the Frost home during several previous visits. Now, staying at the farm to help care for the children in Elinor's absence, she soon began acting in a way that had always vastly irritated her brother, what Frost later called her "strange mixture of hysteria and eccentricity." Particularly, he disliked a certain morbid way she had of speaking to the children, and because of it there were flare-ups of temper on both sides during her visit. Then one day, as Thompson tells the story,

> Jeanie really went into hysterics, skipped out on the porch carrying a cup of coffee in one hand and the saucer in another, hurried out into the drive when her brother tried to get her into the house, and then ran out into the road screaming when he went after her. That was more than he could stand, particularly because he knew it was time for people to be coming home from the shoe shops at Derry Depot. He went back into the house, found his loaded revolver, rushed out to the road, and threatened to kill her if she didn't get back into the house fast. She knew her brother's temper well enough to suspect that he might be telling the truth, and she did as he ordered. Apparently convinced that she was in danger if she stayed there any longer, Jeanie packed her bag and left.

While the picture Thompson gives may be accurate enough in its outlines, a caution must be sounded as to the details, especially the tendency of the last two sentences. Rather than simply recounting the sobering effect of her brother's threat on Jeanie, those sentences manage to insinuate that she would have had good reason to be wary of him, that he really was capable of shooting her down in the road, and that she was justified in feeling unsafe from him even inside the house. It is Thompson's way of putting the thought that is at fault, subtly inviting the reader to believe that Frost might indeed have used the pistol on his distraught sister.

In all of this, Thompson has chosen to make damaging implications about matters which were beyond his knowledge, for Jeanie Frost was dead long before Thompson entered his subject's life. She died in a Maine asylum for the insane in 1929, to which after years of mental deterioration she had been committed by her brother in 1920. This fact would seem pertinent to the story of Jeanie and the revolver, yet in telling it Thompson avoids all reference to the woman's mental condition. Buried in his voluminous notes, cited in a different connection altogether, is a brief statement made in passing that "In 1925, after Jeanie had been committed permanently to a mental hospital . . ."

Everything said so far about the above incident refers to the first volume of the Thompson biography, published in 1966. Four years later a second volume was issued, and there Jeanie's sad story is covered a bit more fully. Again mention is made of the revolver incident of 1907 at the Derry farm. But now her reason for leaving the farm after her brother's threat to shoot her has nothing to do with any fear she may have felt. It is given as a subtle foreshadowing of her own pathetic mental instability: "Jeanie was fascinated by the discovery that her brother had a revolver, and she returned with him, promising to leave town immediately if he would give it to her." Frost's response to his sister's request, as stated by Thompson, is again made to count against the poet: "The offer seemed a bargain, and he gladly gave her the weapon, unloaded, not caring what she might do with it." Just where and how this new version might have originated cannot be said, for Thompson's notes to the second volume have nothing at all to say as to sources for this incident.

The rather startling picture of Frost brandishing a pistol at his own sister inevitably calls up a similar event, also reported by Thompson, that supposedly took place a year or two before. For many readers this incident stands as perhaps the single most damaging personal charge lodged by Thompson against Frost, so this would seem the point at which to examine it. A chilling occurrence, apparently involving the same pistol used on Jeanie, Thompson locates it at the Derry farm when Lesley was "about" six years old, suggesting a date of 1905, more or less. It arose, says Thompson, out of Frost's "intermittent moods of uncertainty and darkness . . . when he was depressed by the notion that he was a failure." If the reality is to be fairly judged, Thompson's entire lengthy account of the brutal scene must be given:

Lesley was never able to forget an even more mysterious performance, the meaning of which nobody ever explained to her. She could remember being awakened by her father abruptly and roughly in the middle of the night, when she was about six years old. She was told to get out of bed and the cold floor under her feet became a vivid reminder that this event occurred on a winter night. She was told to follow her father down the unlit stairs to the parlor, through the parlor to the dining room, and through the dining room toward the kitchen, where she could see a light burning. As she entered she saw her mother sitting at the kitchen table, crying, her hands pressed to her face. Bewildered, Lesley turned to look at her father and noticed for the first time that he had his revolver in his hand. Waving the

revolver toward her mother and then toward himself, he said wildly to
Lesley, "Take your choice. Before morning one of us will be dead."

She wanted both of them, she said, and she started to cry. Her mother
got up from the table, put her arms around Lesley, pushed her out of the
kitchen, led her back to bed, and sat beside her until the child cried herself
to sleep. In the morning she remembered all the facts and wondered if they
had actually happened. Perhaps she had only dreamed them. But no.
There was evidence enough to make her certain that this experience had
not been a dream.

In his notes for this passage Thompson is careful to identify his source
for the shocking incident. Succinctly he states, "This anecdote was told
to LT by Lesley Frost Ballantine on 1 March 1963." The date given
appears to have no special purpose other than demonstrating the author's
scholarly precision, until it is recalled that the death of Lesley's father had
occurred just a month before. In light of that fact, the reason for the date
can be seen as twofold: first, it shows—or better, implies—that Lesley
had dutifully withheld the story so long as her father lived, a reticence
which seems to demonstrate how strongly she believed in its reality.
Second, the date quietly establishes that there would have been no
opportunity for Thompson to test so serious a charge by reviewing it with
Frost himself. The natural effect of all this is to make Thompson appear
objective and conscientious in his role as biographer. At least in this
instance that impression would be quite misleading.

To begin with, the anecdote should not have been presented in such a
bare and downright fashion, dropped into the text as if its truth were
beyond question. Thompson never cited, never even said whether he had
sought and studied, the unspecified "evidence" claimed by Lesley, that
made her so certain, sixty years after the fact, that her childhood experience had been real and not a dream. No context for the incident in the
Frosts' life is suggested, nor is any attempt made to identify causes,
immediate or remote. These oversights are unfortunate, for all the evidence now available tends strongly to mark the painful incident as indeed
one of the impressionable Lesley's childhood nightmares (a possibility
that she herself was the first to raise). And this evidence, it must be said
frankly, was as readily available to Thompson, had he cared to pursue it.

As a young girl, Lesley not only suffered from a definite tendency to
nightmare, but was thoroughly aware of the unpleasant fact. This can be
shown from the pages of one of her own composition books in which she
wrote her daily essays for her parents. At the age of eight, in fact, she

made her dreaming propensity a subject for an essay in itself: "There was once a little girl who never wanted to go to bed . . . She was a very imaginative child, too, and had many day dreams such as I have had in the last few days . . . Now this is one of the reasons why she didn't want to go to bed. At night she always dreamed terrible dreams, but in the day half-fairyland dreams that she liked better than anything else." Several actual dreams are described in her daily compositions, and her fear of nightmares is admitted again in an essay dated December 15, 1907. After being frightened by a howling snowstorm she cried against going to bed because, "I was such a bad dreamer that I was afraid I might dream that thousands of little men were breaking in to carry me off."

The precociously vivid imagination that produced the nightmares is nicely if unintentionally captured by the young girl in another composition, written in May 1908. With the true Frost touch, she entitled it, "Shapes at Night":

> In summer we have to go to bed when it is light, and I ly on my back and think till it gets dark. Sometimes I watch the furniture change into different kinds of figures as it grows darker. I remember once when I slept downstairs in the front room we had a tall coal stove then and it was shaped something like a man, but with no arms. Well, I woke up one night and saw that in the dark and it scared me awfully so I hid my face in the pillow, but it is nice to see the figures on the wallpaper fade away as the light gets dimmer. Flowers have figures too, but pretty ones. Many times I wake up and think the buero is a big giant in the room, but soon faget it by thinking of something else. You watch these things fade away till you are sleepy and then turn on your side and go to sleep.

By what circuitous route Lesley's dream of that night in the Derry kitchen fixed on, transposed, and elaborated some passing quarrel between her parents—not about 1905 as Thompson guessed, but in the summer of 1907 in the days after the depressed Elinor had returned from her confinement in Derry village cannot be fully traced now. The feeling is irresistible, however, that her chilling kitchen dream has borrowed the major part of its content and coloring from that other pistol incident, involving Frost and his sister in that same summer of 1907. (Aside from all else, of course, the dream of awakening in bed at night and arising to wander through the house is by no means uncommon.)

In his description of Jeanie Frost's visit to the farm in 1907, Thompson actually makes the eight-year-old Lesley the unwitting focus of the disagreement that led to the nasty denouement with the pistol in the road. Frost never liked the effect his sister's erratic behavior had on his children, especially when she "dismayed" them with strangely incoherent talk. At the farm during that summer of 1907 there were several incidents of this kind, one of which is reported by Thompson, obviously on Frost's authority:

> Her conversations with the children made his flesh creep. When he saw her, holding Lesley on her lap in the parlor, looking out at the pine grove which covered Klein's Hill, and saying in an almost hysterical voice that there must be a graveyard up there under the pines and soon they would be buried there, all in a row, and wouldn't that be nice; her brother told her to shut up. A little later he found her in the kitchen making a pot of coffee and telling Lesley that she was a coffee drunkard and if Lesley wanted to see her get drunk on coffee, just watch. It was a capacity she did possess and Frost was enraged.

At this point Thompson's narrative becomes fuzzy, and it cannot be decided whether Jeanie's hysterical dash into the road followed that particular coffee incident, though it is likely. In any event, the similarity of this angry eruption, centering on Lesley, to the supposed midnight confrontation in the kitchen between Frost and Elinor, with Lesley again at the center, is all too apparent. That the precocious child, already feeling the ugly strain between her parents over the sudden death of her newborn baby sister, should have projected her anxiety into a nightmare ignited by the all too real quarrel she witnessed between her father and his own sister, is hardly cause for wonder.

As for the pistol, that Frost did possess one is certain. But in this he was no different from other farmers, all of whom kept pistols and shotguns for protection against marauding tramps and other hazards, or for their own hunting. Poultry farmers, especially, needed firearms, with handguns being favored, to scare off the persistent hen hawks that plagued their free-running birds and open-air coops. Many times Lesley must have witnessed her father shooting off a pistol in the tree-fringed field that stretched back behind the farmhouse to scare away some hovering predator.

* * *

SOME weeks after returning to the United States from England in the spring of 1915, Frost told an interviewer that it was "about ten years ago" that he first became really interested in the lives and personalities of his neighbors, seeing in them the stuff of poetry. Initially, he said, the attraction lay in "their tones of speech," but gradually he found that he was drawn quite as much to what people said, as to how they said it: "I remember about when I first began to suspect myself of liking their gossip for its own sake." It is too bad that for once he could not have overcome his casual habits of recollection and been more precise as to names, dates, and circumstances, for the series of steps by which he finally fashioned his very personal poetic idiom are now almost obliterated.

Of greatest moment in this regard is the length of time that passed between the writing of the poultry sketches and his first experiments in verse with the Hall voice and attitude. If the evolution began as early as 1905, as Frost several times was to claim, then the poems that resulted could hardly have been more than feeble anticipations of the later master-pieces, either discarded or kept for later massive reworking, a procedure he seems to have used extensively. The sole poem in which he made direct use of his poultry experience was a straightforward ballad of fourteen quatrains celebrating a champion hen, no doubt one of John Hall's. Devoid of any attempt to catch speaking tones, what is interesting about "A Blue Ribbon at Amesbury" is the deft way it pictures a sight Frost must have witnessed a thousand times in his own backyard, a realistic approach not noticeable in his verse before this. A "fine pullet" has been in competition at the Amesbury show,

> And come with all her ribbons home.
> Her golden leg, her coral comb,
> Her fluff of plumage, white as chalk,
> Her shape, were all the Fancy's talk.

Back up on the roost with the other hens, the pullet "shoulders with a wing so strong," she moves the whole line of birds to make a spot for herself. Then with the night "setting in to blow," she settles down with "a complacent chirr," secure against the "dark and wind and cold."

In the other poems he is known to have written so early, only a stray line or phrase here and there manages to hint at what was to come. "Ghost House," written at the latest by the summer of 1905, affords a good example. Actually his first poem of any real merit—slight enough, it is true—it was also the first in which he attempted consciously to build on his rural experience. "Ghost House" was directly inspired by the old ruins of a family home that stood at the roadside just down from the Frost farm in Derry, a spot Frost walked past hundreds of times, and from which he transplanted wildflowers to his own property. Though graceful, the poem is unoriginal and rather too much on the sentimental side. Yet one whole stanza, the fourth, virtually leaps out of its context, speaking almost a different tongue from the rest of the poem. It sounds, in fact, not unlike some of the lines in *North of Boston*:

> *The whippoorwill is coming to shout*
> *And hush and cluck and flutter about:*
> *I hear him begin far enough away*
> *Full many a time to have his say*
> *Before he arrives to say it out.*

The same may be said for "A Line Storm Song," written by early 1906 at the latest, in which there are some nice touches of the sort he was later to make very much his own. There are clouds that are "tattered and swift," wayside flowers "too wet for the bee," puddles of rainwater in the road "aflutter with wind." But those are all. Whether or not he was writing in earnest during 1904–1907, the real breakthrough did not come until he had absorbed the spirit as well as sense of his rural surroundings and had settled on blank verse as his medium, learning to twine around its more or less regular rhythms the rougher natural cadences of regional speech. (Of course only a definite regional tone, a clear touch of the vernacular, could achieve what Frost was after in his verse. The everyday speech of most Americans lacks sufficient flavor.) Had it not been for the interruption to his writing caused by his teaching at Pinkerton, and by his several years' loss of ambition, that epochal event might well have occurred much sooner than it did. Easily overlooked is still another reason for the delay, one having less to do with his own life and talents than with the formidable task he had set himself—the sheer difficulty, for an outsider, of penetrating to the heart and soul of the Yankee social order, a pattern of daily life in which, as one critic has well observed, "reticence itself is one of the more important principles."

Judging from the handwritten booklet of poems sent to Susan Ward at Christmas 1911, it was during that year, or more probably in the year preceding, that the urge to write poetry had returned on Frost in full force. Whatever it was exactly that brought about the renewal, some part of that fortunate impulse may have been caught from the very thing that had damped his poetic urge in the first place, his involvement with school matters. In May 1910, led by Frost, the Pinkerton students mounted an unusually ambitious drama program, for which Frost also served as producer and director. Personally he undertook to adapt for the students' use no less than five plays: Marlowe's *Faustus*, Milton's *Comus*, Sheridan's *The Rivals*, and two by Yeats, *The Land of Heart's Desire* and *Cathleen ni Houlihan*. The exacting labor of working closely with these texts, condensing scenes and shortening speeches, could well have sparked the reawakening of his dormant artistic drive. Marlowe's supple blank verse, in particular, must have made its own strong appeal.

The return of ambition, however, did not bring with it any marked or immediate advance in ability, a fact which is made evident by the booklet's contents. Yet there is one poem in the little booklet, a poem definitely written at Plymouth in the fall of 1911 (though not published until more than thirty years later), which does carry considerable importance. So far as can be determined, it represents Frost's first surviving attempt to work with a pastoral or rural subject in blank verse. That it fails to come alive is beside the point, for its very existence is enough to prove that he had made a conscious start on the track of his new style more than a year before he went to England.

For anyone whose ear is familiar with the later Frost, the twenty-five-line blank verse monologue "To a Moth Seen in Winter" especially in a first and still unpublished version, offers a peculiar reading experience. It is much like listening to a favorite singer and finding that the well-remembered voice has unaccountably gone flat. Present is the true Frostian attitude toward its rural subject, and there are some typical moments of subtle observation, yet the lines are strangely neuter. Here is a portion lifted from the poem's middle:

> And now, pray tell, what lured you with false hope
> To make the venture of eternity
> And seek the love of kind in wintertime?
> But stay! But stay a little! Hear me out!
> Whither away so soon? Surely I think
> You make a labor of flight for one so airy,
> Spending yourself too much in self-support.
> Nor will you find love, either, nor love you.
> (And I, I pity in you something human,
> The old incurable untimeliness . . .

Though they fall short, what matters is the definite way these blank-verse lines edge close to the feeling of ordinary speech, and in that resides their value to the Frost story. Almost certainly, this was the poem that some friend or acquaintance of Frost's complained of as "sounding too much like talk," a remark which has, in differing forms, but without being linked to a time or person, taken a prominent place in the poet's legend. Though put forward as an objection, meaning that the poem needed the heightening of literary effects, the observation pleased rather than annoyed the author. As he said a few years later, he had long been groping toward something along the lines of talk-in-verse, and the chance remark had brought the subject to the upper levels of consciousness:

> Someone had complained that a little thing of mine was "too near the level of talk." I didn't see why it shouldn't be. So I resolved to go ahead and see what would happen if I went a little nearer with it. It wasn't all obstinacy. It was inspiration. In that criticism I suddenly saw something I had been on the track of ever since I had tasted success in words with a friend I used to sit late with in old high school days. Why was a friend so much more effective than a piece of paper in drawing the living sentences out of me? I thought it might come to my having to remember exactly the shape my sentences took under provocation or under social excitement.

The phrase "having to remember" can also be read as describing the physical effort of actually practicing the living sentences aloud. This practicing, in turn, supplies a link with the previously cited recollections of Sidney Cox and Ernest Silver, both of whom recalled, though unaware, having heard Frost in just such efforts to draw out the "shape" of the living sentences.

The listener who sat up talking with Frost in high school is unidentified. The one who years later complained about some poem as being too near talk is also unknown, but it may well have been the Reverend William Hayes Ward, brother of Susan and former editor of the New York *Independent*. In January 1912 Frost paid a social visit to the Wards, brother and sister, at their home in New Jersey, less than three weeks after sending Susan his little booklet, which includes the full text of "To a Moth Seen in Winter." Coming from Ward, such a comment would have been appropriate, for his taste in poetry ran heavily to its musical qualities, especially as heard in the work of Sidney Lanier. Admittedly the matter appears beyond proof, yet this much at least can be said: if it was not Ward who made the comment, and if "Moth" was not the poem that called it forth, it will be hard to find another candidate for either honor. Before this period—the fall of 1911—there is no other poem of record that could conceivably have prompted a comment on its qualities as "talk." Afterward, any such remark would have been a mere description of a technique to which Frost had already committed himself, thus of no shaping force in his career.

From the materials at hand, it may be concluded, there is no certain way of uncovering the magical moment when Frost first learned to write with confidence in his new voice. Perhaps such a rare and rarified artistic culmination will always be reserved by nature to the unbreachable privacy of the human mind. But there is one further step that might be taken in the search, a step which brings the elusive denouement a little nearer.

Not included in the 1911 booklet, and of no definite provenance, but prominent among the entries in *North of Boston*, is a poem so unlike any other published by Frost that it has always called perplexed attention to itself as something of a maverick. This is the 105-line "Blueberries," which preserves the memory of the Frost family's berrying expeditions in Derry. This curious poem must now be seen for what it is, not a full-fledged performance, but another early experiment, and what is more pertinent, also a failed one (it hardly deserves its place in *North of Boston*, where it functions as little more than a change of pace). In isolated phrases and passages "Blueberries" does, as was seen by a few early readers, catch some of the authentic flavor. Yet as a whole it fails badly, for it is not couched in the calm, flexible rhythms of blank verse, but in the bounce and jiggle of anapaestic tetrameter, made even noisier and more awkward by rhymed couplets. Instead of coiling around the words in a delicate union of sound and sense, the triple meter insistently pulls and tugs opposite to the meaning and nuance, preventing the lines from achieving the veritable air of talk. A sample will reveal the misdirected tension:

> "I've told you how once, not long after we came,
> I almost provoked poor Loren to mirth
> By going to him of all people on earth
> To ask if he knew any fruit to be had
> For the picking. The rascal, he said he'd be glad
> To tell if he knew. But the year had been bad.
> There had *been* some berries—but those were all gone.
> He didn't say where they had been. He went on:
> 'I'm sure—I'm sure'—as polite as could be.
> He spoke to his wife in the door, 'Let me see,

Mame, we don't know any good berrying place?'
It was all he could do to keep a straight face."

At some time not long after he wrote "Blueberries," Frost must have recognized his mistake. When he did so, when he at last saw clearly what it was he was seeking, he achieved it by making a masterful coalescence of his two separate experiments—the form of one with the content and manner of the other, the blank verse of "To a Moth Seen in Winter," with the rural attitudes and Yankee voice of "Blueberries." The identity of the poem in which this happened may never be known with certainty, but a guess may not be out of order: "The Housekeeper," in which Frost celebrates the memory of old John Hall, then dead some five years.

As a lad of eighteen, in 1894, having just sold his first poem to the New York *Independent*, Frost impulsively wrote a letter of thanks to the paper's editor, saying that as a true lover of poetry he felt an "inflexible ambition" to become a full-fledged poet himself. With the prodigal self-assurance of youth he added that in pursuit of his goal he was quite prepared to "idle away an age accumulating a greater inspiration." The age that the youthful dreamer offered up so glibly on the altar of art had lasted for a much longer time than he could ever have predicted, nearly twenty years. Now, as he resigned his position at the Normal school—closing his ears to his friends' warnings about so drastic a move for a family man, and at his age—stored his furniture, packed his crates and bags, and with his wife and children faced toward the Boston waterfront, he was on his way to a renewal of the freedom he had so grudgingly surrendered when he joined the teaching staff at Pinkerton. This time, however, there was a vital difference—which is why in his letter of March 1912 to his friend Mosher, he could so confidently talk of the poems he had "still under cover that more nearly represent what I'm going to be."

Considering the varied manuscripts reposing in his trunk—mostly rough, tentative, and incomplete as they no doubt were—his confidence was no more than proper. Before his foot touched British soil, Robert Frost was satisfied that he had succeeded in accumulating that greater inspiration, and knew pretty well the sort of poet he was going to be.

F I V E

THE SHOP
ON DEVONSHIRE STREET

RISING early in the Bungalow on the morning of Friday, October
25, Elinor Frost vowed that, despite her household chores and the
daily classes for Carol and Marjorie, before going to bed again she would
write no less than four letters to neglected friends back in the United
States. After getting the children up and fed, and Lesley and Irma off to
school, she settled down at the living-room table and succeeded in finish-
ing at least two of the promised four. In one of these she provides a
fleeting glimpse of the Frosts behind their vine-covered stucco walls, just
as they were trying to get comfortable in their English surroundings and
still perhaps feeling a trifle uneasy.

"It is seven weeks since we landed on this shore," she wrote, "and six
since we came to this little house, and I can scarcely believe it, the time
has passed so swiftly." She again refers to her "dear little cottage,"
indicating that she has not yet begun to feel hemmed in by the narrow
hallways, and says that in the days since they arrived all sorts of beautiful
flowers have bloomed in the back yard. The children, though mostly
happy and content, are already beginning to feel "homesick sometimes,"
which may indicate some initial difficulty over making friends among the
local children (there is no sign that for their time in Beaconsfield the
Frost children had any special playmates). It is the frank observation with
which she closes the letter that reveals most, showing how slight had

76

been the contact between the Frosts and their neighbors in those six weeks. Still standoffish, Elinor at least is not yet able to see past surface differences: "I wish I had time to write you all my impressions. We find everything most interesting. The people are very polite—but they are different from Americans. I would say that the majority I have had an opportunity to observe seem inferior to me, if I was not afraid of being prejudiced." (She means "seem to me to be inferior," of course, not "inferior to me.")

Though they were to live on Reynolds Road for a year and a half, the Frosts never did get to know any of their neighbors intimately. There is record, in fact, of only one sustained contact of any sort with a neighbor, a young wife who lived in the cottage called Clevedon, four houses down. This was Effie Solomon, who until shortly before her recent death at the age of ninety-two still lived at Clevedon and often spoke of her friendship with the Frosts. She was aware that Frost wrote poetry, and she remembered how on her visits to the Bungalow he would sometimes read his verses aloud. In this there is nothing improbable, for Frost later was to become well known for the easy way he would volunteer to read his poems, published and unpublished, for even casual visitors. Effie Solomon, it appears, was the first outside the Frost family to have had the privilege of hearing some of the work that was soon to command the delighted attention of literary circles in both England and America. The first quiet hint of that epochal development arrived at the Bungalow late in October in the form of a note from the firm of David Nutt.

Despite some careful probing, it still cannot be said with any precision just how long the manuscript of A Boy's Will lay unread in Mrs. Nutt's Bloomsbury Street office. Frost's own later estimates of all that transpired at this time altered slightly at each telling to fit the mood of the moment, a talker's privilege. Four or five days, or three, sometimes two, were his casual estimates of the interval that passed between his leaving the manuscript in London and the arrival of Nutt's note in the mail announcing acceptance. Matters did not transpire quite that rapidly, however, for a close look at all the surrounding events shows that the suspense must have lasted about two weeks, certainly no less than ten days.

Whether Mrs. Nutt was the only reader of the manuscript, or even the principal reader, is a more pertinent question and one no easier to settle. Frost himself professed to know nothing definite, though he admitted being curious about the matter, and once he asked Mrs. Nutt who her advisors were. For some unspecified reason, according to Frost, the woman refused to say. Long afterward, he seems to have decided that the reader of his manuscript was the young John Drinkwater, also a Nutt author and then very much a part of London's literary scene. If Nutt's reader was indeed Drinkwater, admittedly a logical choice, then it is strange that he overlooked the fact when writing his autobiography twenty years later. About Frost's poetry he has nothing to say, and refers to him only once, in passing and inaccurately, as "an American poet who was then a young wanderer in England." Still, Drinkwater remains a possibility, especially in view of the fact that some weeks after receiving the good news from Mrs. Nutt, Frost would actually meet the thirty-year-old dramatist.

In any case, it was no more than two days after Elinor carried out her letter-writing resolve that there arrived at the Bungalow a stiffish envelope bearing the return address of David Nutt. In it was a card signed by Mrs. Nutt and carrying her hurried scrawl on both sides. Many of the words were nearly unreadable and would have needed close study to decipher, especially the crucial phrase, "I am therefore disposed to bring out your poems." Curiously, of the moment when Frost managed to extract from the scrawl the meaning of those words, aided no doubt by an excited Elinor, only a single record remains. In a 1915 interview he said that after all those long years of trying, "The day my poetry was accepted in England was one of the happiest days of my life." In his many other interviews, and in the multitude of his remembered conversations, he never again reverted to that happy moment.

Some of the more subtle references in Mrs. Nutt's short, businesslike note could not have been evident to either of the Frosts on that first reading, but they are pertinent to the full story of his belated triumph. In its entirety the card reads:

17, Grape Street,
New Oxford Street
London W.C.

Editorial Office:—
6, Bloomsbury St., W.C.

26th October 1912

Dear Mr. Frost

I have looked through your manuscript and I am personally interested in the treatment of your theme. I am therefore disposed to bring out your poems if the proposal I can put before you and which would be on the principal of a royalty payment will suit you. I cannot put a dry and cut proposal before you as yet, as I want to think a little about the most suitable form to give to the book but I hope to be in a position to do so very soon.

Faithfully Yours
M. L. Nutt
David Nutt

Quite noticeable is the fact that Mrs. Nutt says nothing about the poems themselves, but only expresses a personal interest in the book's theme and its "treatment." This guarded way of stating her opinion (and her mistake with the idiomatic "cut and dried"), may indicate some lack of competence, as well as confidence, in the field of English poetry. Frost himself at some point became wary of her abilities in that direction, later recalling that "she didn't seem very literary herself." Still, as her novel shows, she did take an interest in adolescent psychology, so she may have been sincere in placing emphasis on the book's theme. But the rest of her note reveals the businesswoman, working patiently to bring Frost to the point where he would be willing to "help bear expenses," by giving up part of his royalties. A less blatant form of vanity publishing, this arrangement was one accepted by many authors at the time since it did not require them to make a cash payment in advance. For the Nutt firm, it also offered a satisfactory arrangement since it reduced the risk, and at the same time promised a larger profit should the book sell even moderately well. Of course, it could work only where a book showed some legitimate promise.

Stating her readiness to enter a royalty contract, on which Frost had insisted, she says she needs time to work up a proper offer, to be based on "the most suitable form to give the book." This was nothing more than a delaying tactic, designed to keep the eager author dangling. From the start, Frost's little volume was clearly meant for inclusion in Nutt's established line, "The Shilling Series of Modern Poets" (some of these still survive and most can be seen all too plainly as outright vanity items). First putting publication within his reach, the woman then makes him wait an indefinite length of time before unveiling her proposal. Especially since this would be Frost's first book, it was expected that as each anxious day passed he would edge closer to acceptance of certain clauses he would find embedded in the formal contract. Not surprisingly, the tactic worked as planned, though once fully unveiled it took a month or so to bring Frost to heel.

After the arrival of the first note, many days passed in silence, and for Frost no doubt in painful slowness. When a second note finally arrived—

as much as two weeks after the first, it would appear—it bore an invitation for him to call at the Nutt office to discuss a contract. At that second meeting he found that Mrs. Nutt was making some strong demands: she wanted world rights in the English language, and also expected to be given an exclusive option not just on his next book, but on his next four books, prose or verse. The royalty she offered was the day's usual rate for a first book, a straight twelve percent, but it would take effect only after sales had passed 250 copies. Until that figure was reached he would receive nothing. Finally, the first edition would be small, only a thousand copies, a safe total to start with.

Draft contract in hand, Frost went home to study the details and at this juncture, suspecting that the proposal was not a good one, he seems to have slowed matters somewhat. By mid-November, his head spinning, he had reached the conclusion that the contract was downright unfair. Yet at the same time he was also becoming very fearful of losing the chance for which he had hungered so long. His puzzlement was severe and at last it found an outlet in a letter he wrote on November 19 to a friend in the United States: "I have signed no contract as yet, but after what has passed, I suppose I am bound to sign, if pressed, almost anything that doesn't seem too one-sided . . . I suppose I ought to be proud to be so much in demand: the embarrassment is so novel in my experience . . . Am I too far committed to draw back? I am nearly the worst person in the world in a muddle like this." Of less immediate concern, if equally disturbing, was his natural apprehension that having all his first poetry issued by an English publisher might seem "traitorously un-American."

All too apparent are the contradictory feelings of being sorely beyond his depth yet anxious not to mishandle his great chance. In the end, as might be expected, his artistic ambition won out over his business instincts, and on December 16 he signed Nutt's contract, a one-page, typed document with nine short clauses. It was not long, however, before he awoke to his blunder in accepting, as he called it contemptuously, "a fool's contract." Even the clause which specified how often an accounting of sales should be rendered—"annually to the 31st December"—did not give a date by which this should be done each year. This meant, according to the loosely worded clause, that Nutt was not obligated to pay any royalties for fully fifteen months after the close of the first calendar year of sale.

Whether Frost really understood the import of the 250-copy exemption from his royalties is uncertain but may be taken as doubtful. In reality, it meant that for a book whose price was to be fixed at one shilling sixpence, he was handing over to Mrs. Nutt the first twenty-four pounds of the author's share of his book's earnings, a sum equal to several months rent on the Bungalow. But it was the option clause that represented his most grievous misstep. Not only did it tie him to Nutt for his next four books, each of which the publisher might or might not decide to publish, it did so "on the same terms" as the first volume. Frost's acceptance of that rapacious condition may serve as the final indication of how badly he wanted to see a volume in the bookstores with his name on it.

And yet his signing of the one-sided contract, with all its defects, must have yielded him a measure of real joy, especially when he found that so small a volume—at most it would hardly exceed fifty pages—needed no time at all to print, bind, and distribute. Before the month of February 1913 was done, as Mrs. Nutt informed him, he could expect to see his book on the shelves.

*   *   *

ONE of the burdens carried by Frost throughout the period of his early struggles, felt heavily or lightly according to mood and circumstance, was the generally overlooked fact of his artistic isolation. At no time during his youthful meandering in the nineties, or during his years in poultry farming or in teaching, had he enjoyed even brief contact with other artists. The sympathetic understanding of another practicing poet, or of any mind with a creative force to match his own, had been entirely denied him. For any artist attempting to fashion work of the high originality of Frost's, such isolation so long continued must have been a severe handicap. For Frost this would have proved particularly true, for it was to a large degree by means of the give-and-take of freewheeling discussion on an intellectual plane that he was best able to control and organize his thoughts, in the process generating the necessary self-confidence. Especially in the period after 1910, as he entered his mid-thirties and began groping, still vaguely but with some realizing sense of purpose, toward his true poetic identity would this lack have made itself felt, and there are signs that this is very much what happened.

In England, during his first months, that isolation had continued unbroken, Frost having no contact with writers or literary circles beyond his friend at *T. P.'s Weekly* and any others he may have met at the weekly's office. But then, early in the new year, some three weeks after signing the Nutt contract, his lonely road took a sudden turning. With heady speed he found himself a participant, far beyond anything he could have expected, in the bustle of literary London, enjoying ready access to many of the leading poets of the day. This abrupt shift in his fortunes came at just the right moment in his career, when he needed it most, and the day of its beginning can be stated exactly: Wednesday, January 8, 1913. It was on that day, at about four in the afternoon, that The Poetry Bookshop, a unique venture of the British editor-poet, Harold Monro, was given its formal opening in London. Crowding the narrow premises in Devonshire Street to talk, drink tea, listen to speakers and to poetry being read aloud, and to celebrate what everyone hoped would be a new day for British poetry, was a noisy gathering of three hundred. Included were writers, poets, playwrights, editors, journalists, and sundry *litterateurs* of all kinds and degrees. Among them, feeling just a bit giddy as he brushed elbows with the elite of contemporary English literature, was Frost.

Devonshire Street in 1913 was not a location that could be expected to harbor bookshops, let alone a shop devoted entirely to the field of poetry. A short, narrow span, it ran on a straight line between heavily traveled Theobold's Road at its southern end, and the "decayed elegance" of small, quiet Queen Square to the north. Though it lay close to the British Museum, no more than five minutes away on foot, it was part of a seedy, run-down enclave whose rows of eighteenth-century houses sheltered large numbers of poor families. Short as the street was—it stretched for only some two hundred yards—among its faded house fronts it boasted many shops, as well as three pubs. In daylight hours and through a good part of the night, the darkness relieved only by the dingy glow of gas lamps standing at intervals, the sidewalks and gutters were crowded with ragged children, "grubby urchins" in the phrase of the day.

The offbeat location had been deliberately chosen, not only because it lay near the University of London and other large institutions and office buildings, but with an eye toward the appeal of the picturesque. For many of the shop's customers, as Monro admitted, "the novelty of the idea and the obscurity of the street were the principal appeal," at least at first. So struck was one enthusiast by the combination of literature and lowlife that he wrote a sonnet entitled, "The Bookshop in the Slum." This hint of the romantic in the shop's location was lost on more practical natures, including Monro's wife, who saw Devonshire Street as "a shabby little thoroughfare . . . where rubbish sometimes hurtled down from upper story windows on the heads of unwary pedestrians." The bookshop (unfortunately destroyed in a bombing raid in 1943), stood at about the street's midpoint, exactly opposite a covered alleyway called Gage Street (still there and still covered). Its black-painted wooden front, framing a many-paned display window, usually bore a tangle of crude chalk decorations contributed by the urchins.

Entered by a door to the left, the ground floor presented a longish, high-ceilinged main room resembling a quiet, comfortable study in some elegant residence. The walls, and the tiers of bookshelves built into them, were of gleaming dark brown wood. Scattered round on thick carpets were tables and chairs, and one or two sofas, all of heavy oak. On the right was a large fireplace, and round the three other walls, halfway up, ran a small gallery, below which were hung framed woodcuts. At the rear a curtained doorway led to an office and a flight of stairs. The upper floors of the three-story building, all a part of the shop, were planned as meeting rooms and cheap accommodations for transient artists (Frost himself, with the family, was to make use of the rooms a year later).

Though not opened formally until January 1913, the bookshop was doing business as early as the previous November, and it was then, or perhaps in December, that Frost first encountered it. Mrs. Nutt, or someone in her office, would have called his attention to it simply as a matter of good business, but in any case it received wide attention in papers and magazines, including *T. P.'s Weekly*. Early in December Frost was in town to discuss his contract, and it may have been then that he paid his first visit to the bookshop, which was only a short walk from the Nutt office on Bloomsbury Street.

"You are not asked to buy poetry when you enter the shop," reported *T. P.'s Weekly*. "You are left quite alone and permitted to handle the volumes and to sit down on the excellent Romney Green settles and read and loiter to your heart's content." It was just this relaxed atmosphere, as Frost later recalled, that he encountered on the occasion of his first visit. A shop assistant looking down from his perch on one of the wall ladders gave him a nod of welcome, then turned back to his shelves, leaving Frost to browse. Knowing of the planned opening festivities, Frost asked the assistant if they were open to the public, and was told that admission was by special invitation only. Still, the man added, if Frost were to come round on the night in question he probably would not be turned away. It was in that haphazard fashion that he was led to make the trip to London on January 8, and at the shop door was relieved and gratified to find himself courteously admitted. Making his way through the noisy crush he found a seat with several others on the narrow iron stairway that spiraled its way up to the gallery.

After the company had been treated to two or three speeches, followed by several poetry readings, one by John Drinkwater, tea was served. It was during this relaxed period, with the guests mingling freely in the narrow room, that Frost made two acquaintances, both of whom in different ways were to prove of decisive importance to him. The first of the two, British poet Frank S. Flint, was to become a good friend, and would open to Frost the whole active world of English poetry, as well as introducing him to a little known poet-critic, T. E. Hulme, who would help him achieve a final formulation of his poetic theories. The second, an aspiring poetess named Mary Gardner, wife of one of the country's leading archaeologists, was to play a role even more important in Frost's literary career. She would be instrumental in providing the setting, far to the north in Scotland, from which would come one of Frost's most memorable poems, "Mending Wall."

Apparently it was the twenty-seven-year-old Flint, who had taken a seat on the iron steps just below Frost, who made the first move. A thin-faced, bespectacled civil servant, friendly but diffident in manner, Flint looked up and inquired pleasantly if he was correct in thinking that Frost was an American. Frost answered yes, and asked how his questioner had guessed. His glance dropping to a level with Frost's feet, Flint replied, "Your shoes." In England men's shoes were not so square-toed, he explained. The two introduced themselves and before long they discovered that they were fellow poets, Flint already with a book to his credit. Called *In the Net of the Stars*, it had been published three years before, by the respected firm of Elkin Matthews. Perhaps a bit defensively, Frost explained that he too had a volume, or would have when it was issued by Nutt in a few weeks.

At some point that evening Flint performed his first important service for Frost, asking whether he was acquainted with another young American poet then living and working in London, named Ezra Pound. As a reviewer of poetry, Flint said, Pound had access to several literary periodicals, including the new American monthly *Poetry,* so it wouldn't hurt to know him. When Frost admitted that he had not heard Pound's name before, Flint laughingly warned him never to let Pound hear him say that, a light remark but one which must have put Frost somewhat on his guard. Volunteering to arrange a meeting between Frost and his countryman, Flint went even further in his efforts to be helpful, saying that he would himself look for a chance to review Frost's book.

With Flint's friendly offer, and his advice about Pound, all that Frost had been told about the special nature of book reviewing in London—that it was largely through personal contact with the leading names that books of poetry were able to find reviewers at all, and that the Poetry Bookshop was fast becoming a center where any number of reviewers might be met at any time—was confirmed. (Another American hopeful then in England, J. G. Fletcher, put the matter bluntly when he recalled that literary success at that time "lay less in merit than in cleverly handled contacts with the dominant figures of the day.") Thus the exchange with Flint, alone, accomplished a large part of Frost's purpose in attending the shop's opening.

Just how, in that milling crowd, Frost managed to meet and become friendly with the bright, articulate Mary Gardner, and her daughter Phyllis who had accompanied her, it would be interesting to know. Perhaps the introduction came through Flint, who was on intimate terms with a great number of those present, starting with Monro himself. As it turned out, the two had something in common, for Mrs. Gardner also had a small volume of poems about to be published, illustrated with woodcuts by her daughter. Her publisher was J. M. Dent, a name that carried considerably more weight than that of David Nutt (from all the signs, her book was an outright vanity item, something Frost would later discover to his intense discomfort). The Gardners had two other children, a daughter, Delphis, and a son, Christopher, who were about the same age as Lesley and Carol. However it may have happened, when Frost left the shop that day he took with him Mrs. Gardner's invitation for the Frosts and their children to visit the Gardner's at their home just south of London, at Tadworth in Surrey.

As the crowd began to break up, Frost found that Flint's book was on sale in the shop. In what appears a deliberate, none-too-subtle bid for closer acquaintance, but which perhaps was also prompted by a certain amount of curiosity, with its shy author looking on he bought a copy. Flint responded by handing Frost his card and asking to have Nutt send him a review copy of *A Boy's Will*. If Frost met anyone beyond Flint and the two Gardner women that evening, other than in passing, it has escaped the record. In any case, what did happen to him, and what it led to, was sufficient to bear out the truth of an observation made by another writer intimately acquainted with pre–World War I London. In those days, Ford Madox Ford fondly remarked, London "was unrivalled in its powers of assimilation—the great, easy-going, tolerant, lovable, old dressing-gown of a place that it was then, but was never more to be."

It had been a highly successful outing for Frost, not only for the contacts he had made, but equally for the sheer enjoyment he felt at being among his artistic peers. Something of that response can be gleaned from an unusual letter he wrote Flint two weeks later, in which he mixed several different, even contradictory moods. Rather awkwardly, he combines a rare personal note of confession with a tortuous attempt to give his honest opinion of Flint's poems—which could not have been high—without offending the younger man. The letter's opening paragraph, even discounting its overstatement, shows just how deeply he had been affected in prior years by the deprivation of artistic sympathy. It shows, as well, that during the festivities at the bookshop he had made no effort to conceal his joy, amounting almost to bubbling high spirits, over hearing poetry read and discussed with serious intent as a natural part of life:

Dear Mr. Flint:—

I trust there was nothing ambiguous in my rather frank enjoyment of an unusual situation the other night. Considering certain gentle jibes you dealt me, I am not quite sure in the retrospect that you didn't think I was laughing at someone or something, as the American papers laughed (some of them) at Yeats. You will take my word for it that there was nothing in my sleeve: I showed just what I felt. I was only too childishly happy in being allowed to make one for a moment in a company in which I hadn't to be ashamed of having written verse. Perhaps it will help you to understand my state of mind if I tell you that I have lived for the most part in villages where it were better that a millstone were hanged about your neck than that you should own yourself a minor poet.

Having admitted so much about himself, he then launches directly into his reaction to Flint's *In the Net of the Stars*. Even without a knowledge of what must in all honesty be called Flint's lackluster verse, a reader would have no trouble in detecting Frost's intellectual contortions. Nonplussed at the pedestrian air of his new friend's writing, he gropes for something good to say, and it is with a surprising degree of obfuscation that he broaches the subject at all:

About your book. Promise not to suspect me of reviewing it as of obligation, because I bought it so ostentatiously under your eyes, and I will tell you in a word what I think of it. Poet-like you are going to resent my praising what I want to praise in it, when it comes to details. But you wont mind my saying in general that the best of it is where it came from. And the next best is the beautiful sad figure of the title, which recurring in the body of the book, and, if I recollect aright, in the poem in the English Review, gives to the whole significance. We are in the net of the stars to our sorrow as inexorably as the Olympian pair were in another net to their shame.

All his life Frost was drawn to the subject of astronomy, so that his liking for Flint's figurative title may be taken as sincere. But when he says of the volume that "the best of it is where it came from," he is walking the fine edge of critical double-talk, involving no possible compliment to Flint. His next comments, making a brave effort to be specific, could only have been penned in some anguish of soul, or perhaps in a mood of simple abandon. At this precise moment, it must be remembered, he was himself engaged in writing some of the most original, powerful, down-to-earth poetry of this century:

> I don't know what theory you may be committed or dedicated to as an affiliated poet of Devonshire St., but for my part give me an out-and-out metaphor. If that is old-fashioned, make the most of it. And give me a generous sprinkling of words like "brindled" for the bees, "gauze" for the sea-haze, "little mouths" for the half-opened lilac flowers, "wafer" for the moon, "silver streak" for the swan's mirrored neck and "tarnished copper" for her beak. (And by the way wasn't streak with beak a fruitful rhyme?)

Except for an aptitude for languages and an unusual depth of sincerity, Flint was a man of limited artistic abilities (though he has, because of his link with the beginnings of the Imagist movement, been accorded a fair amount of attention in histories of the period). Anyone today who glances through *In the Net of the Stars* will appreciate the quandary in which Frost found himself, wanting to offer a sincere opinion but not at the risk of giving offense. Not a few of the poems in Flint's thin volume, reading rather like Yeatsian parody, cross the line to the simplistic and Frost must have smiled if not winced at some of the sentiments ("O love, your little bosoms are/ more to me than the death of a star;/ And the wet grass beneath your feet/ I will gather to take with me to sleep"). Still, determined to remain on good terms with the first published poet he had ever met, one who was able to open doors, he ends his critical excursion (the first he had made on the work of a living poet), with a last attempt to cover his tepid response. "All this is uncalled-for, I know," he writes. "The more reason, from my point of view for saying it. I had your book, I had your card, I had the impression of your prevailing mood, I was impelled to write, and I have written." At that he drops the subject, but he does not bring his long letter to a close without adding a masterstroke, clearly meant to pique Flint's further interest in this middle-aged American poet. Making a veiled reference to his years of isolation on the Derry farm, he confides archly,

You make me long to ask you a question that your book only makes a lovely pretext of answering. When the life of the streets perplexed me a long time ago I attempted to find an answer to it for myself by going literally into the wilderness, where I was so lost to friends and everyone that not five people crossed my threshold in as many years. I came back to do my day's work in its day none the wiser.

Taken broadly—the only proper way to take Frost in such moments—and despite what has been charged, there is no real untruth in those words, only what might be called subjective reemphasis. Circumstances, artistic and personal, really did "perplex" him and drive him to move to farming country with his wife and, at that time, one child. In its contrast to the city of Lawrence, where he had lived since the age of ten, the rural Derry of 1900 might well have seemed to a young dreamer to be a veritable wilderness. Callers during the first phase at the Derry farm may have numbered more than five, but, as can be shown, not many more. And he did "come back" from the farm, to a teaching job at the Derry high school, without having found the answer to what it was that had perplexed him—success as a poet—a detail he prefers not to specify. And in that last, elaborate oversight is the paragraph's beauty.

It is noticeable that the question Frost says he longs to ask is nowhere stated, so it would have been natural for Flint to inquire about it at his next opportunity. In his answer, dated January 30, that is just what he did. And while he thanks Frost for the comment on his poems, a dubious form of "praise" which he apparently found gratifying, he was not wholly taken in. In silent rebuttal he goes to the trouble of enclosing a laudatory notice of his poems from another hand:

Dear Mr. Frost,

I apologize to you for not writing before to thank you for your very kind letter. I have added you to Arnold Bennett and a chemist's assistant in New Foundland, making three strangers to me who have understood what I was about in my little book. You will see what Arnold Bennett wrote from the enclosed sheet . . . Why did you not ask the question my book is only a pretense of answering? Why be so timid in these things? Why, for instance, did you run away when you heard that a woman was coming with us? She did not come after all. I like your letter immensely, though, it is the sort of praise that pleases one. I only wish my poems were more worthy of it.

Since the surviving Flint-Frost correspondence is interrupted at this point, not resuming until early summer, that particular question seems destined to remain unasked.

In the same letter, Flint kept his word about putting Frost in touch with the young American writer, Ezra Pound. A calling card was enclosed bearing Pound's name and address—10 Church Walk, Kensington—all printed in red. No specific message of invitation appeared on or with the card. Instead, Pound had scrawled in pencil across the card's bottom the brusque phrase, "At home—sometimes." The glib inference that the privilege of seeing its author would be worth any trouble taken to find him at home (no telephone number appeared) struck Frost as very much in keeping with what Flint had already said of Pound's crudities. Still, he decided, if Pound was someone who could help provide publicity for A Boy's Will, then he would be able to put up with a good deal of the man's nonsense. Awaiting the proper moment for its use, he placed the card in his wallet.

In closing his letter, Flint asked in friendly fashion, "Do you ever come to London?" an invitation Frost would certainly have answered in the affirmative. From what is known of the movements of the two in the following weeks, however, it appears that their next meeting did not take place until late February, again at the Poetry Bookshop, when Frost may have attended some poetry readings. From the first these were one of the shop's regular features, held every Tuesday and Thursday evening at six, in an upstairs room. (Public readings were an integral part of Monro's original design for the shop's character, but he was frequently guilty of exaggerated claims as to their value. Once, carried completely away, he insisted that books of poetry should be regarded as no more than "printed scores" to refresh the memory of public readers.)

The first few readings at the bookshop seem to have gotten off to a slow start. One by the popular Rupert Brooke, given three weeks after the opening, drew less than a dozen listeners. Interest soon picked up, however, and within a year, regularly attracting crowds of thirty or forty and more, they had become a fixture of London's literary scene. In the course of the next few years most of England's poets, of high and low degree, were invited to read at the shop their own as well as others' works. Frost, though he was certainly available and within reach for most of the ensuing two years, never made such an appearance, not even when his English reputation had reached its height in 1914 with the publication of North of Boston. Since throughout his stay in England he remained on good terms with Monro and the bookshop, it is hard to think that he was never invited. More likely, he was invited more than once but, moved by whatever nervous apprehension about his then untried abilities as a reader of verse, declined. In view of the enormous reputation he was to gain as a platform performer, beginning on his return to the United States, Monro's missed opportunity is ironic.

In the first days of February 1913, perhaps in the same mail that brought Flint's letter since they were posted in London on the same day, there arrived at the Bungalow a small package containing something infinitely more welcome than the letter, the proofs of A Boy's Will. At that time Frost was caught up in what, from the evidence of his own statements and the actual work completed, must have been a veritable fever of composition. "You have no idea," he had written a friend at Christmas in discussing his writing habits, "of the way I mismanage myself since I broke loose and ceased to keep hours." But with the arrival of the proofs, which were badly behind schedule for February publication, poetry was put aside.

As may still be seen today, the proofs were surprisingly clean, and his reading of the fifty-two pages, even if he brooded over them repeatedly, not unlikely for an author with a first book, would have taken no more than two or three days. No changes were made in the texts of the poems themselves, and the only addition was an acknowledgment of the several American magazines in which nine of the thirty-two poems had been published initially. These names Nutt grouped inconspicuously on the final page, by oversight omitting one of the four names Frost had listed. When the corrected proofs were returned to the Nutt office, by mail or by Frost in person, he had the satisfaction of knowing that one short month would see the completed book in his hands.

That brief interruption to his writing was followed a few days later by another, less happy interruption when Lesley was brought home from school with a severely sprained ankle. Advised by a local doctor to have the injury looked at by a specialist, Frost took his daughter to London where the foot was x-rayed, with the result that the sprain was pronounced "a very bad case. She may be two months off her feet." The prognosis proved correct, and it was the last days of March before the disappointed girl was allowed to walk again. Meantime, as her mother commented in a letter, "She is very nervous, of course, and it is difficult to make her days pass pleasantly."

These winter months early in 1913, during which Frost was steadily producing the revolutionary poetry that would go into his second volume, must have been unusually trying ones for him. During weeks at a stretch the weather continued dismal, bringing long periods of dark days and cold rain, or dank skies full of threatening clouds, a state of things that Elinor confessed she found to be particularly depressing. Since the other three children were also kept indoors by the wet and the chill, joining their sister who occupied a chair in the living room with her bandaged ankle propped up, her reaction is not surprising.

Frost, hunting for a quiet spot in the Bungalow to do his writing, hemmed in by the few small rooms and the narrow hallway, at last began to feel a little desperate. Now in heading his letters he customarily gave as his address not his usual breezy, "The Bungalow, Beaks, Bucks," but another joking phrase, "The Bung. Hole." When a correspondent mistakenly used that phrase as a legitimate address, Frost corrected him and explained drily that the words meant "The Bung for short and Hole by discourtesy." Often in these weeks of clammy weather and crowded rooms he was able to find the necessary solitude only by staying up long past the time when the others were asleep, writing poetry until two or three in the morning at the dining table in the silence of the firelit living room.

SIX

ALL SORTS OF A GAME

A WEEK or so before the planned publication date of *A Boy's Will*—now set for March 13—Frost put aside his writing and took the train from Beaconsfield to London. This time, instead of heading for his usual haunts in the area around the British Museum and the Poetry Bookshop, he turned in the opposite direction and made for the residential neighborhood crowding against the southwest corner of spacious Kensington Gardens. The house he was seeking would not have been easy to find for it stood in a narrow little jumble of streets at the back of gray-walled, high-steepled St. Mary Abbott's Church. Turning off Kensington High Street he skirted an ancient graveyard at the rear of the church, then swung into a shallow, dead-end spur. At a dingy-looking, three-story building of yellowed brick, the last on the right, he pressed the buzzer. Ringing through No. 10 Church Walk, the sound of the doorbell signalled the opening of Frost's personal publicity campaign on behalf of his forthcoming book.

In reality, he was rather late in getting started. No doubt it had taken time to overcome the feeling that a certain crassness was involved in openly seeking attention for his book. But with publication so near, and perhaps urged by Mrs. Nutt, he could no longer resist making use of the card Ezra Pound had sent him through Flint. The energetic, twenty-seven-year-old Pound, besides contributing a review, could also furnish introductions to a good many of London's leading literary names. Whatever lingering reluctance Frost may have felt would have been dispelled by his awareness that, for him, time was running out: a bare two weeks after the appearance of his book he would celebrate his thirty-ninth birthday. As it happened, once he was aboard London's literary merry-go-round it seems that he came to enjoy the challenge. "Getting reviewed for poetry over here is all sorts of a game," he remarked buoyantly in a letter soon after starting his campaign.

The ringing bell of No. 10 brought the landlady, who directed him up a narrow flight of stairs to a closed door on the second-floor landing. His knock was answered by a muffled shout to wait, and a few seconds later the door was opened by a fresh-faced, gray-eyed young man sporting a mounting shock of reddish hair and a trim, pointed beard. He had been having a wash, Pound apologized as he knotted the belt of a purple silk dressing gown.

The one-room flat in which Frost found himself was small and cluttered. To the right of the entrance door a white enamel bedstead stood along the wall. Set against the other walls, all hung with pictures, were a tall cupboard, a large wardrobe, a nondescript couch, and some leather trunks. Between two windows at the further end of the room stood an oak table heaped with papers, magazines, and books, and a battered typewriter. In the room's far corner were a mahogany washstand and a cast-iron stove, and filling its center was a square table with several cane chairs.

Pound's opening remark, as Frost would later recall it, quickly bore out Flint's warnings about the young man's manner: in a tone that was far too brusque, he asked why his visitor had taken so long to call round. Then came an abrupt request, more like a demand, to see a copy of the new book. Frost had not yet received his advance copies of A Boy's Will, and even if he had thought of stopping off at Nutt's to get one, carrying it directly to Pound would have seemed too much like begging. Explaining to Pound that he'd be glad to have a copy sent, he was surprised to hear his host announce that together they would immediately make the trip over to Nutt's and get one. Gratified by such eagerness, Frost agreed.

When the two started off they may have intended going by motor-bus or by Underground. For whatever reason—it may have been one of those marvelously crisp and mild London days of early spring, and in any case both men were athletic and fond of walking—they decided to make the journey on foot. Their most probable route would have taken them through the length of Kensington Gardens and Hyde Park, along tree-shaded Rotten Row to Hyde Park Corner, next along wide Piccadilly, then north on Charing Cross Road. At a normally brisk pace, something over an hour would have been needed to get them to Bloomsbury Street. (This route readily suggests itself as the obvious one from Pound's flat. A point is made of it because some few critics, preferring to believe that Frost lied about not having the book with him, have rejected his claim that the two actually walked the whole distance to get it. On a mild day it is still a pleasant walk, especially through the park, by Rotten Row or beside the Serpentine, and the distance can easily be covered in an hour and a quarter. The return to the flat may also have been done on foot, or the two may have chosen to ride.)

At the Nutt office, for some reason they were given only a single copy of the book, and it went not to its author but into the reaching hands of Pound. Long remembered by Frost from that day was a single fact: he never touched the thin, bronze-colored volume clutched so tantalizingly in his companion's hand. Pound, perhaps assuming that Frost had already examined a copy, never thought to offer.

In all of this, Pound's eagerness to see Frost's book deserves some notice, for it was not, as is usually assumed, motivated solely by a wish to further the career of a fellow American, or to aid the cause of literature. At that time in London Pound had just begun serving as European correspondent for the new American monthly, *Poetry*, founded in Chicago only six months before by Harriet Monroe. The post paid a negligible and uncertain salary, but it gave him at a stroke what he wanted most, literary standing in the eyes of his English friends, as well as an assured American outlet for his own verse. Eager to establish itself, the magazine sought to take the lead in discovering new talent, and Pound was soon caught up in the effort. Tirelessly he worked to provide the Chicago office with frequent "scoops," as he called them. "We must be taken seriously, and *at once*," he insisted to Harriet Monroe. "We must be the voice not only for the U.S. but internationally." When he repeated that eager sentiment in a later note to Miss Monroe he again stressed the need for avoiding delay: "We have got to be taken seriously, and *at once*." Given this purpose, his quick interest in Frost comes into focus as a natural part of the magazine's policy.

Back at the Church Walk flat no time was wasted in talk. Telling Frost to find something to read, Pound said he would have a look through *A Boy's Will*. In the subsequent silence, while Frost sat paging through a magazine, there came a slight chuckle from Pound who, without looking up and omitting to specify the poem, asked, "You don't mind our liking this?" Amused by the youthful pomposity, Frost replied, "No, go ahead and like it." Then he ventured to guess which of the poems had brought the chuckle, and Pound confirmed it: "In Neglect." Occurring at the volume's middle, the poem consisted of only five lines:

> *They leave us so to the way we took,*
> *As two in whom they were proved mistaken,*
> *That we sit sometimes in the wayside nook,*
> *With mischievous, vagrant, seraphic look*
> *And try if we cannot feel forsaken.*

With that, it is said, Frost abruptly volunteered the information that there was "quite a story behind those lines." According to Lawrance Thompson, he then began "pouring out an overdramatized and not too accurate version" of the supposed story, how his grandfather and his uncle, both dead, had "mistreated" him by depriving him of his rightful legacy. But that view of what happened is most improbable. Frost would hardly have offered a blanket indictment of his grandfather and uncle, for his view of each was necessarily quite different.

Frost's grandfather had died in 1901 at the age of seventy-eight, having retired from the important position of overseer in a Lawrence textile mill. Instead of leaving a regular share of his fairly substantial estate to his only grandson, whom he viewed as unstable—not without cause, it must be admitted—he had set up a trust fund paying an annuity (which might have been larger except that a part of the estate was allotted to Jeanie Frost). He also deeded his grandson habitation rights to the Derry farm, withholding full ownership for a period of ten years—by which time, he hoped, his grandson would have settled down to something more substantial than poetry. Frost's granduncle, Elihu Colcord, his grandmother's brother, was also a man of some wealth, from whom Frost also expected to inherit. But Colcord, who died shortly after the grandfather, left his entire estate, some $15,000, to a New Hampshire Congregationalist seminary. Perhaps with some justification, Frost felt that his career would have been very different, his fulfillment not so long delayed, had he received a regular portion from his uncle. For one thing, he would not have suffered the serious interruption to his developing abilities that began in 1906, when he left the farm to spend five years as a teacher at Pinkerton.

Some hint of these matters Frost certainly did reveal during his visit at Church Walk, no doubt rambling on in that outspoken and indiscreet style that was to become one of his most fascinating, and alarming, conversational traits. He could hardly have realized how closely Pound was taking it all in.

They parted that day when Pound announced that he would immediately, that very moment, start a review of *A Boy's Will* for the Chicago magazine, and Frost "had better run along home" so he could get to work. Leaving Church Walk, Frost carried with him presentation copies of two of Pound's own most recent books of poetry, as well as an invitation that they meet again for lunch.

Very quickly Pound was reporting his new find to Chicago. "Have just discovered another Amur'kn," he wrote Harriet Monroe around March 8. "Vurry Amur'kn, with, I think, the seeds of grace. Have reviewed an advance copy of his book, but have run it out too long. Will send it as soon as I've tried to condense it—also some of his stuff if it isn't all in the book." When he wrote again several days afterward he enclosed the shortened review. "It's our second scoop," he explained, "for I only found the man by accident and I think I've about the only copy of the book that has left the shop . . . We should print this notice at once as we ought to be first and some of the reviewers here are sure to make fuss enough to get quoted in N.Y." (What he says about having the only copy can hardly be accurate, for *A Boy's Will* was published only a few days after the date of this letter.)

During the remainder of March and into the first days of April, while he waited anxiously for the first reviews, Frost had the heady experience of meeting, through Pound and Flint, at least a half-dozen of England's best-known writers, novelists, and poets. Among them were Ford Madox Ford (then Heuffer), Maurice Hewlett, Richard Aldington, Hilda Doolittle, Ernest Rhys, and May Sinclair, a parade of names that culminated with an invitation from William Butler Yeats (conveyed through Pound), to attend one of the regular Monday night gatherings at his London apartment. While he was grateful for their interest in his work, and very much alive to the good they could do him, Frost was well past the age where he might have been awed by such people. Of these early acquaintances, it was only with Yeats and May Sinclair that he managed to find reason for further meetings.

The contact with Yeats began when Pound relayed the exciting news that his friend had not only read *A Boy's Will*, but had pronounced it nothing less than "the best poetry written in America for a long time." Coming from the leading poet in English, this was far more than anyone could have hoped for, and if Yeats would allow his opinion to be quoted, then Frost might have the start of at least a small triumph. Happily he went, with Pound, to attend a gathering at Yeats' apartment, at No. 18 Woburn Buildings, probably on the evening of Monday, March 31. Just off Russell Square, it was only around the corner from the Premier Hotel, where the Frosts had stopped on first reaching London.

From the beginning of his residence in the flat twenty years before, Yeats had welcomed to it the great and near-great of English literature, as well as many young hopefuls, and the experience had become dear in the memories of many writers. A good description of it is to be found in the words of a staff reporter from *T. P.'s Weekly,* who went there to interview the poet in the very week of Frost's own first visit. Occupying a full page, the interview was printed on April 4, 1913. It shows that the reporter approached the assignment in a properly reverential mood:

> I had dreamed of a subdued atmosphere free of the disillusioning effects of electric light and all the latest improvements—and I found it. The house was reticent; the poet himself opened the door and led me up the narrow, dark staircase till we reached his own bachelor room, dimly lighted by the red coals cuddled together in the grate, and two candles in tall, green candlesticks set upon the table. The pictures on the wall looked sleepily through the shadows, and as I sank down in a low armchair in front of the fire, I felt with relief that this was a fitting house for a poet and a mystic . . . Mr. Yeats seated himself upon an old wooden settle opposite me, a tall, dark man, with an almost Spanish type of face, and a quiet, modulated voice.

The pictures on the walls of the sitting room, according to frequent visitor, John Masefield, included several engravings by Blake, as well as original paintings by Yeats's father and others. Masefield also mentioned the high-backed wooden settle and the ornate candles, as well as a low divan and many bookcases. Between two other candles, both huge, there stood a stout wooden lectern on which an oversize volume of Chaucer lay open. At the center of the room a round table held various jars containing water, wine, and cigarettes. The walls were papered dark brown, creating an atmosphere that was decidedly somber.

Yeats himself played the dominant part at these special evenings, a fact vividly recalled by Masefield, who described Yeats' talk—which tended to run to monologue—as "brilliant and unfailing, coming from some undying source of wisdom and wit, never bitter, often merry, always generous, helpful and inspiring; wholly delightful to his hearers." Some others, less prone to reverence, recalled Yeats as remote and superior, even rather affected. One regular attendant at these Monday nights, a

subeditor for the *English Review*, recalled how on his first visit he had
been slow to catch the prevailing mood. Sitting beside Yeats on the
wooden settle, he listened politely as a young Indian woman in a sari at
his feet begged the poet to sing one of the lyrics he had composed to an old
Irish air. Yeats, who was tone-deaf, readily complied by using "a sort of
dirgelike incantation, calculated to send any unhappy giggler into hys-
terics. I bore it as long as I could, but at last the back of the settle began to
shake and I received the impact of one of the poet's nasty glances from
behind his pince-nez. Mercifully I recovered but it was an awful experience." Both views of the Irish poet were to be confirmed by Frost, who
always afterward thought of Yeats as perhaps the best talker he had ever
heard, but a man terribly lost in affectation.

Of Frost's personal experience that night little survives. The older
man's plays were discussed, but not at any length, and the closest the two
came to an exchange of literary interest occurred when Frost made bold
to assert that he could usually tell whether a particular poem had been
written quickly under a sudden impulse or had been much labored over.
Giving an example, he made a guess that one of Yeats' best-known lyrics,
"The Song of Wandering Aengus," had been completed swiftly at a single
sitting. Sighing, Yeats answered that the brief poem had cost him at least
nine agonizing hours, and had been composed "during his terrible years,"
which all present took as referring to his long and frustrated pursuit of
Maude Gonne. If Frost's own book was mentioned there is no record of
what was said, nor apparently did Yeats repeat his high opinion of it. On
his departure, a bit disheartened that he had not made more of an
impression on his famous host, Frost was mildly surprised to have Yeats
invite him back, "to make one of his circle at his Monday Nights when he
is in London," as he proudly wrote to Bartlett. Getting an endorsement
from Yeats for *A Boy's Will* might be like pulling teeth, but it was worth
waiting for.

It was a day or two later that Frost met May Sinclair, at her home in
fashionable Edwardes Square, a few blocks west of Kensington Gardens.
With her transatlantic reputation as novelist and poet, Miss Sinclair
wielded considerable influence, so Frost was pleased to have her say she
had detected "something unusual" in his book—though just what this
was, either she never said or Frost failed to record. Her several invitations
to tea during the following weeks seemed to promise that her interest
would not be fleeting, and in fact she was shortly to play a role in
procuring some important publicity for *A Boy's Will*.

Despite all the attention he was receiving personally, Frost was very much aware that two weeks after publication his book had not been given even a single notice, and his growing anxiety was put into another letter to Bartlett. "I am in mortal fear now," he confessed, "lest the reviewers should fail to take any notice of it. Such a work isn't sold in bookstores but through the notices in the papers entirely. It is going the rounds now and it remains to be seen whether it will fall flat or not." Within a day or two of writing those words, he had his first notice of sorts. It could have done little to cheer him.

On the back page of the *Athenaeum*, a prominent literary weekly, tucked in with some fourteen other titles, he came upon his name in boldface type: "Frost (Robert), A Boy's Will, 1/6 net. Nutt." None of the titles listed was accorded more than two or three sentences of comment. In its entirety, Frost's read: "These poems are intended by the author to possess a certain sequence, and to depict the various stages of a young man's outlook upon life. The author is only half successful in this, possibly because many of his verses do not rise above the ordinary, though here or there a happy line or phrase lingers gratefully in the memory." That sixty-word comment, the first appraisal of Frost's poetry ever printed, must have brought some real gloom to the Bungalow.

Five days later the blow was lightened somewhat when the *Times Literary Supplement* gave its own roundup of new books. This time no less than sixty-two titles were crowded on a single large page, and more than half were dismissed with a lone sentence. Frost's was accorded two: "There is an agreeable individuality about these pieces: the writer is not afraid to voice the simplest of his thoughts and fancies, and these, springing from a capacity of complete absorption in the influences of nature and the open air, are often naively engaging. Sometimes, too, in a vein of reflection, he makes one stop and think, though the thought may be feebly or obscurely expressed (as in the last stanza of a poem, otherwise striking, called 'The Trial By Existence')." This was a little better, but as later became clear the references to the naive and simple nature of the verse did not please him.

All too quickly the remainder of April slipped past with nothing further appearing. At this juncture, fully two months after publication, Nutt seems to have taken a hand, suggesting that Frost make use of his contacts in the British dependency of Vancouver. All that is known of this attempt to spark attention is contained in a letter Frost wrote about mid-May to John Bartlett, who was himself just starting on a career as a journalist. Bartlett, Frost instructed, must immediately order twenty copies of the book: "You must do this of the publisher and not of me so as to make it look as if I had taken hold in the far west (why, God only knows). Then you must get me a notice in the most literary of the Vancouver dailies or weeklies. Make it personal if you like, a sort of news item. Like this: Jaunty Bart., the popular and ever censorious fakeer of the Sun staff is in receipt of etc. etc. till you get to 'allow me to sell you a couple' (quoting Alice). You know the sort of thing. Be sure to say, This is hot stuff. A few choice copies left . . . Can't you ring me into one of your columns in the Montreal Star?"

The high spirits in the letter are misleading. Frost's real mood at the time was quite opposite, something clearly evident to Elinor, who wrote home that "Rob has been altogether discouraged at times." Revealingly, it was also at this precise moment, eight months after leaving the United States, that Frost began to acknowledge the first pangs of homesickness. Sending a copy of his book to Susan Ward, he proudly tells how it has attracted the attention of some of England's leading literary minds, and he pointedly adds that his contract with Nutt is on a royalty basis. But suddenly he breaks into a confession that, despite his book's good fortune, not all is right with him in England: "And yet we are very, very homesick in this English mud. We can't hope to be happy long out of New England. I never knew how much of a Yankee I was till I had been out of New Hampshire a few months. I suppose the life in such towns as Plymouth and Derry and South Berwick is the best on earth." With his book facing imminent failure, the familiar, comfortable life from which he ran away six months before with such brave hopes, now begins to seem dearer and more desirable than ever.

Late in May the suspense broke, and there came a small flood of notices, all prompted by the personal contacts Frost had made. Probably the first of these to reach Beaconsfield was Pound's, in *Poetry*. Though Frost would have been glad to see it—his first experience of a lengthy discussion of his poetry by a qualified fellow poet—he could not have been entirely happy with what he read. Because of its importance in the Frost story, and Pound's later rise as critic, this review deserves to be looked at in detail.

For some reason not explained, Pound headed his remarks with a two-line quotation from one of the sonnets in the volume, and the second of these lines he had, without permission, shortened in accord with his own Imagist principles,

I had withdrawn in forest and my song
Was swallowed up in leaves

chopping off the phrase "that blew alway," and destroying both rhythm and rhyme. But the mangled quotation was the least of the shocks in store.

An offhand, disjointed air—probably not so deliberate as is assumed, since it was dashed off in a great hurry—pervades the text, and the praise was not only muted, it took a form for which Frost was not prepared.

> There is another personality in the realm of verse, another American, found, as is usual, on this side of the water, by an English publisher long known as a lover of good books. David Nutt publishes at his own expense *A Boy's Will* by Robert Frost, the latter having long been scorned by the "great American editors." It is the old story.
>
> Mr. Frost's book is a little raw, and it has in it a number of infelicities; underneath them it has the tang of the New Hampshire woods, and it has just this utter sincerity. It is not post-Miltonic or post-Swinburnian or post-Kiplonian. This man has the good sense to speak naturally and to paint the thing, the thing as he sees it. And to do this is a very different matter from gunning about for the circumplectious polysyllable.
>
> It is almost on this account that it is a difficult book to quote from.

> *She's glad her simple worsted gray*
> *Is silver now with clinging mist—*

> does not catch your attention. The lady is praising the autumn rain, and he ends the poem, letting her talk.

> *Not yesterday I learned to know*
> *The love of bare November days,*
> *Before the coming of the snow;*
> *But it were vain to tell her so,*
> *And they are better for her praise.*

Or again:

> *There was never a sound beside the wood but one,*
> *And that was my long scythe whispering to the ground.*
>
> . . . .
>
> *My long scythe whispered and left the hay to make.*

I remember that I was once canoeing and thirsty and I put into a shanty for water and found a man there who had no water and gave me cold coffee instead. And he didn't understand it, he was from a minor city and he "just set there watchin' the river" and didn't "seem to want to go back," and he didn't care for anything else. And so I presume he entered into Anunda. And I remember Joseph Campbell telling me of meeting a man on a desolate waste of bogs, and he said to him, "It's rather dull here"; and the man said, "Faith, ye can sit on a middan and dream stars."

And that is the essence of folk poetry with distinction between America and Ireland. And Frost's book reminded me of these things.

There is perhaps as much of Frost's personal tone in the following little catch, which is short enough to quote, as in anything else. It is to his wife, written when his grandfather and his uncle had disinherited him of a comfortable fortune and left him in poverty because he was a useless poet instead of a money-getter. [Quotes "In Neglect"]

There are graver things, but they suffer too much by making excerpts. One reads the book for the "tone," which is homely, by intent, and pleasing, never doubting that it comes direct from his own life, and that no two lives are the same.

He has now and then such a swift and bold expression as "The whimper of hawks beside the sun." He has now and then a beautiful simile, well used, but he is for the most part as simple as the lines I have quoted in opening or as in the poem of mowing. He is without sham and without affectation.

Careless in both thought and expression the review certainly is. Worst by far, however, was the heedless bad taste of openly referring to intimate family matters, more so when discussing the poetry of an unknown. Moreover, the facts as given by Pound are almost certainly wrong, for Frost would hardly have claimed that his grandfather had "disinherited" him. If that word was used at all by Frost it concerned only the uncle's estate. In lumping grandfather and uncle together, Pound made Frost appear to be guilty both of lying and of shameful ingratitude. Elinor Frost, on reading the passage, and remembering all that the dead grandfather's annuity had meant in their lives, could not hold back tears of embarrassment and anger.

Had Pound been less intent on achieving a "scoop" over his rivals, he might have written a review of some insight, and of better service to Frost at the time. As it is, the usual defects resulting from haste are plainly in evidence. The bare mentions of Milton, Swinburne, and Kipling are too cryptic and far drawn, and might have been spared. The references to the man who gave Pound the cold coffee, and to the Irishman in the bog, lack firm connection to anything said before or after, so it is hard to decide just what Pound was "reminded" of in the realm of "folk poetry." That phrase itself, it need scarcely be said, is very wide of the mark to describe the late-Romantic air of the verses in A Boy's Will. Where Pound praises Frost for avoiding orotund language, the thought as professional criticism is merely trite, as if he were instructing a schoolboy. He says the book is difficult to quote from, and he then proceeds to give two lines from "My

November Guest," but only in order to show that they are not worth quoting. Of the single whole stanza given, he says the lines are spoken by the woman ("letting her talk"), when in reality they are Frost's own closing comments. He admits that there are "graver things" in the volume, but decides that they would suffer from excerpting, which is decidedly untrue, but which is the hurried reviewer's usual excuse. At last Pound's headlong pace rushed him, in his final sentence, into a glaring tautology, of the sort he frequently railed at in the work of other writers. But perhaps the real fault lies with Harriet Monroe, who might have held Pound's notice back for rewriting, if she too had not been more concerned with a scoop.

For Frost, far worse than these deficiencies of thought and style was the shock of finding his poetry classed as naïve and unsophisticated: the "utter" sincerity, the "direct" speaking out of an autobiographical context, the barnyard implication of the Irish saying, the veiled reference to the "natural" man in that last sentence, the rawness, the infelicity, the tang of the woods—all these strongly reinforced the portrait of Frost's work as "folk poetry," with all that the phrase implied as to lack of conscious art. It was the manure pile image that hurt most, and it soon brought from Frost an angry rejection of the idea of himself as an uncomplicated versifier of simple rural themes. "Who will show me the correlation," he burst out in a letter to Flint, "of anything I ever wrote and his quotation from the Irish, You may sit on a middan and dream stars. You may sit on a sofa and dream garters. But tell me I implore what on earth is a middan if it isn't a midden, and where the hell is the fitness of a word like that in connection with what I wrote on a not inexpensive farm."

In a letter to Flint two weeks earlier, he had been more explicit, asserting roundly that "Ezra Pound manifestly made a mistake when he thought he knew how to praise my poems for the right thing. What he saw in them isn't there and what is there he couldn't have seen or he wouldn't have liked them." Behind these outbursts lay Frost's belated awakening to the danger of having his poetry dismissed as the spontaneous overflow of a heart and intellect essentially countrified and primitive, devoid of literary sophistication—and he was only too aware that the new poetry he was writing, with its colloquial air and unemphatic style, would be even more liable to just such misinterpretation. The *Times* had been first to sound this note, with its "naively engaging" remark, but it was not until he read Pound's more extended opinion that he began to understand the impression that was taking hold.

Somewhat surprisingly, Flint's judgment of *A Boy's Will*, in *Poetry and*

Drama, did little to soothe Frost's anxiety. Prominent was a reference to his "simplicity of utterance," which, as Flint went on to explain, arose from "a candid heart," recognizable by its "spontaneity." Almost as if describing a rustic, Flint drew on his acquaintance with Frost to provide some personal comment: "But behind all is the heart and life of a man, and the more you ponder his poems, the more convinced you become that the heart is pure and the life not lived in vain." Flint redeemed himself, however, by finding something more in the poems than simplicity, and he went on to concede "subtlety in evocation of moods, humour, and an ear for silences." On this fleeting judgment Frost pounced gratefully: "I have to thank you for the word 'subtlety' in your review," he wrote. "The poems are open. I am not so sure that the best of them are simple. If they are they are subtle too. I thank you, too, for seeing the humour."

A third notice showed up in *T. P.'s Weekly,* buried in a rambling treatment of six new volumes of poetry. It was written by one of the magazine's regulars, Reginald Buckley, with whom Frost seems to have had some acquaintance. This time *A Boy's Will* was identified not as a farm product, but more circumspectly as "a book of verse afield," a designation which, while still evoking a rural setting, allows for a somewhat higher level of culture. It is tempting to see this phrase, used nowhere else in reviews of the volume, as coming from Frost himself, perhaps suggested in conversation with Buckley at the weekly's office. The remainder of the Buckley notice also manages to blend the idea of rustic origins with something higher: "there is a fragrance here, and now and then a little turn of quiet humour like a sudden ruffle of the breeze on still water. 'In a Vale' could not have been written by anyone but a close companion of flowers and night and mist. 'Into My Own,' the opening poem, has the confidence not learned in cities."

In reality, it appears, a more substantial notice had been expected from *T. P.'s,* for when Bartlett, a faithful reader of the paper, inquired about the review's short, offhand character, Frost went out of his way to offer an explanation, and it smacks of resentment. Buckley, he wrote, "has recently issued a book with David Nutt, but at his own expense, whereas in my case David Nutt assumed the risks [not entirely true, of course]. And these other people Buckley reviewed are his personal friends or friends of his friends or if not that simply examples of the kind of wrong horse most fools put their money on." (Any idea that Buckley may have been the accommodating ex-bobby who aided Frost initially seems negated by the variety and relative sophistication of his contributions to the magazine.)

What mattered most to Frost about a fourth notice, in the *English Review*, was the source itself. "A leading literary monthly," he called it proudly in a letter, explaining that it was the magazine "that found Masefield and Conrad." It was another roundup review, however, and while a little more effusive than that in *T. P.'s*, it also expressed a strong sense of the poetry's "simple" origins. Frost was mentioned third, after the *Gitanjali* of Rabindranath Tagore, then the rage of London ("Mr. Yeats tells us that this volume has stirred his blood as nothing else has done for years"). Frost's book received the briefest mention, and its juxtaposition with Tagore brought it no benefit:

> After the subtle refinements of *Gitanjali* it does one good to glance awhile into the simple woodland philosophy of Mr. Frost. Nowhere on earth, we fancy, is there more outrageous nonsense printed under the name of poetry than in America; and our author, we are told, is an American. All the more credit to him for breaking away from this tradition—if such it can be called—and giving us not derivative, hypersensuous drivel, but an image of things really heard and seen. There is a wild, racy flavour in his poems; they sound that inevitable response to nature which is the hallmark of true lyric feeling.

Frost must have winced at the "simple woodland philosophy," and also the "wild, racy flavour," catchwords for primitivism. But he may also have realized what was probably the truth, that the opinion expressed in the *English Review* reflected the direct influence of Ezra Pound, who was an intimate of the magazine's editor.

The notice that would have jarred most came in the glossy, oversize pages of London's leading popular literary journal, the *Bookman*. The June issue brought a seven-line mention of *A Boy's Will*, in still another group review, this one written by Katharine Tynan, a busy journalist well known for her own verse. Surprisingly casual in its bored dismissal of Frost's volume, the review affords a perfect example in brief of a reviewer's abuse of privilege. In fact the impression is strong that Miss Tynan did no more than flip through Frost's pages, then penned her remarks in a most hurried and thoughtless fashion:

> None of these three young poets is without promise. One may even have hopes of them as the poets of tomorrow, although they are not the poets but the disciples of today. Mr. Frost is apparently an American, so one would like to be kind to him as a stranger. So far his achievement is no great matter: but he has a way of keeping one expectant, as though something

good were sure to come. We shall look for it in another volume. *A Boy's Will*
suggests young work. We shall hope to meet Mr. Frost another day.

The last three sentences betray the heedless attitude: aside from the
outright repetition, there is the fatuousness of the remark about young
work, as if the fact was not openly stated in the volume itself.

As it happens, recompense for this shoddy treatment was not long in
coming. May Sinclair was a close acquaintance of the *Bookman*'s editor, St.
John Adcock, and on June 4, some days after the appearance of the Tynan
review, she invited Frost by letter to meet her for lunch at the Albemarle
Club in Dover Street, just off Piccadilly. She forgot to post her letter,
however, and it was this circumstance that preserved the record of her part
in the arrangements for a second *Bookman* review. Two days after writing
her first note, still not aware she had neglected to send it, she wrote again:

> Dear Mr Frost
>
> I was so sorry you didn't turn up today. I hope I didn't address my letter
> all wrong. Mr. St. John Adcock was also very sorry he missed you. I showed
> him your poems and Ezra Pound's review of them, and he asked me if you
> would send him your portrait and a personal note to go with the review of
> them in the "Bookman." He does not yet know if a copy has been sent to the
> "Bookman" offices, perhaps you will see that this is done? His address is A.
> St. John Adcock Esq. Editor of "The Bookman," Warwick Square.
>
> I hope you will come some other day to meet him. Meanwhile he would
> be glad if you would call to see him at the office. You'll find him an awfully
> good sort.

Frost did pay an early visit to Adcock in his office, where he was told
that a more adequate notice of his book would appear in the *Bookman*'s
August issue. For some reason he took his time about supplying the
portrait, actually waiting until almost the last moment. Then, on June
30, attired in suit, vest, white shirt with cuff links, and stiff collar and
tie, he went the four miles from Beaconsfield to High Wycombe, to
Sweetland's Photographic Studio. No doubt it was Elinor who selected
the pose sent to the *Bookman*: full face, seated at a table, left hand
pensively to brow.

*   *   *

WHATEVER his reasons, and overlooking the defects of his review, it
is beyond question that Ezra Pound, in taking notice of *A Boy's Will*,

in supplying introductions, and in his offers of sympathy and encouragement, rendered Frost timely service. Despite this, the friendship between the two lasted only a short time, less than four months (and for a third of the period Pound was out of London traveling on the continent). While the details of this curious friendship, and its termination, would in any case be of interest, there exists another, equally compelling reason for tracing out its course. Lawrance Thompson in treating of these events does not hesitate to assign blame for the break, and he lays it all on Frost, casting him in the role of ingrate. Moved by "jealousy" and a vague "dark resentment," says Thompson, Frost coldly betrayed his benefactor. Whether that is true, and to what extent, is a question to be judged on the facts.

That Pound was a "difficult" individual, is a point today scarcely disputed. Even in his more obscure youth, before World War I, he managed at one time or another to annoy, anger, and disappoint almost every acquaintance, ally, and friend that he had, including those who stood ready to excuse his faults. Frank Flint, originally one of Pound's sincerest admirers, eventually fell out with him and was led to say frankly in a letter to his former friend, "You are indeed a disagreeable person, as you say; it is one of the regrets of all those who have ever known you that this should be so."

Fiercely and profoundly involved with all manner of literature Pound certainly was. But it was an extremely personal involvement, often unpleasant when seen close up, and its least attractive side can be summed up in his own inadvertent words, uttered shortly before the first meeting with Frost. "We're in such a beautiful position," he wrote Harriet Monroe in discussing the low state of literature in America, "to save the public's soul by punching its face that it seems a crime not to do so." Particularly during his London days it was not always possible to say which of these two activities—saving souls or punching faces—was more strongly at work in him. It was an attitude the advancing years did little to soften.

Some three weeks after he and Frost first met, Pound left London for a visit to Paris. He returned about mid-May, and his first action with regard to Frost was to ask Harriet Monroe about some poems of Frost's that had supposedly been rejected by *Poetry* while Frost was still in America. The fact of that rejection had been discovered by Miss Monroe in her magazine's files, and she had instructed Pound to "apologize for us and say we are very contrite and would like some more some day." Acting on this invitation, well before the first of June 1913, Pound had in his possession the original manuscript of "The Death of the Hired Man" (which may have been the very poem declined by *Poetry*). Impressed, Pound shrewdly judged this dramatic narrative to be far superior to anything in *A Boy's Will*. Yet it was with this poem that he began his effort, quite seriously intended, to capture Frost as a disciple—and he did succeed in persuading him to drop "a line or two" from the poem, as Frost later admitted, lines now lost. For Pound this was nothing new, for he was then indulging in a similar pedagogic pursuit with several other poets, including Amy Lowell (in England for the summer), Richard Aldington, Hilda Doolittle, Frank Flint, and J. G. Fletcher, all of whom tended to a rather uncritical acceptance of his pronouncements. In Frost, however, he had encountered a fully developed artist, one whose strong individuality could not be controlled or diverted, a fact, it seems, that Pound never came close to grasping. For Pound, Frost was never much more than talent in the raw.

The easygoing, accommodating Frost, impressed by the sharp, energetic mind, bemused by the furious temperament and the wide knowledge of literature, was at first drawn to his compatriot. He was even a bit fascinated by the haughty rudeness, continually flaunted by Pound almost as a weapon. The crude behavior, like the outlandish dress (clothes of exotic material and loudly clashing colors, flamboyant ties, a single earring), Frost tended to excuse on the ground of youth. But soon after Pound's return from the continent Frost finally decided that he had had enough of the posturing, a change in attitude that was probably inevitable, but which was hastened by three separate and more or less embarrassing incidents that happened in quick succession. Known only in their essentials, nothing can be said about dates or locations, though all were connected with public restaurants. Some casual remarks of Frost's made many years later are all that survive by way of elaboration: "Among the things that Pound did was show me Bohemia . . . he'd take me to restaurants and things." Again: "Don't forget that our first moments together—Pound's and mine—were happy, even romantic. Pound showed me London's Bohemia—he was boyish about it."

The most fleeting of these restaurant incidents has Pound engaging in some loud and boisterous behavior accompanied by obnoxious language, perhaps a result of too much wine. Complaints from other patrons caused a waiter to set up a screen around the two. The second incident was more definitely embarrassing. Pound, at that time an avid tennis player and proud of his athletic abilities, was also taking lessons in judo. Lunching with Frost, he began explaining the intricacies of his new enthusiasm, and he insisted on demonstrating a hold. Rising from his chair, he invited Frost to stand up. As Frost rose hesitantly, without warning Pound grabbed one of his wrists, then turned and bent down in the standard shoulder throw. Taken unaware, Frost was pulled off his feet and dragged over Pound's crouching back, landing heavily on the floor, where he lay sprawled under the questioning stares of all in the restaurant. What he may have done or said on rising he never mentioned, but talking of the incident years later he said he had taken it all in good spirits and had not gotten angry—though he did insist that he was as strong as Pound, and it had been only the use of surprise that had put him down.

Other guests may or may not have been present at the first two incidents. At the third there were two women (neither has been identified), and it appears that on this occasion Pound was in a truculent mood from the start. During the meal he became steadily more annoyed with the women's talk, and at last he jumped to his feet, knocking over his chair. Loudly and disdainfully he announced, "I leave these women to *you*." To Frost's consternation, he then turned and pranced out the door.

During this same period—mid-May to mid-June—Pound continued to press Frost on the question of writing free verse, an interference that Frost simply laughed off. Then came a day when Pound blandly announced that unless Frost espoused Imagist principles he would no longer enjoy Pound's sponsorship—the threat also implied the severing of all the important contacts already made, starting with Yeats, and others in prospect. In a letter Frost tries to make light of this new development, but underneath the breeziness can be heard a note of annoyed surprise, if not actual anger: "You will be amused to hear that Pound has taken to bullying me . . . He says I must write something much more like *vers libre* or he will let me perish of neglect. He really threatens."

The more the two were together, the more Frost became aware of some uglier traits in the Pound personality. There was a certain deviousness, not obtrusive before, and that he now proceeded to discuss with Flint. All that is known of this exchange is contained in a letter Frost received from Flint after a visit the Englishman paid to Beaconsfield late in June. It appears that during the visit Frost revealed some things about Pound which took the other man by surprise. This is evident from Flint's letter, written the next evening from his home in Highbury, London: "I think over all we said yesterday. I am very angry about E. P. . . . there is much that I feel and understand in the E. P. case that sickens. I admit now and avow now that I had always lurking doubts about E. P. . . . I have always hated and loathed insincerity, hypocrisy, and *arrivisme*. I have always wanted to find nobility in men and have been heartsick when one by one they have deceived me . . . there is no envy in all this, only sickness that another illusion is gone."

Another result of the long talk that Sunday with Flint at the Bungalow was some burlesque *vers libre* by Frost. Besides the threat to abandon him, he also made fun of Pound's frenetic efforts to direct the work of other poets, in this case the newly married pair Hilda Doolittle and Richard Aldington. Having dashed off the twenty-two-line verse he sent it to Flint for his amusement, saying he could show it to Pound "if you think it won't get me into any worse trouble than I deserve to get into." As Flint would have understood, the caution referred to Pound's ability to influence the fortunes of *A Boy's Will*, as well as possible later volumes. The parody was written on a separate sheet:

POETS ARE BORN NOT MADE

My nose is out of joint
For my father-in-letters—
My Father mind you—
Has been brought to bed of another poet,
And I not nine months old.
It is twins this time
And they came into the world prodigiously
    United in wedlock
(Don't try to visualize this)
Already they have written their first poem in
    vers libre
And sold it within twenty-four hours.
My father-in-letters was the affluent American
    Buyer
There was no one to bid against him.
The merit of the poem is the new convention
That definitely locates an emotion in the belly,
Instead of scientifically in the viscera at large,
Or mid-Victorianly in the heart.
It voices a desire to grin
With the grin of a beast more scared than frightened.

For Why?
Because it is a cinch that twins so well born
Will be able to sell almost anything they write.

The lines neatly impale their target, not least in showing how Pound's methods as an editor tended to reduce poetry to just another commodity. But Frost was reluctant to be the cause of Flint's lost illusions, so in a letter sent with the parody he responded to the younger man's agonizing by suggesting that his estimate of Pound had swung too far in the opposite direction. "I shouldn't take his unmasking too much to heart," he cautioned, ". . . and whatever you do don't judge him too hardly on my authority." The admonition had its effect, and a calmer Flint in his turn began counseling patience toward the faults of their irritating friend: "Your 'poem' is very amusing! I think it might annoy him! . . . You know I think his bark is much worse than his bite; and that much that seems offensive to us externally is merely external and a kind of outer defense—a mask . . . All the same he irritates; and we mustn't allow ourselves to be irritated, don't you think? Don't you feel it as a weakness?"

To this, Frost returned a last comment concerning Flint's tendency toward shyness and his allowing himself to be unduly manipulated by Pound. "The only fault I find with you," he wrote, "is that you speak with too much diffidence. You are afraid of yourself. I was impatient with you when you used that word 'weakness' for Pound's perfidy. You are in awe of that great intellect abloom in hair. You saw me first but you had to pass me over for him to discover." Flint's reply to that outright criticism supports Frost's reading of the situation. Some things about Pound, Flint repeated, increase his resentment, "yet all the time I'm wishing to remain friends with him." This exchange with Flint was closed out by Frost on June 26 when in a much softened mood he suggested, "You take Ezra sadly and I angrily. But what is the use. We will hate the arrivist in him and like what there is left to like. He wants to be good to us all. And having fired myself off in about five poems like the one I sent you I feel better toward him."

The manuscript of another of those five poems fired off by Frost has survived, and it affords ample evidence to show that his effort to see Pound's good side arose, as always, from a concern over the welfare of his books. He knew that Pound, if provoked, might well turn nasty. Only the last half of the poem is needed here:

I suspected though that in praising me
You were not concerned so much with my desert

As with your power,
And that you praised me arbitrarily
And took credit to yourself
In demonstrating that you could thrust anything
* upon the world,*
Were it never so humble,
And bid your will avouch it.
And here we come close to what I demanded of you.
* I did not want the money you were disbursing*
* Among your favorites*
* For two American editors.*
*   Not that.*
All I asked was that you should hold to one thing:
That you considered me a poet.
That was why I clung to you
* As one clings to a group of insincere friends*
* For fear they shall turn their thoughts against him*
* The moment he is out of hearing.*
The truth is I was afraid of you.

Parody of free verse though it is, this poem contains none of the jocular note that underlies the first one. Here there is a degree of actual bitterness.

In the midst of these discontents Frost made still another discovery about Pound's "perfidy," and it was enough to push matters to a conclusion. The manuscript of "The Death of The Hired Man," given to Pound in May, had not been sent to Chicago for use in *Poetry*, as Frost had expected. Instead, Pound had quietly sent it to a New York magazine with which he had a close connection, *The Smart Set*. Not a little aggravated by the presumption, Frost was firm in his decision that he did not want his poem to appear in such company (probably he was put off by the deliberately flaunted air of superiority, an understandable reaction for the time). But when he gave orders that the manuscript be withdrawn he was astonished to hear Pound refuse. Shortly after, as Frost took some pains to tell Flint, he tried again, this time by mail, and was again repulsed: "I wrote him—I may as well confess—a rather wild letter demanding my manuscript back for no assigned reason. He told me I was having a fit of nerves and refused to comply. The terms on which we are likely to meet next are problematic."

Wishing to avoid upsetting the unstable Pound, Frost delayed doing anything further about the poem, and for a while the situation hung fire. About the middle of August the impasse was solved when the editor of *The Smart Set,* against all expectation, returned the manuscript. By then Frost and Pound had not met or corresponded in more than a month. For Frost, the initially helpful but finally troublesome figure of Ezra Pound— "an incredible ass," was Frost's final word for him later that fall—had begun receding into the past.

SEVEN

SEEKING ACHE OF MEMORY

P ERSISTING drearily week after week, the gloom and chill of winter lasted through April. Then early May brought an abrupt change in the weather, bestowing on Beaconsfield a long succession of mild, sunny days. By June, as Elinor noted, the trees and bushes around the Bungalow had begun to blossom: in the front yard a profusion of roses, at the rear, apple and pear trees flowering in the midst of currant and raspberry bushes. Gratefully, the Frosts took advantage of the improvement, frequently packing lunches and going off on day-long hikes. It was their first experience of the English countryside in its best summer dress, and Elinor especially welcomed the change, since it allowed the family to escape the small rooms and narrow halls. Joyfully in her letters she hails the "perfect" weather, calling it "charming" and "very lovely." When the returning birds began singing in the trees around the Bungalow she listed some she had never heard before: skylark, cuckoo, the English blackbird.

By now Frost's contacts had widened considerably and had grown easier, and when he visited the homes of friends in town, or joined them at restaurants, the shy Elinor sometimes went along. With the Gardners in particular both Frosts had quickly become intimate, and on the arrival of good weather the two families began exchanging visits to each other's homes. At least once Mary's busy archaeologist-husband, Ernest, then a professor at the University of London, was included. Unfortunately, when the two elder Gardners passed from the scene (both died in the late thirties), they left nothing explicit on record about their link with the

Frosts, nor did their three children later. Because of this, an intenser interest settles on the five brief letters that did survive, all of them written to the Frosts by the Gardners. Two, by Mary Gardner, are dated May and June 1913, and while implying more than they state, they provide a tantalizing glimpse into some of Frost's activities that first spring in England. Both were written from Farm Corner, the Gardner's home in Tadworth, Surrey. The first, dated May 28, follows a visit the Frosts had paid to Tadworth the previous Sunday:

Dear Mr. Frost

The thanks are really all on my side. Yes, I thought that would sting, that beastly minor poet remark. How *does* she know you are minor? And how is the distinction between major and minor in poetry assured, or [how is it] more important than in say politics or philanthropy. Never mind.

I fear I bored you on Sunday. The truth is I was trying to understand. But I didn't notice much logic, & Truth is so elusive, too. What is true today is so horribly untrue tomorrow. But one thing remains clear. America is waiting for a poet to indicate to her her true ambitions, and to help her to that coherence that only common ideals give. Are you he, major or minor?

One day next week will you let Phyllis and Delphis and me come to see your children? Tuesday is the best day, for then I can either bring Ernest and Christopher, or if Boy can't get leave from his schoolmaster, leave the one to mind the other. But any day that would suit you we would come.

It was jolly on Sunday. I liked the Whitman bit you read as well as anything there is.

> Yours Most Sincerely,
> Mary Gardner

P.S. I saw a copy of "Poetry." The tone *is* rather personal of the review of you. I am reproved by your categoricalness. Don't forget about Ezra Pound. Could he come June 14, do you think?

Who the "she" might have been who labeled Frost minor, and in what circumstances, is not discoverable (does the reference indicate an overlooked review of A *Boy's Will*?). What the note in its assured and breezy tone does bear out is a description of Mary Gardner penned at this time by Elinor, who had found her new friend to be "very kind-hearted, clever, and impulsive." The invitation in the postscript would have come to nothing for it was just at this time that Pound and Frost had begun their falling out.

The second surviving note of this spring was written by Mrs. Gardner two weeks later. Its joking salutation refers to a poem in *A Boy's Will* entitled "Pan with Us," which had probably been discussed between them. The drawings mentioned were probably pencil sketches in an earlier letter by Frost, a sometime habit of his:

Dear Pan;

How amusing life is! Your drawings caused great exhilaration in this family and produced pretty much the same effect as the cupboard and boxes at the "Omega" shop.

I want you to meet my friend Mrs. Mair who lives at 14 Campden Hills Gardens, Kensington. You would like her very much.

I ran up hard against another Futurist, and told him my opinions, hard and good, about a picture he invited me to admire. Items: the drawing was bad, the colouring dirty, the pattern—save the mark—ill-conditioned and unnatural; and so on. Strange to say, we parted on quite good terms. Suppose now we of the non-existent art of literature threw over the alphabet. It is just possible to start too far back, & yet hold on to too much.

I see the English Review likes your Boy's Will, & for some of the right reasons, of which I am glad. I don't think quite a large dose of success would spoil you.

Judging by the contents of "Pan with Us," Mrs. Gardner's use of the name for Frost intended nothing very abstruse, only a light reference to him in his role as America's neglected poet. (The joke may have miscarried, for the poem's opening lines come rather too close to making a point of Frost's age, at least a decade more advanced than that of most "new" poets. When Pan emerged from the woods one day, Frost had written, "His skin and his hair and his eyes were gray.") The invitation to meet Mrs. Jessie Mair, wife of a member of the Civil Service Commission (and afterward Lady Beveridge), was accepted. It was a fateful introduction, for Mrs. Mair was to prove of great if accidental importance to Frost. It was she who introduced him to the man, her brother-in-law, who would play a now-forgotten part in the inspiration of "Mending Wall."

Even such normal socializing as this by the Frosts, where it called for any sort of financial outlay, was severely limited. By spring the family finances had reached their lowest ebb, with no further income in prospect until mid-July, when the $800 annuity was due. But that annual windfall now would need careful husbanding against an ever more uncertain future, so that it provided no relief from the accustomed close budgeting. Visitors to the Bungalow, noticing the plain food, sparse furniture, and other signs of restricted finances, must have suspected the truth. One who definitely did notice, and who undertook to do something about it, was Frank Flint. After visiting the Bungalow with his wife and baby daughter in late June, he suggested to Frost that he could stretch his budget, food especially, by joining the Civil Service Supply Association (an early form of cooperative), and he sent detailed instructions for applying. "Forgive this perhaps unmannerly intrusion into your private affairs," he apologized in his letter. "I do it because I think you may be helped thereby." Surprised and perhaps a bit uncomfortable at having such private family matters brought into the open, Frost laconically returned Flint his thanks "for all the information of your letter of this morning. We have to consider such things. Very thoughtful of you and your wife."

Of greater concern than finances at this same time was Frost's anxiety over his poetry, his growing fear that it was being perceived as the work of an essentially self-taught rustic devoid of true literary skills. The more he thought of it, the more worried he grew that his new poetry, because of its peculiar absence of rhetorical effect, its air of ordinary talk—all the result of much painstaking art!—might be taken as merely primitive. Doubts might even be raised as to whether this new style was poetry at all, and not just tricked-up prose. Some initial sense of this reaction had already begun to reach him from the friends who were reading his new work in manuscript, passed around as early as April or May.

At last in mid-July he put the fear into words for his Maine friend, Thomas Mosher. Alluding to the greatly simplified diction and syntax he was using in his poetry, he assures Mosher that such low-key language "is appropriate to the virtues I celebrate." Cautioning his correspondent, he adds that he is fully aware of the daring transformation he has achieved: "At least I am sure I can count on you to give me credit for knowing what I am about. You are not going to make the mistake that Pound makes of assuming my simplicity is that of the untutored child. I am not undesigning." Still more pointed was a complaining remark in a subsequent letter to Richard Garnett, in which Frost offers thanks for a pivotal review of *North of Boston*. "What you are good enough to call my method they haven't noticed. I am not supposed to have a method. I am a naive person." That comment was written four months after Frost's return to the United States, a fact that demonstrates how real and abiding, and perhaps how well-founded, was this particular fear.

It as in some such apprehensive state of mind that he decided, late in

June 1913, to emulate the self-protective step that had been taken by Wordsworth in his *Lyrical Ballads*: he would insert a preface in his new volume, putting on record a reasoned exposition of all the conscious literary principles, the metrical sophistication, that underlay his bold new technique. That, in any case, seems to have been the main purpose of the active, even intense interest he now took in formal theories of prosody, an analytical concern not greatly in evidence before this. Reasonably enough, he began by seeking help in organizing his ideas, sending a request to Frank Flint that he set up a meeting with a particular member of London's loose literary groups, T. E. Hulme.

Already known as a translator of Bergson, (whose work was then of much interest to Frost), the twenty-nine-year-old Hulme had begun making a name, both as an author and in private, for his broadly philosophic approach to literary criticism. His rooms at 67 Frith Street, Soho Square, in a building of "decaying grandeur" that had once housed the Venetian Embassy, had been the site of many of the meetings that gave rise to Imagism, a movement in which Hulme played a principal role. By Frost's time these meetings had become regular weekly gatherings, often including Flint and Pound, at which groups of poets and other artists read and criticized newly written verse.

Frost and Hulme had already met, probably in April through Flint, and Frost had been impressed enough to ask Hulme for an opinion of the poems planned for *North of Boston*. Now he wanted to bring Hulme's abilities to bear on the more specific technical ideas that had been simmering at the back of his mind for two or three years. A postcard to Flint, dated June 24, makes clear that he is not seeking to be heard by the full Tuesday evening tribunal of Frith Street, but by a more intimate audience. "Do you suppose" he asks, "you could get Hulme to listen with you some night to my theory of what would be pure form in poetry? I don't want to talk to a salon, but to a couple of clear heads who will listen and will give my idea its due. I will be greatly helped in what is before me by a little honest criticism."

The meeting took place on July 1. Regrettably, all that is known of it is Frost's brief note of thanks to Flint a few days later. "My ideas got just the rub they needed," he says gratefully. It may also have been at this meeting that there was born the effective phrase Frost was to employ from then on to describe his new poetic practice, "the sound of sense." The first traceable use of the words occurs in a letter he wrote three days after that meeting.

At Frith Street Frost had left some of his poems in manuscript with

Hulme and Flint, to be read at their leisure. Hulme's response is lost, but Flint soon sent his opinion, and since his letter offers the first written comment on poems that were to gain the attention of the English-speaking world, it deserves preservation in its entirety:

My Dear Frost,

I have read your little dramas—they are drama—and I like them very much. (It occurs to me typing this from a rough note that you might try your hand at a play later on when you are well known.) You have a lode there from which you ought to extract quantities of good clean ore. But, to drop that image, I need not say to you that you must avoid monotony of treatment in a book full of pieces like the four I have seen. I do not mean that I have felt such monotony; but I wondered what the effect of—say— another dozen would be read right off on end—a silly thing to do, however, by the way. But you can easily avoid that monotony, I think. Your technical skill is equal to that, and I should say that you were still making discoveries.

One thing seemed to strike me, however, and that was your overfondness for the rhythm of single lines; you would get variety and add to the compulsion of your work if you threw the rhythm over several lines. You can catch a reader up at the beginning of a line, for instance, and drop him, excited and wondering, some twelve lines further on. Browning does so. And this, I think, without sacrificing that simplicity of diction which you are after: indeed, by refining on that simplicity, so that the reader has a secret unapprehended astonishment at the rise and fall of the rhythm and the emotion it translates. This requires great skill and emotional impulsion from the poet.

I feel, however, that I have nothing to say to you about these poems, except: go on! Get it all out of you; Hew at it; shape it! You have found a vein, and you are not working it to waste. You know your instruments and the use you may put them to; and what I have said above may be presumption. No man has the right, really, to carp and criticise, and say this is wrong and that has no place here, when a poet is working consciously and conscientiously and well in the stuff of life; and for this I praise you. You must now, you can only, go to the end.

I told Hulme that you had still more to say. He said he was sorry he stopped you on a point of logic, as he did, which he did because he thought you were at the end. He says, come up again next Tuesday, at the same time, and we will continue. Let us both know if you will not.

Yours ever,
F. S. Flint

P.S. The feeling behind the foregoing was that you would have to fight things out for yourself. There is nobody on earth who can help you.

Though the letter evidently means to offer sympathy and encouragement, it also gives off a peculiar air of restraint, as if the writer out of kindness were suppressing more negative feelings. That may or may not be true, so it is only fair to set beside the letter Frost's own words about Flint's reaction to one of the more important of the poems, words written the following year but which obviously refer to this time: "I shan't forget the day I tried the Hired Man on you and you waxed prophetic."

Whatever course it took exactly, the talk at Hulme's place on the subject of pure form in poetry had a rare stimulating effect on Frost's brimming thoughts, for three days later they spilled over in a memorable letter to John Bartlett. There is excitement in what he says, even some giddiness, yet he is serious too, and very much in earnest as he pursues his novel theme—the impression is strong, in fact, that he is here consciously drafting a formal essay. Talking of the different usages of the word "craftsman," he slides without warning into a playfully boastful mood that prepares the way for his real topic: "To be perfectly frank with you I am one of the most notable craftsmen of my time. That will transpire presently. I am possibly the only person going who works on any but a worn-out theory (principle I had better say) of versification . . . I alone of English writers have consciously set myself to make music out of what I may call the sound of sense."

While he writes as if expressing radically new ideas, in his soberer moments he must have been aware that he was simply dressing up old truths, though his fresh and evocative way of restating those truths does wonderfully reinvigorate them, even makes them more applicable to his personal practice. In his own poetry the speaking voice, the sound of sense, really does take precedence over the cadence or the meter, as if the only purpose of the blank verse was to provide quiet background music. His distinctive way of combining the two rhythms, natural speech and artificial meter, really did create something new in world literature, a voice that at the same time both talks and sings:

Now it is possible to have sense without the sound of sense (as in much prose that is supposed to pass muster but which makes very dull reading). The best place to get the abstract sound of sense is from voices behind a door that cuts off the words . . . [Such] sounds are summoned by the audial imagination, and they must be positive, strong, and definitely and unmistakeably indicated by the context. The reader must be at no loss to give his voice the posture proper to the sentence. The simple declarative sentence used in making a statement is one thing. But Lord love ye it mustn't be worked to death. It is against the law of nature that whole poems should be written in it. If they are written they won't be read. The sound of sense, then. You get that. It is the abstract vitality of our speech. It is pure sound, pure form.

As he continues, his tendency to exaggeration, so typical of its author in certain moods, becomes prominent, though it is now combined with a rapid analysis of the skills at work in his own practice:

But remember we are still talking of the raw material of poetry. An ear and an appetite for these sounds of sense is the first qualification of a writer, be it of prose or verse. But if one is to be a poet he must learn to get cadences by skillfully breaking the sounds of sense with all their irregularity of accent across the regular beat of the meter . . . We depend for variety on the infinite play of accents in the sounds of sense. The high possibility of emotional expression all lets in this mingling [with the meter] of sound-sense and word-accent. A curious thing. And all this has its bearing on your prose me boy . . . Never if you can help it write down a sentence in which the voice will not know how to posture specially.

It is in making his claim so sweeping, of course, that Frost at last goes somewhat awry. Whether in prose or in poetry (though in the nature of the case less with poetry), overt intellectual content is independent of any form of vocal pattern. Above a certain level, meaning can never depend to any large extent on variation in sound, for the posture a voice takes is most often determined by factors that are quite aside from sense— situation, mood, background, personal quirks of the speaker, and so on. The earnestness of Frost's advice to his friend, remembering that Bartlett was a working journalist concerned mainly with straight reporting, often of an agricultural nature, must have made the younger man smile.

In closing, Frost takes the uncharacteristic step of inviting Bartlett to save the letter for future reference: "Maybe you'll keep this discourse on the sound of sense till I can say more on it." Eight months were to pass, however, before he returned to the subject, and when he does it is at once obvious that the lengthy interim has witnessed some very deliberate study—in fact, Frost now admits that he has it in mind to write an essay on the topic. The central emphasis of his theory has been ingeniously shifted, and he now identifies the *sentence* as the basic unit by which the sense-sounds make themselves heard, an idea which really did have something new to offer. A sampling will show that what he has to say this time is not the impulsive commentary of the first letter, but is very well thought out, almost congealing into aphorisms:

> I give you a new definition of a sentence: A sentence is a sound in itself on which other sounds called words may be strung. You may string words together without a sentence-sound to string them on, just as you may tie clothes together by the sleeves and stretch them without a clothes-line between two trees, but—it is bad for the clothes . . .
>
> The sentence-sounds are very definite entities. (This is no literary mysticism I am preaching.) They are as definite as words . . . I think no writer invents them. The most original writer only catches them fresh from talk, where they grow spontaneously.
>
> A man is all a writer if *all* his words are strung on definite recognizable sentence sounds. The voice of the imagination, the speaking voice must know certainly how to behave, how to posture in every sentence . . . A man is a marked writer if his words are largely strung on the more striking sentence sounds . . .
>
> It is so and not otherwise that we get the variety that makes it fun to write and read. *The ear does it.* The ear is the only true writer and the only true reader . . . Remember that the sentence-sound often says more than the words. It may even as in irony convey a meaning opposite to the words . . .
>
> I wouldn't be writing this if I didn't think it the most important thing I know. I write it partly for my own benefit, to clarify my ideas for an essay or two I am going to write some fine day (not far distant) . . .

In two later instances he went even further in elucidating this new idea of the sentence (again, perhaps a bit too far). To Cox in December 1914 he insisted, "Just so many sentence sounds belong to a man as just so many vocal runs belong to one kind of bird. We come into the world with them and create none of them." About a year after that observation was made he reached his most extreme position on the topic, expressed in another letter, this time to Harvard critic Walter Eaton:

> What bothers people in my blank verse is that I have tried to see what I could do with boasting tones and quizzical tones and shrugging tones (for there are such) and forty eleven other tones. All I care a cent for is to catch sentence tones that haven't been brought to book. I don't say to make them, mind you but to catch them. No one makes them or adds to them. They are

always there—living in the cave of the mouth. They are real cave things:
they were before words were. And they are as definitely things as any
image of sight. The most creative imagination is only their summoner. But
summoning them is not all. They are only lovely when thrown and drawn
and displayed across spaces of the footed line . . .

In the end, no preface appeared in *North of Boston*, nor did Frost ever
get around to writing those essays (another time he thought he would do a
book on sentence-sounds for the field of education, but that project also
was dropped). Perhaps the most interesting aspect of this whole theoretical interlude is the fact that ultimately it played no real part at all in his
career. For a while the sound-of-sense theory stayed vibrant in his mind,
but the interval was not long, making its final public appearances in
interviews and talks he gave during the year after his return to the United
States. Thereafter, though he raised the topic in private now and then,
the formal theory became a desultory concern, and in less than a decade
it had faded entirely away.

The reason for Frost's abandonment of an idea that had so deeply
occupied him is no mystery. By means of it he had thought to defend
himself and his work, to demonstrate that he was not naïve, was not just
an unskilled purveyor of rural scenes and sentiment. When at last his
poetry began to find acceptance as a major accomplishment, he no longer
cared to insist on or even discuss its complexity or depth, or the extent of
its technical niceties. Actually, he went the other way. Increasingly
through the remainder of his life he made a habit of ignoring, in some
cases deprecating, the highly sophisticated art that lay at the core of his
simple-seeming verse.

*   *   *

LATE July brought to Beaconsfield the August 1913 number of the
Bookman. After the long wait, its treatment of *A Boy's Will* turned out to
be something of a disappointment. It was not a formal review but a short,
sketchy presentation of book and author, and the fact that a photograph
accompanied it was not as impressive as the invitation had made it seem.
Heavily illustrated, the *Bookman* made a practice of carrying photos of
nearly every writer and personality, known or unknown, whose name or
work showed up in its glossy pages. What must have been even more
annoying, Frost's picture did not accompany the story, but was pushed
two pages back by the magazine's crowded layout.

Opening with some comment on the unusual number of American

writers then active in London, the *Bookman* writer (probably Adcock himself) soon launched into the first description of Frost's life ever printed. In putting on record the place of Frost's birth, though, he missed a chance to explain that Frost's father, a Harvard graduate, was one of those ambitious young men of the 1870s who, restless in the sedate East, had gone west to seek his fortune. Sadly, after a short, hectic career as a journalist and budding politician, the elder Frost died of tuberculosis before he was forty:

> Born in San Francisco, where his father, a friend of Henry George, edited a newspaper, Mr. Frost was educated at Boston, and became an occasional contributor to The Forum, the New York Independent, and other American publications. But he disliked city life and did not number the profitable business instincts among his gifts. After his marriage he cut himself off from all his other belongings, and for several years lived with his wife and four children on a lonely farm in a forest clearing; he was nothing much of a farmer, but contrived to make enough by it for the needs of himself and his family whilst he was giving his soul room and time to grow and developing his poetic gifts.
>
> Much of his first volume was written in those days, and reveals his love of nature and of the loneliness of the woods and fields, touches in pictures of the everyday life that lay about him, and is filled with musings on the mysteries of existence, his dreams of what lies behind him, and his hopes of the future. His verse has a strong individual note, and is marked by an unaffected simplicity and a stark directness of utterance that breathes of austere living and the open air . . .

From Frost himself, of course, had come the exaggeration of that "lonely farm in a forest clearing," since it echoes the sense of what he had earlier written Flint about going "literally into the wilderness." However, "forest clearing" stretches things a bit, even for Frost's brand of hyperbole, and perhaps the phrase is Adcock's own, reflecting a tendency of the time among educated Britons to view everything outside America's major cities as uncleared forest. While Frost could hardly have welcomed the manner in which his poetry was characterized — simple, stark, austere— this attention from the *Bookman* was certainly the most important given his volume to then, and its sympathetic and approving nature could only have provided his drooping spirits with a decided lift. It was encouragement he sorely needed.

All during June and July he had been nagged and irritated by a complicated mixture of depressed feelings. Crowding on top of doubts and apprehension, even confusion, as to his poetic future, came nervousness as to his family's welfare, all giving rise to—but perhaps also to some degree arising from—a bad case of homesickness. First mentioned in May, the homesickness showed up again in July when he wrote Silver about seeing in London "lots of Americans, as I go about, with their box-toed shoes, but they are mostly of the personally conducted variety. I yearn towards them just the same. I'm a Yank from Yankville." With the lease of the Bungalow up for renewal in September, he was also faced with the necessity of deciding whether to stay longer in England, go over to France for a while, or perhaps return to America. In such circumstances, especially recalling the shaky finances, staying or going could not have been an easy choice to make, and what seems to have decided him on staying was his second volume, just then rounding into shape for publication in the fall. Mrs. Nutt had already agreed to a contract, and a tentative title had been chosen: *Farm Servants and Other People*.

Of most concern was a sudden and severe outbreak of self-doubt over his poetry. What brought it on is uncertain, but that it was real, and that it represented for him an anxious interlude, can be seen from passages in several letters he wrote Flint. In the first, written on June 19, he asks his friend to inquire after some manuscripts he had left with Hulme, and his request betrays an apprehension quite removed from his usual epistolary calm: "Don't say anything to make me seem impatient. But if you could find out from him about it. Lord Lord I live in a state of suspense when I have manuscript out." A week later he apologizes to Flint for not sending some promised poems, meant for reading by both Flint and Hulme. General nervousness over some unnamed cause, he explains, has kept him from typing them: "I have been in such a fever of what-shall-I-call-it that I haven't had application enough to sit down to two hundred lines on the Blick." Two weeks later still, having finally dispatched the manuscripts, he abruptly changed his mind: "Please don't show those poems to Hulme till you hear from me again if it is not till this month next year. I am suffering from uncertainty with regard both to the poems and to myself. Sometimes I despair of myself for several kinds of a fool. Never ask me why." It was in this unsettled mood, as he brooded in a ferment of doubt and discomfort, that he wrote "Birches," that flowing blank-verse monologue in which he openly yearns for the uncomplicated life he had known on the Derry Farm.

Frost himself volunteered little specific about how or when the poem was written, only saying that it came to him during a bout with homesickness, "while tramping the muddy yard at the Bungalow." Much later, some forty years after the fact, he explained that the final version was "two fragments soldered together so long ago that I have forgotten where the joint is." The version quoted below appears to be the main fragment, written, as the evidence indicates, at the Bungalow in late July. The fragment omitted here, a twenty-line digression on ice storms, had probably been written in another connection altogether—and perhaps it will always remain a question as to whether he improved the poem by the addition. The two fragments were probably not brought together until a couple of years later, in time for the poem's first publication in the *Atlantic* in August 1915. Interesting is the fact that deletion of the digression (lines 4–24 in the original), requires only one very slight change in punctuation, the dropping of a period at the end of the third line, giving to the result the smoothness of first composition. True poems, Frost once observed, never begin in deliberate fashion, as a well-defined thought in the poet's mind, but tentatively, vaguely, "as a lump in the throat, a sense of wrong, a homesickness, a lovesickness." Of all his poems, "Birches," in conception and execution, may stand as the epitome of that dictum:

> When I see birches bend to left and right
> Across the lines of straighter darker trees,
> I like to think some boy's been swinging them
> As he went out and in to fetch the cows—
> Some boy too far from town to learn baseball,
> Whose only play was what he found himself,
> Summer or winter, and could play alone.
> One by one he subdued his father's trees
> By riding them down over and over again
> Until he took the stiffness out of them,
> And not one but hung limp, not one was left
> For him to conquer. He learned all there was
> To learn about not launching out too soon
> And so not carrying the tree away
> Clear to the ground. He always kept his poise
> To the top branches, climbing carefully
> With the same pains you use to fill a cup
> Up to the brim, and even above the brim.
> Then he flung outward, feet first, with a swish,
> Kicking his way down through the air to the ground.
> So was I once myself a swinger of birches.

And so I dream of going back to be.
It's when I'm weary of considerations,
And life is too much like a pathless wood
Where your face burns and tickles with the cobwebs
Broken across it, and one eye is weeping
From a twig's having lashed across it open.
I'd like to get away from earth awhile
And then come back to it and begin over.
May no fate willfully misunderstand me
And half grant what I wish and snatch me away
Not to return. Earth's the right place for love:
I don't know where it's likely to go better.
I'd like to go by climbing a birch tree,
And climb black branches up a snow-white trunk
Toward *heaven,* till the tree could bear no more,
But dipped its top and set me down again.
That would be good both going and coming back.
One could do worse than be a swinger of birches.

When Frost says he dreams of "going back" to be a swinger of birches, the dream was not a poetic invention. It can be shown, indeed, that the line deliberately recalls his own indulgence in the exhilarating game of swinging on birch trees, and not only in his youth, for he taught the trick to his children. The proof of all this, once again, is Lesley. In two of her daily compositions, both written when she was not quite seven, she mentions her own liking for the little game, though still at that age slightly fearful of it, and her father's as well. In October 1905, Frost took his daughter to hunt for chestnuts in the thick woods at the back of the Derry farm. That evening Lesley used the outing as the theme of her composition, which she ends: "We started home and on the way home i climbed up a hi birch and came down with it and i stopped in the air about three feet and papa cout me." Two days after that, apparently lacking fresh inspiration, she expanded on the topic:

i like to climb trees very much but mama doesnt like me to becose i tare my stocings so i have to stop i do not like to but i have to at first i was scared to swing with birchis but now i am not so much scared if it swings down with me if it goes klere down with me i dont like it if it dosunt i climb uther trees but they dont swing as the birchis do so i dont like them as well i climb oak and mapel but they swing with me i like that to but not as well but papa likes to swing beter [than I do] i climb apale trees but those dont swing at all do they.

Whatever it was that sent Frost's thoughts winging back to his old farm as he stood in the muddy yard of the house on Reynolds Road, it is just possible that the initial spark came from a rereading of his daughter's old composition. That suggestion is not so arbitrary as it may seem, for examination of Lesley's copybook shows that as many as fifteen or twenty of her father's poems coincide with specific topics or incidents treated in her daily compositions of 1905–1907. It is easy to see how Frost, at different times through the years, might have browsed in his daughter's carefully preserved copybooks (and those of the other children), deliberately using them to refresh his memory of a time when he was just beginning to open himself to the strange new influence of a life he had not really known before, and when, as the *Bookman* phrased it, he was "giving his soul room and time to grow." If so, it was part of his new approach in general to his poetry, a final and firm decision to treat only of real people and events, to handle only those situations he had actually encountered in life, especially during his Derry days.

Not once but many times in the ensuing years Frost was to insist that every one of his poems after that first volume was "based on an actual experience." All were drawn, he added, or nearly all, from the life he had lived in "a little circle that runs from Derry down to Lawrence, Massachusetts." A fuller statement made in the 1930s brings the two claims together, making very apparent what he meant to convey: "I always drew for my poetry, wherever I might find myself, or what might put something into my head, on the experiences of my past, long ago, out of that and out of Derry." That precise claim, expressed in more general terms, he had already made while still in England, and in fact he had very soon proposed to himself a special label for his new practice. "I am not a realist but an actualist," he jotted in the notebook kept through 1914. "A realist is satisfied if what he writes seems as if it must have happened. I set down nothing that hasn't to my knowledge actually happened." Then, taking the idea another step further—apparently at about the same time as the notebook jotting—he scribbled a passage in a letter to Cox which expresses the ultimate conscious artistry of the goal he had set himself: "We write of things we see and we write in accents we hear. Thus we gather both our material and technique with the imagination from life;

The Beaconsfield cottage, called the Bungalow, with the Frost children posing in front (l. to r.): Marjorie, Carol, Lesley, Irma. The photo, made in spring 1913, is on the reverse of a postcard sent home by Irma. (Courtesy of Plymouth State College Library, New Hampshire)

Beaconsfield New Town, about the time of Frost's residence, showing Penn Road at its junction with Reynolds Road, to the left. The Frosts' cottage stood on Reynolds Road five minutes' walk from this corner.

Beaconsfield New Town as Frost knew it. *Above:* Penn Road looking toward town from near the corner of Reynolds Road. In the distance is the sign of estate agent A. C. Frost. *Below:* Station Road, looking from the town center toward the turn-off for Reynolds Road. The railroad ran (and runs) through a cut just past the row of buildings.

The Bungalow today. Missing are the half-circles at the tops of the porch columns. Otherwise the building remains virtually the same, inside and out, as it was in Frost's time. (1985 photo)

Rear of the Bungalow today. The large back garden is still enclosed by tall hedges, one of which is the same laurel hedge (below) mentioned by Frost. (1985 photo)

Robert Frost in a photo made at High Wycombe, June 1913. The picture appeared in the London *Bookman* for August, the first photograph of Frost as poet ever published. (Courtesy of Jones Library, Amherst)

Robert Frost at his favorite writing desk, a board laid across the arms of his Morris chair. A lifelong possession, the chair was carried to England and back. (1915 photo, courtesy of Jones Library, Amherst)

Frank S. Flint, early contributor to the Imagist movement, and the man who "opened England" to Frost by introducing him to other writers and editors. He remained a close friend, even advising Frost on how the family budget in England might be stretched. (Courtesy of O. Flint)

Robert Frost's only sister, Jeanie Frost. Date of the photo is unknown, but apparently about the turn of the century, when Jeanie would have been in her early twenties. (Courtesy of James E. Newdick)

Church Walk, Kensington, showing the short spur off Church Walk proper, which contained Ezra Pound's apartment building, the furthest in on the right, one flight up. (1985 photo)

The London flat of W. B. Yeats, at No. 18 Woburn Buildings, where Frost met the poet several times in 1913: the middle building, second from right, one flight up. (1985 photo)

Lascelles Abercrombie with his two sons, about 1914, at the Gallows, his home in Ryton, Gloucestershire, which was the Frost family's last residence in England. (Courtesy of Barbara Davis, Ryton)

Wilfrid Gibson, one of England's leading pre–World War I poets, but who provided Frost with his most disappointing English friendship.

The village of Kingsbarns, near St. Andrews in Fifeshire, Scotland, where the Frost family vacationed in 1913, probably boarding at one of the houses shown. (1985 photo)

Constantine's Cave on the shore at Fife Ness, Scotland, where Frost was shown ancient rock cuttings by his friend, archaeologist Ernest Gardner. (1985 photo)

One of two stone walls—"dry stone dykes"—in the fields outside the village of Kingsbarns, the sight of which inspired Frost to write "Mending Wall." The spire of Kingsbarns's 17th-century church can be seen in the distance. The view is north, toward the mouth of the Firth of Tay. (1985 photo)

Little Iddens, the Frost family's home in Ledington, Gloucestershire, during April–September 1914. The house was part of a 100-acre farm called Henberrow, which is still intact today. *Left*: The front door and facade of Little Iddens. (1985 photo)

Some of Frost's English friends and acquaintances in a photo of 1914 (l. to r.): John Drinkwater, Wilfrid Gibson, Edward Marsh (originator of the *Georgian Anthology*, and then secretary to Winston Churchill), Lascelles Abercrombie, Mrs. Gibson, Mrs. Abercrombie. (Courtesy of Barbara Davis, Ryton)

Two views of The Old Nail Shop, home of the Wilfrid Gibsons in Greenway, Gloucestershire, the site of many visits by Frost and his family during 1914. (1985 photos)

Edward Thomas about the time
he first met Frost, in 1913, just
after completing his book *In
Pursuit of Spring. Below:*
Edward Thomas as a second
Lieutenant of Artillery,
December 1916. (Courtesy of
Myfanwy Thomas)

Robert Frost a few weeks after his return from England in 1915. The photo was made at Eaton's Studio, Littleton, New Hampshire, and was the first picture of Frost to reach the American public. It appeared with a long article in *Boston Evening Transcript*, 8 May 1915. (Courtesy of James E. Newdick)

and our technique becomes as much material as material itself." His creative imagination, all these comments proclaim, had acquired the singular knack of blending all stimulus, of whatever source and nature, with his vivid remembrance of a single, unifying, fructifying period of his early life.

Translating these loose recollections into firm chronology, it is seen that Frost here speaks of a time that covers almost exactly a decade—from October 1900 when he took over the old Magoun place in Derry, to August 1911 when he left Derry and moved north to join the staff of the Plymouth Normal School (an earlier move in the summer of 1909 from the farm to an apartment in Derry Village brought no real interruption in his outlook). During that single decade he stocked his memory with enough in the way of incident, insight, and personality to serve as the basis for the great bulk of his writing over no less than half a century. It is remarkable that, barring only a poem or two, all of his best and best-known work can be traced, directly or indirectly, to some experience of that memorable, long ago decade.

The gathering in of his Derry impressions had no doubt begun as a largely unconscious process. Only toward the end of the period, as technique and material were impelled toward, and then sought each other, becoming one, taking definite shape in actual poems, did he see clearly into his artistic future. From then on, it may be said, he consciously hoarded his memories, keeping them safe from trivial disturbance, becoming reluctant to call them up for any reason other than serious poetry. In light of all this, it is easy to sympathize with his well-known uneasiness, almost fright, at the intrusions of early would-be biographers, threatening with their questions and active research the silent integrity of his cherished past. The extensive probing of Robert Newdick especially filled him at times with consternation, a feeling that at one point was relayed to Newdick through a common friend: "He said he had spent his life heaping up piles of building material—friends, experiences, memories—and leaving them behind him unused to be used sometime when, as, and how he wished . . . this material he feels is his possibly for poems, and that once shaped by another hand isn't quite his anymore." It was mainly this jealously protective attitude, during the twenties and thirties in particular, that set up the strangely contradictory situation in which he warmly welcomed writing about himself, while at the same time he seemed to discourage and prohibit it.

This thoroughly calculated use of his farm past—remote past—is an aspect of Frost's career not sufficiently understood. At least its deliberate aspect has not been given its due weight in studies on the development of his art. Here, to say truth, is a rather serious omission, for in that same direction it is possible to go one important step further, uncovering thereby the primary emotional state, the deep well, from which he consistently drew inspiration for all his finest work, those twenty or so poems that rest secure at the core of his achievement. Literally all of these, it now can be seen, come straight out of his memory of one particular segment of that farm decade, the very earliest, when he was still an outsider, still living in daily resentment of the hard fate that had driven him "into the wilderness" (the word itself surely was intended by Frost to mean more than forest). Never doubting that he was an alien in the rural world of southern New Hampshire, questioning whether he would ever belong to it in any intimate or permanent way, yet increasingly fascinated by the earthy life he found there, he was held in a restless, unstable equilibrium. By looking at the life around him through the medium of his perplexity, subtly picturing it at work in himself against a background of real people and real events, he was able to shape his unique vision.

These were the years, roughly 1901–1905, when his own moody temperament, combined with the taciturnity of his neighbors, virtually isolated him, and he had only the talkative hen fancier, John Hall, to give him comfort. When at various times, moved by who knows what obscure prompting, he wrote out of his memory of those five crucial years he was able to create immortal poetry, with "Stopping by Woods on a Snowy Evening," perhaps the supreme example of the process. Though this best known of all Frost's poems was written as late as 1922, it actually recalls in a veiled way a sudden moment of personal anguish that took place no less than seventeen years before, at the Christmas of 1905. (Returning from town after having failed to sell a batch of eggs, the money meant to buy Christmas presents for his four children, he stopped his buggy on the road where it was screened from the Frost house by trees. Alone in the driving snow, the memory of his years of hopeful but frustrated struggle welled up, and he let his long-pent feelings out in tears.)

During the second half of his Derry period, 1906–1911, while he taught school and met a widening circle of people, his life opened up, his naturally gregarious temperament blossomed, and gradually he came to accept his place in the common humanity of the region—a place not quite assimilated, of course, and necessarily unique, given what he was. The poetry that came out of this later, more expansive period breathes a different atmosphere, more serene, more confident—and somehow less compelling. Still frequently memorable, it is somehow not as liable, in Frost's own phrase, "to stick like burrs."

It was in November 1911 that the Derry farm was sold, passing out of Frost's life forever. After the sale, as he prepared to leave for Plymouth with his family, he was impelled to commemorate in verse the surrender of the house and land that had meant so much to him:

> *Well-away and be it so,*
> *To the stranger let them go.*
> *Even cheerfully I yield*
> *Pasture and chard, or mowing-field,*
> *Yea and wish him all the gain*
> *I required of them in vain.*
>
> .   .   .   .   .   .
>
> *Only be it understood*
> *It shall be no trespassing*
> *If I come again some spring*
> *In the gray disguise of years*
> *Seeking ache of memory here.*

Only once in all the years afterward did Frost make an actual return to the Derry farm, indeed in gray disguise, when he thought of spreading on the land the ashes of the dead Elinor (an indifferent greeting by the then owners made him change his mind). But there were many hundreds of times in the half-century that followed his departure from Derry in which he went back in spirit, seeking to arouse the heartfelt ache of memory that alone could supply him with true inspiration. Of his meditative lyrics, probably the sonnet "Mowing" was the first to receive birth in this way. "Birches" apparently was second. Both of these poems had been sparked by recollections of a particular activity pursued on the farm, one involving work, the other play. Less than a month after the writing of "Birches," a third memorable lyric would appear, also based on a vivid memory of the farm. This time it concerned a pursuit that was in a sense both work and play: springtime repairs on the stone boundary that enclosed his old piece of land. The immediate spark would come in, of all places, a wide green field on the Scottish coast near the Firth of Tay.

EIGHT

DRY STONE WALLS

ABOUT the middle of August all the Frosts packed their bags and went down to London where they joined a coasting steamer bound north for Dundee. With the decision made to stay in England for another year, and the lease renewed on the Bungalow, they were taking their first trip of any length since arriving in Beaconsfield. A holiday in France had been their first thought, but at the urging of Mrs. Gardner the plans had been changed. For the last two weeks of August the six Frosts were to join the five Gardners in the small village of Kingsbarns on the northern coast of Fife, the broad jut of land just above Edinburgh. Sun, sand, swimming, boating, and relaxing were to be the main attractions, with literature to occupy the evenings. Unfortunately, personal strains were quick to develop between Frost and his hosts, so that the holiday for a time at least lost much of its fun.

For all the easy friendship that had sprung up so rapidly between the two families, on Frost's part there seems to have been some holding back from the start. This is strongly implied by some later comments of his, but also by one particular piece of evidence, the letter in which Mrs. Gardner offered her suggestion about the joint holiday.

Late in July, one day after they dined with the Frosts at the Athenaeum Club, the Gardners left London for their rented cottage in Kingsbarns, intending to spend a month. Immediately on their arrival Mrs. Gardner sent Frost her apologies for what appears to have been some abrasive behavior: "I hope that I have not fallen into disgrace on account of my wild talk at the club the other night. Perhaps I meant some of what I said; I think I did . . . But I fear I was full of *hubris* the other night, and wish I could have put forward my thoughts more gently and seductively instead of snapping them out like a bear with a sore head. Forgive me if it offended you." In closing, she extends her invitation to the Frosts for a Scottish holiday, but the tone suggests it is not the first time she had brought up the idea: "We hope that you and your family will make this little trip and come to Fife before we return. We could *lend* you this cottage for the last week in August as I want to go jaunting around. Let us know if you are coming north and when, and we could arrange a lodging. I will find out what is available anyhow." The Frosts willingly agreed and lodgings were soon found for them in the village. After reaching Dundee by steamer they went by train across the Firth of Tay, past the ancient town of St. Andrews, then six miles further on to Kingsbarns.

Relations between the two families at first were cordial, everyone being occupied with little else than "bathing and basking in the sun." Then came a rapid sequence of two incidents which, for the grown-ups at least, threw a cloud over the pleasant outing. The first incident touched Mary Gardner's just-published volume of poetry, the second concerned her husband's professional competence, or appeared to do so. Since it was only Frost who made any record of these events, and then only in passing, any reconstruction may tend to be one-sided. Yet sufficient detail is available to show what happened—and to show as well that the highly critical view taken by Lawrance Thompson of Frost's behavior, in both instances, is at least excessive.

It was only a few days after his arrival that Frost unwisely allowed himself to be drawn into a free-wheeling discussion of Mrs. Gardner's book, published the month before. Entitled *Plain Themes*, it carried woodcut illustrations by her daughter Phyllis, an aspiring artist of some talent. Presenting Frost with a copy of the sixty-five-page book, Mrs. Gardner in some subtle manner let it be known that she hoped or expected Frost would write a review, and would place it in some periodical. While Frost was still reading, or soon after he had finished, Mrs. Gardner sought his verdict. Apparently she did this not in private but in company with others, her family and perhaps some friends. Caught off guard when given the book to read, Frost would have found it at once distressingly obvious that Mrs. Gardner's volume, though issued by the respected firm of Dent, was an outright vanity item, wholly subsidized. The woman had gained not the least recognition as a poet, had reached print only in a newspaper or two, yet Dent had gone to the extreme of presenting her poems in a sumptuous, heavily illustrated format. Six months before, in commenting on Flint's poetry, Frost had permitted himself to say some things by way of approval that he could not have felt. But that had been done in writing, in a private letter, where there was opportunity to shade the insincerity. In this instance, confronted by his hostess in company with others, he could not find a graceful way to dissemble. His description of what happened next, written within a week, shows how inexperienced he was in such delicate matters: "Well, I haul off and start to say what I don't think with appropriate sops to my conscience. But such integrity as I have is all literary. I make a poor liar where the worth of books is concerned. I flounder and am lost." The result of his tactless fumbling, it appears, was a dismissal of his opinion by both Gardners, in a mood of resentment barely concealed.

Embarrassed and resentful, before long Frost's anger boiled over in a letter to John Bartlett. "These Gardners are the kind that hunt lions," he wrote heatedly, "and they picked me up cheap as a sort of bargain before I was as yet made . . . They are a one–hoss poet themselves and at the present moment they are particularly keen on lions as creatures who may be put under obligation to review them in the papers." In a cooler moment he would readily have admitted that he was nowhere near being a lion, and had no literary largesse to dispense, but in his anger he had convinced himself for the moment that Mrs. Gardner's whole purpose in bringing him to Scotland was a scheme to exact favors. Of course, neither of the two can be blamed for the depressing outcome. With sincere and enthusiastic, but inexperienced individuals, the result was nearly inevitable. (Frost, it might be noted, was able to remedy his deficiency of sophistication, becoming an adroit avoider of such literary quicksands.)

Only a day or two later there occurred the second incident, compounding matters, and regrettably, it seems to have arisen from a brave attempt by Ernest Gardner to smooth things over between Frost and his wife. One of the country's leading classical archaeologists, as well as a teacher of note, Gardner also took an interest, if a casual one, in British prehistory. To Frost he now disclosed the confidential news that an exciting discovery had recently been made in the vicinity, not five miles from the village of Kingsbarns. In a cave on the shore at the easternmost tip of Fife, several wall carvings, supposed to be by paleolithic man, had been found, the first of their kind in the British Isles. Tentatively identified as showing a horse, an ass, and an "elephant," the carvings were still officially a secret. But, if Frost liked, Gardner would be pleased to take him to the cave for a private showing. An armchair archaeologist of sorts, Frost eagerly accepted.

The cave in question, a rather shallow one, sat facing north on the windswept shore of Fife Ness, ten feet or so above a boulder-strewn beach of rough sand. Inside, Gardner led Frost to the sloping rear wall. In a recess at the wall's base he pointed out a number of small, faint carvings or cuttings in the bare rock, crude outline drawings. Crouching to inspect the prize, Frost felt an immediate disappointment. His description of the sight, penned the next day, shows the pains he took to observe both cave and markings:

> There were many marks on the cave wall, some wavy grooves due to water, some sharp-edged depressions due to the flaking off of the sandstone strata. It would have been strange if some of the marks hadn't accidentally looked like something. The sandstone was so soft and moist that a little rubbing easily made them look more like something. Animals are always the better for rubbing. And think of it—tracery like that in such a substance assumed to have lasted for ten–twenty thousand years. Why I'd be willing to leave it to the cave men as to whether they had anything to do with the elephant the horse or the ass. I'll bet the layer of sandstone they are on hasn't been uncovered five hundred years if it has been a hundred. I begin to think I must be some archaeologist myself, I doubted the authenticity of this prehistoric managerie so easily. The beasts left me cold. I tried to rise to the moment, but the cave was clammy and there were other things, principally the literary literature. Still I have no doubt a rumpus will be raised over Gardner's discovery . . . Not a word to your city editor about all this. I am betraying a confidence in consigning it to paper. But damn—

Though Frost doesn't say so, it appears that in some manner Gardner was made aware of his agitation in the cave and of his low opinion of the discovery, so that the ride back to Kingsbarns became a glum affair for both men. The discomfort probably also transferred itself to the wives, perhaps also reaching the children. No doubt it was something of a relief for all concerned when the Gardners, a few days later, left on their planned jaunting around before returning home to Surrey.

In his fleeting treatment of this cave incident, Lawrance Thompson sees the poet's behavior as having been caused by leftover anger. Basing his remarks on Frost's own description in the letter to Bartlett (he gives no sign of having dug deeper), Thompson condemns Frost's outburst as simple spite—an unworthy attempt to "assert his own archaeological superiority over the distinguished expert." Since Frost certainly did not possess anything like real competence in the field, nothing that would entitle him to oppose the views of a leading professional, it does appear that Thompson's strictures are justified. Yet it requires only a little searching through the literature to demonstrate that Frost, while not wholly correct, was exactly right in his instinctive rejection of a paleolithic origin for the cuttings. To what extent this reflects on Gardner's professional competence is less easy to judge, though it should be recalled that his expertise was classical, and Greek more than Roman. (Again, only Frost's version is available, and some of what he reports in his letter is definitely inaccurate: these were not the first cave cuttings found in Fife, nor had they been discovered by Gardner.)

The cave at Fife Ness—known as Constantine's Cave from once having sheltered a Pictish king of that name—was not the only shoreline cave in the vicinity. Just to the west along the coast, on the outskirts of St. Andrews, were two similar caves, and six even larger caves lay on the southern shore of Fife, near the village of Wemyss. All these caves had been known to the public for centuries, and active scholarly interest in them dated to the 1850s. But up to the time of Frost's visit that interest had been desultory, and it is true that no serious study had been made either of caves or contents. The first excavation, at Kinkell Cave close to St. Andrews, had been carried out in the summer of 1913, only weeks before Frost's arrival in Kingsbarns. Digging at Constantine's Cave was planned for the following summer, so that when Gardner took Frost to the site little was known of it professionally. There was only a single brief reference to it in print at the time, published some forty years before, along with a sketch of one of the animal carvings from the walls. This showed the supposed "elephant," which was not the actual animal but a Pictish symbol, another example of which had been found in one of the caves at Wemyss.

Results of the excavations at Constantine's Cave (completed 1914) conclusively dated its earliest occupation to Roman times (agreeing with what had already been established at Kinkell Cave). Specifically, the date was fixed at the second century A.D., ruling out any possibility of stone age habitation, neolithic or paleolithic. The crude cuttings in the rock were related not to the Roman era but to a later period still, some as late as A.D. 800. They were definitely man-made, so Frost was wrong as to their origin. But his rejection of so great an age as ten thousand years for the cuttings was proved surprisingly sound. The wavy grooves he noticed on the walls, obviously formed by the action of water, are still very much in evidence today and, in all truth, they should have alerted Gardner to the fact that the cave had been underwater, or subject to frequent inundation, not so very long before.

The final decision on all these caves round the shore of Fife, in geologic terms, is that they are of comparatively recent origin, having been above water for hardly more than two thousand years. No "rumpus" was raised over any of them, and it was not until quite recently that a call was issued for preservation of their more interesting features. Results of the completed work at Constantine's Cave were published in full by the Society of Antiquaries of Scotland, in their *Proceedings* of 1915, by which time Frost had left England. It is more than probable that Gardner would have seen this publication (a friend of his was one of the archaeologists involved), but if he sent a copy to Frost the fact has escaped notice.

None of this would have much significance for the Frost story, except that the unpleasantness does seem to have impaired the intimacy between the two families. No sudden break is detectable, however, only a drifting apart after Kingsbarns, with Mary Gardner making what appears to be one last effort in the fall to keep up contact. In mid-December she sent a short note to Elinor offering to lighten the Frosts' burden during the school holidays: she has heard that two of the Frost children are to spend the Christmas vacation with the Mairs, "and it has just struck me that if you send the other two to us, you and Mr. Frost could have a sort of little honeymoon together. Will you let me know how this strikes you. I think it a lovely idea." There is no sign that the generous offer was accepted and in fact the two families may never have met again, though this is not certain. Neither is there any sign that Mary Gardner (died 1936), ever came to realize that her Yankee bard had indeed become the poet America was waiting for.

*   *   *

FOR at least a part of their stay in Kingsbarns the Frosts were not restricted for companionship to the Gardners. Quite a little group of holidaymakers was on hand during August, all old friends or relations of the Gardners and each other. Jessie Mair, whom Frost had met at the Poetry Bookshop in June, came up from London, bringing her four young children. A sister of Mrs. Mair, Edith Smith, came from Edinburgh along with her husband, James Cruikshank Smith, and their four teenage daughters. There were also two young girls from a family by the name of Adamson, friends of the Smiths. It was this J. C. Smith, an inspector of schools in Edinburgh and a literary scholar in his own right, whom fate chose to place at Frost's side when he was visited by the inspiration for "Mending Wall."

That Frost was from the first impressed by Smith as a scholar can be seen from their later correspondence, but at Kingsbarns he had good reason to be grateful for one of the Scotsman's more practical qualities, his presence of mind. It was Smith's prompt action one day on the beach that saved Frost from what could have been a dangerous situation. While swimming offshore Frost was caught by an unexpectedly strong current that rapidly swept him out past the safe point. Fast becoming exhausted, he was just able to reach a shoal, where he clung to some rocks. No boats were in sight, and while watchers at the water's edge debated how to bring him ashore, Smith came along and speedily organized a human chain of swimmers. The poet was soon safely on the beach.

Smith, as it appears, never made any deliberate record of his part in the conception of "Mending Wall." A letter of his to Frost, however, contains a reference which, when coupled with a passing mention by Frost himself, permits at least an outline of the event to be recovered. Whether it happened before or after the rescue cannot be said, though a good guess would place it afterward.

The evidence begins with Frost: less than two weeks after his return to Beaconsfield, in a letter to Cox he briefly mentions the Scottish holiday, lists some of the sights encountered, then remarks, "and there are stone walls (dry stone dykes) in the north: I liked those." Linked with that admission is Smith's letter, dated November 24, 1913, in which he thanks Frost for having sent him a batch of manuscript poems for reading. He has thoroughly enjoyed the poems, he reports, and he then goes on with a tantalizing brevity: "Of course I recognized 'Mending Wall' at once as the poem which had been suggested by our walk at Kingsbarns." To start with, that remark at once provides a more precise dating for the poem's composition, for according to Smith it had by then been read not only by himself but by certain friends as well. This claim certainly throws back the writing of "Mending Wall" to October and, remembering Frost's notorious slowness in composition, very likely to September, matching it with his mention of stone walls in the letter to Cox. Moreover, if Smith's remark is to be taken at face value, it seems that at least a first draft of the poem was in existence before Frost left Kingsbarns.

It was on a walk into the countryside around the village, at any rate, that the two men came upon stone walls, "dry stone dykes," of the loosely heaped, unmortared variety Frost had known in New Hampshire, and which bordered his own old farm in Derry. Such walls may be found generally in Fife today, and cutting across the wide, green fields that hem the tidy village of Kingsbarns on the south, two ancient examples can still be seen. Both stretch conspicuously for hundreds of yards straight across open fields toward the light blue waters of the North Sea, and cannot be missed by anyone walking the area's few roads. Strolling with his friend beside or through these fields, Frost would have spotted these same two walls, and perhaps he could not resist comparing them for Smith's benefit with the old walls he had known back home. Subsequently, Frost was to recall that he wrote his poem in a mood of homesickness—as he had "Birches" in July—and while "thinking of the old wall that I hadn't mended in several years and which must be in a terrible condition." Talking with Smith in the broad, windy field above Kingsbarns, no doubt he explained exactly the way in which he and his neighbors in Derry went about caring for their boundary walls, neighbor helping neighbor (in this instance a French-Canadian named Napoleon Guy, who had the farm next to Frost). It was a homely task in which Frost would have joined on many occasions during his decade on the farm, and perhaps all that the poem does is expand on the homely details he provided for Smith that day:

> Something there is that doesn't love a wall,
> That sends the frozen-ground-swell under it
> And spills the upper boulders in the sun,
> And makes gaps even two can pass abreast.
> The work of hunters is another thing:
> I have come after them and made repair
> Where they have left not one stone on a stone,
> But they would have the rabbit out of hiding,
> To please the yelping dogs. The gaps I mean,
> No one has seen them made or heard them made,
> But at spring mending-time we find them there.
> I let my neighbor know beyond the hill;
> And on a day we meet to walk the line
> And set the wall between us once again.
> We keep the wall between us as we go.
> To each the boulders that have fallen to each.
> And some are loaves and some so nearly balls
> We have to use a spell to make them balance:
> "Stay where you are until our backs are turned!"

We wear our fingers rough with handling them.
Oh, just another kind of outdoor game,
One on a side. It comes to little more:
There where it is we do not need the wall:
He is all pine and I am apple orchard.
My apple trees will never get across
And eat the cones under his pines, I tell him.
He only says, "Good fences make good neighbors."
Spring is the mischief in me, and I wonder
If I could put a notion in his head:
"Why do they make good neighbors? Isn't it
Where there are cows? But here there are no cows.
Before I built a wall I'd ask to know
What I was walling in or walling out,
And to whom I was like to give offense.
Something there is that doesn't love a wall,
That wants it down." I could say "Elves" to him,
But it's not elves exactly, and I'd rather
He said it for himself. I see him there,
Bringing a stone grasped firmly by the top
In each hand, like an old-stone savage armed.
He moves in darkness as it seems to me,
Not of woods only and the shade of trees.
He will not go behind his father's saying,
And he likes having thought of it so well
He says again, "Good fences make good neighbors."

The opening image, peculiarly effective, in which the imperceptibly heaving, frost-impelled earth spills loose stones off the wall's top and sloping sides, may or may not accord with strict geologic truth. Yet the notion of swells or waves passing through the ground as they pass through water had been in Frost's mind for a year, ever since he pictured a rain-soaked hill in Beaconsfield as an "undergoing wave." That early lyric had been born in the first place out of his keen awareness that he had reached England, had actually brought about the wished for upheaval in his life. Once aboard England's island-ship, launched on what he knew would be his final voyage of self-discovery, the solid earth of Beaconsfield had

briefly metamorphosed to take its place in the new excitement stirring
his thoughts. In the earlier poem the facile image, opposing reality, had
come to nothing. Now, linked to the genuine inspiration of "Mending
Wall," it had found its true expression—the fact was still the sweetest
dream, especially, as always, when it opened the way to something
beyond.

Hard fact does indeed remain the grounding of "Mending Wall."
Where Frost complains about the damage caused to the walls by hunters,
for example, he is not fictionalizing, but being faithful to his own personal experience. The proof again resides in his daughter's composition
book where, some seven years before going to England, she made mention
of the depredations left by hunters in the stone walls of the Derry farm.
On a Sunday in October 1905 Frost took the whole family on a picnic to a
large grove at one corner of the farm. Walking happily through the fields
they made an annoying discovery, as reported by Lesley: "On the way ofer
we fond the ston wall knokt down in to plasys and Carol fond a shell that
they empty out after the little bulits have gone out . . . i wisht i had won
but i fond won on the way home and it was like a rele won." Hunters in
the Derry woods had always been something of an annoyance and worry
for Frost, concerned as he was for the safety of the four children who
were accustomed to have the free run of the farm and surrounding lands.
(Not all the poem's images came from recollections of the Derry farm,
however. The old-stone savage, very likely, was contributed by Frost's
talks with Gardner over the cave at Fife Ness.)

Frost's part in looking after the walls on his farm would have begun in
the spring of 1901, six months after he and his family moved in, certainly
by the next year. It is the mood of those earliest wall-mending excursions
that is reflected in the poem. Afterward, having gotten to know and to
truly appreciate the best in his farm neighbors, he would not have been
inclined to picture any of them as a simple-minded primitive, one who

> . . . *moves in darkness as it seems to me,*
> *Not of woods only and the shade of trees.*

Only during those beginning years on the farm would he have reacted to a
neighbor as he does in "Mending Wall," stressing what appeared to be the
low culture and lack of imagination. Yet in sketching the well-remembered scene he makes the aphorism about good fences and good neighbors
tell with as much force as his own derision of unneeded walls, so that in
the poem the two points of view remain fixed in opposition—as they lay

unresolved in Frost's own accurate memory of his early wall mending. The result is a subtly powerful presentation of one of life's central conflicts, in which both sides are equally worthy. On the one hand is acceptance of tradition, of the good in things as they are, and on the other, a continual, unsatisfied striving after change and betterment.

Certainly it does seem reasonable and eminently civilized to assert that

> *Before I built a wall I'd ask to know*
> *What I was walling in or walling out,*
> *And to whom I was like to give offense.*

Yet there is also a virtue in refusing to go behind time-tested wisdom, of the sort reflected in the widely held bit of folk philosophy quoted in the poem. The old saying itself—picked up by Frost from the talk of his New Hampshire neighbors, and found also in the pages of a 1906 *Farmer's Almanac* he apparently owned—recognizes the truth that man-made barriers, in effects and purposes, are as much psychological as physical. By putting personal questions in the hands of a silent arbiter, taking away the fear of encroachment, boundaries can actually serve to bring people closer.

It is in the bantering of the passage on apples-pinecones-cows (lines 23–31) that the poem comes closest to recalling the youthful Frost. It wonderfully captures his feeling during those days and months "in the wilderness," when he first hesitantly began to see the human reality beneath the rawer surface conditions of country living, and to find in them, if grudgingly, something that was somehow poetic. "I don't think anyone understands people," he was to say years later in roguish understatement, "unless he has learned from country life that lots of people are smarter than they look." One indication of his slowly changing outlook, skillfully planted in the poem, lies in the tone used by the mischievous, slightly superior speaker. Even as he thinks of putting a notion in the head of his supposedly dullard companion, he has himself begun to talk with something of the colorful ease and idiomatic bite of the rustic people around him.

This biographical reading of the poem in no way denies those abstruser levels of meaning that have been so finely elucidated by able critics. But those profundities, it can be fairly said, are not the ones that have given these simple lines their surprising hold on the affections of so many readers in the two generations just past. Rather, their perennial appeal resides in the tension that, even on a hundredth reading, gently tugs a reader first toward the comfort and safety of proven wisdom, then back toward the idea of change, freedom, possibility. Here, in a gently compelling parable of country ways, is one of life's familiar moods, shared by all men and women, a recurring mood that poses a question never or seldom finally answered. Here is youth guessing at its future, age looking wistfully over its shoulder.

* * *

OF all the men Frost came to know in England during his first full year, the one who impressed him most was his Kingsbarns companion, J. C. Smith. For this Scotsman he quickly developed a special feeling of kinship, apparently because of the way he managed to combine strong artistic leanings with the demanding profession of an educator and the care of a large family. Those precise conditions had operated in Frost's own past, and he knew that they must continue to order his future. His admiration for the man who had already so well succeeded in the same difficult task he touched on in a letter written after he had reached the quiet of Beaconsfield: "With all the work he must have to do [as an inspector of schools], he still finds time to edit Shakespeare for the Oxford Press and run after everything new in English literature. Like all of them over here he reads in half a dozen languages and like all the educated ones I have met over here he is so utterly unassuming that you might look and not see him . . . I don't mean that Smith's knowledge doesn't show when and where it should. The last time I saw him I don't know how many poems by all sorts of great poets he recited whole."

Frost did not exaggerate. For various educational journals, as well as the *Manchester Guardian*, Smith wrote regularly. He was a recognized Wordsworth expert, had edited the complete works of Edmund Spencer, had written several book-length studies on English and Scottish literature, and had prepared anthologies of verse for use in schools. When he and Frost met he was in the midst of editing a massive new three-volume edition of Shakespeare.

Perhaps not surprisingly, one of Frost's first actions on returning to Beaconsfield was to mail Smith a copy of *A Boy's Will*. The little volume was quickly read by the whole Smith family, and the Scotsman's response was sent in a letter of September 15. Since it is one of the very few surviving documents relating to this period, a few of its more personal references may also hold some interest:

Dear Mr. Frost:

There's no doubt about it. You've got the poetic gift. We spent two delightful evenings reading your book aloud after dinner—Mrs. Mair and the Adamson girls with us. (Sarah Adamson reads beautifully). For myself, I think on the whole 'October' is my favorite; but other poems won other suffrages. My own taste is fairly simple, and I like you best when you are most objective. And I rather suspect that you are travelling in that direction yourself. I told them that your forthcoming volume wd. be probably be more objective and austere . . . Margot [Adamson] has been showing me her poems and reading some of them to me. She has no art as yet—she's only 15—but she has the lyric temperament . . . at present she is too much enraptured with the hectic genius of Francis Thompson . . .

Well, I thank you most warmly for sending me your book, & I shall proclaim it wherever I get the chance. It's so genuine and so original . . . let me know when to look for your second volume.

To pass from that, we suddenly concluded on Saturday that we were all weary of Kingsbarns, & came here to my father-in-law's for a couple of nights. We go to Edinburgh tomorrow where at 20 Braid Avenue I shall hope to hear from you soon. Must stop to catch post. Best wishes to Mrs. Frost and from my girls to yours.

Within days of hearing from Smith, Frost had sent him another batch of manuscript poems, all from the new book which was just then rounding into shape. From a close reading of Smith's subsequent comments it is evident that in sending these particular poems Frost was seeking to bolster some nagging doubts of his own as to their quality. Smith's reaction to two of them was not especially encouraging, and in his remarks he sounds for the first time a basic question regarding the form of Frost's narratives, echoes of which reverberate even now. The question is one that perhaps can be settled only in the mind of the individual reader:

I am of opinion that "Blueberries" is all right. But the "Self-Seeker" is quite the best of the bunch. It strikes a higher note. Only both Grierson and I—we read it together—were some little time in getting the exact hang of it; and perhaps you might make the opening situation a little clearer for the benefit of those of us who are strange to shafts and wheel pits. And yet, I don't know: rereading makes the situation plain enough.

The one poem I'm not quite clear about is "The Hundred Collars." I know, because you told me, what the central idea is—the dilemma of the theoretical democrat when he's brought up against the real thing—man and brother, [word illegible] and equal, but a little drunk, and wanting to present you—as a token of his brotherhood and equality—with a hundred old collars. The idea's all right, and quite important—it *is* a real dilemma for the likes of us, but is it a *poetic* idea? Wouldn't you make a better thing of it in prose?

There now, it's out; and perhaps I have hit a fundamental difference of opinion. But at any rate you can give me your view. Mine is quite old-fashioned, viz., that the only reason for verse is that one has something to say that can't be said in prose.

In addition to this commentary of Smith's on his new poetry, Frost at the same time unexpectedly found himself reading the final review attention he was to receive on his old verse. Three new notices of A Boy's Will reached him in late September, and all three would have heartened him. But one, the *Academy*, then perhaps England's leading literary journal, must have left him a bit breathless.

The first of the three to reach him, the *Nation*, offered little more than a few bland phrases, but ended by pronouncing its opinion that the book had "more promise than is usual in a first venture." The *Dial*, originating in Chicago, went in the other direction, seeing the book in surprisingly visionary terms, perhaps not altogether inappropriate: "A dream world of elusive shapes and tremulous imaginings . . . a world in which passion has been stilled and the soul grown quiet . . . The sun does not shine, but the pale grey of twilight enfolds nature with a more gracious charm." It quoted two poems whole ("Reluctance" and "Flower-Gathering," as well as the first stanza of "Revelation," not the best choices possible), and closed by making a favorable comparison with the verse of Lawrence Housman.

The remarks that appeared in the *Academy* present another of those enduring minor mysteries connected with Frost's overseas stay. Its praise, nothing short of lavish, was couched in a tone that came near being adulatory. The review was not signed, and to this day its author has managed to go unidentified. Frost in his published letters and public remarks, left no comment whatever on this best by far of all his early reviews, a strange enough omission in itself. In those years the London presses poured out poetry in something of an avalanche, fueled by the willingness of even legitimate authors to pay part or all of the costs, so that only a minuscule portion of it spoke with anything like a commanding voice. That fact, alluded to in the *Academy*'s opening sentence, probably goes some way toward explaining the extravagance of the review:

We wish we could fitly express the difference which marks off *A Boy's Will* from all the other books here noticed. Perhaps it is best hinted by stating that the poems combine, with a rare sufficiency, the essential qualities of inevitability and surprise. We have read every line with that amazement and delight which are too seldom evoked by books of modern verse . . . It is so simple, lucid, and experimental that, reading a poem, one can see clearly with the poet's own swift eyes, and follow the trail of his glancing thought. One feels that this man has *seen* and *felt*; seen with a revelatory, a creative vision; felt personally and intensely; and he simply writes down, without confusion or affectation, the results thereof. Rarely today is it our fortune to fall in with a new poet expressing himself in so pure a vein. No one who cares for poetry should miss this little book.

Interestingly, this was the only notice of *A Boy's Will* with enough delicacy of insight to pick up an aspect of the volume that should have been evident to any practiced reviewer. Referring to the poet's supposed youth—plainly announced in the title but equally evident, as the writer observed, "in the dew and the ecstasy, the audacity too" of the contents— the reviewer points out unerringly that the poems are curiously free from youthful excess. There is "no insistent obtrusion of self-consciousness, no labored painting of lilies, nothing of the plunge and strain after superthings." No effort is made to account for this apparent contradic- tion and the bemused reviewer certainly never guessed the truth, that this youthful poetry was written by a man standing on the threshold of middle age.

After quoting the effective "Storm Fear," the review closes with a confident prediction that Frost's future writing will prove "far worthier than much which passes for front-rank poetry at the present time." Any suspicion that the reviewer had met Frost, or had already seen and been influenced by some of his new poetry as it went the rounds in manu- script, must be rejected. The anonymous voice takes pains to make it known that "We have not the slightest idea who Mr. Robert Frost may be." That simple disclaimer would have been enough, in the London of those days, to establish that the review was not a case of logrolling, for its falsity would have been easily uncovered.

Perhaps the leading fact about this somewhat startling notice is the immediate and very practical effect it had on Frost's fortunes. Almost certainly it was the one factor that convinced a still doubtful Mrs. Nutt that she really had discovered a poet of rare promise, moving her to make firm plans for issuing a second volume, and in a more sumptuous dress. By themselves, the earlier notices of *A Boy's Will* might not have convinced a small publisher to renew the risk, even with Frost sharing the expenses. Less easy to trace is the rousing effect the *Academy* review must have had on Frost's drooping spirits, and on the bout of homesickness he had suffered through the summer, as well as on his private estimate of himself.

Barring some accidental revelation, it seems that the identity of Frost's earliest true champion is destined to remain unknown. A pity.

N I N E

A POET AND NOTHING ELSE

WITHIN a day or two of his return from Scotland early in September, Frost was again in London, apparently to see Mrs. Nutt about the contract for his next volume. Little but a signature would have been required for that transaction, since the restrictive option clause in the old contract left next to nothing to be arranged. By this time, as his letters make clear, Frost had awakened to the blatant unfairness of the original agreement, but there was little of a practical nature to be done. In any case, he was now vastly more concerned with getting his second book into print without further delay—publication had already been moved back once, from fall 1913 to spring 1914. His impatience had good cause: encouraged by the reception of A Boy's Will and by his friends' highly favorable comment on his new writing, no doubt also stimulated to new exertion by his holiday, he had made up his mind about his future, and it involved no small or tentative ambition.

As with so many before him, Frost now eagerly began to glimpse the possibility of an untrammeled existence, one in which he would enjoy endless freedom to do nothing but think and write. A dream of earning much the greater part of his living from poetry had taken possession of him, and in the fall of 1913 he began acting very much as if such an artist's paradise would for him indeed come to pass. Inevitably, the demands of reality, principally in the form of four rapidly growing children, would soon bring him to admit the futility of such a hope. But for several months that fall he was quite serious about it, even convincing himself that his personal goals and the future welfare of his family were identical. Writing to John Bartlett, then a new father, about the responsibilities of raising children, he counsels, "All I say is don't let them influence you or divert you from your chosen way. Don't let them reduce you to the ranks. Only then will they live and grow up to thank you." Of course, all this was mostly brave hyperbole, as Frost himself knew in his heart when he wrote the words. In large ways and small his life for almost a decade and a half had been repeatedly influenced, and diverted, by the needs of his children, most notably in 1906 when he gave up his easy, poetic life on the Derry farm for the salary of a teacher.

The first definite sign of his new attitude, leaving no doubt as to his sentiments, occurs in a letter of early November, and it appears that he almost surprises himself in putting the idea on paper:

> You mustn't take me too seriously if I now proceed to brag a bit about my exploits as a poet. There is one qualifying fact always to bear in mind: there is a kind of success called "of estime," and it butters no parsnips. It means a success with the critical few who are supposed to know. But really to arrive where I can stand on my legs as a poet and nothing else I must get outside that circle to the general reader who buys books in their thousands. I may not be able to do that. I believe in doing it—don't you doubt me there. I want to be a poet for all sorts and kinds. I could never make a merit of being caviare to the crowd the way my quasi-friend Pound does. I want to reach out, and would if it were a thing I could do by taking thought.

Something audacious speaks out of that passage, with its bland dismissal of the *success d'estime* scored by *A Boy's Will*, and its confident hope of appealing to "all sorts and kinds." But his plans for reaching that always mythical market in which volumes of poetry readily sold by the thousand were not so naive as they sound. He did not really believe that he could derive from poetry alone an adequate income for a family of six, and his real intention becomes clear a month later when to a friend back in Plymouth he briefly mentions an indispensable part of his plan: "My dream would be to get the thing started in London and then do the rest of it from a farm in New England where I could live cheap and get Yankier and Yankier." What he had in mind was nothing less than a return to the idyllic life he had enjoyed as a farmer in Derry, but with one essential difference. Now he would possess an established reputation allowing him to publish whatever he wrote pretty much where and when he wished. Thus his hope of becoming "a poet and nothing else" meant not so much a farmer-poet as it did a successful poet with an assured income—from the annuity and his writing, however small—who chose to live on a farm in order to mix on familiar terms with the people and the things he would write about. (Curiously, he still had not the least inkling of the prominent part to be taken in his subsequent career by his lecturing, both as to personal fame and finances.)

Integral to the process of achieving all this was a solid English reputation, and this required winning as wide personal acceptance as possible in the free flow of London's literary society. Within a few weeks of his return from Kingsbarns, traveling frequently into town, he managed to "reach out" to no less than a dozen leading figures whom he had not met before—among them were Walter de la Mare, Rupert Brooke, Laurence Binyon, Gordon Bottomley, W. H. Davies, Ford Madox Ford, W. H. Hudson, John Freeman, John Masefield, Wilfrid Gibson, Lascelles Abercrombie, and the newly appointed poet laureate Robert Bridges. He also resumed attendance at the weekly gatherings in the homes of Hulme and Yeats, thereby meeting many more if lesser names. This part of the task he had set himself imposed no special difficulty, given the camaraderie that then existed among London writers. Once begun, it would have been hard to avoid being drawn further and further into the steady round of meetings at homes, clubs, and restaurants.

It was Harold Monro who set in motion one of the most important of these introductions, for it was he who brought Frost together with Wilfrid Gibson, a prolific and much admired poet then held in high esteem on both sides of the Atlantic, whose brief but surprising influence on Frost has been overlooked. Through Gibson Frost would meet two other poets of standing, Lascelles Abercrombie and Ralph Hodgson, and it was through Hodgson that he was brought to know the journalist-critic Edward Thomas, with whom he was destined to have the most important by far of all his English friendships.

Two brief notes from Hodgson to Frost still survive, and they show how easy and casual was the process of being folded into English literary circles at the time. Meeting Hodgson for a lunch that had been arranged by Gibson, Frost left with his new acquaintance a manuscript of one of his new poems (probably "The Death of the Hired Man"). Less than a week later the mail brought Hodgson's reaction: "Forgive me for keeping your poem a day or two longer than I ought to have done. I very much like it, and imagine it must be unique in American poetry; it is like nothing I have seen from your country, and I foresee a welcome for it in ours. It was a great pleasure to meet you the other day. I owe Gibson a good turn for that." Another two weeks and Hodgson in his turn set up a meeting with the busy Edward Thomas, who had asked for an introduction. "My dear Frost," Hodgson wrote, "Shall you by chance be in town on Tuesday? If so you might turn up at St. George's Restaurant, next to the Coliseum in St. Martin's Lane close by Trafalgar Square—at about 4. Edward Thomas will be up and I think you'd both like to know each other. This just on the chance that you might happen to be in London. I hope very much your wife is well again."

The renewed attendance at Yeats' Monday nights, unfortunately brought no greater success in cultivating the renowned Irishman. The reason for the failure, which disappointed Frost more than he cared to admit, was again simply the marked difference in temperament between the two. This is made quite plain by what happened at one mid-September visit, during which Frost became irritated by what he saw as a display of the Irish poet's childish superstition. Yeats, it seems, had told the assembled company a little story in which he showed himself in Frost's phrase, "perilously near" an actual belief in fairies and leprechauns, his voice betraying "the strangest accent of wistful half-belief." He had visited the cottage of two oldsters in Ireland, Yeats explained, where he was told of a captured leprechaun they had kept in a cage on their wall. "The little fellow was fine and sleek when they trapped him, but he had pined in captivity." Outside the house another little fellow kept vigil, and when the elderly couple, moved by remorse, finally released their tiny prisoner the two sprites hurried off together hand-in-hand. Acidly Frost remarks in his letter telling of the evening that his host "was in a state of mind to resent being asked point blank what he thought of such a story. And it wouldn't have been best for anyone to go on the assumption that he told it to be amusing." The fact that Frost himself did not ask the question is the best indicator of his diffidence in that company, though his holding back may have been just the better part of valor, since he probably still hoped for a public word on his poetry from Yeats.

His encounter with Robert Bridges, which occurred a week or so after the leprechaun evening with Yeats, came about somewhat by accident. Frost's Scottish friend, J. C. Smith, had earlier sent a copy of A Boy's Will to Laurence Binyon. Impressed, and no doubt prompted by Smith, Binyon invited Frost at his convenience to call round to his London lodgings. When Frost did so he found that his host that day was to meet Bridges for lunch. Invited along, Frost soon found himself seated at a table with Binyon and the elderly Bridges in the Vienna Cafe in Soho, a favorite watering place for writers. The meeting led nowhere, however, perhaps because Frost this time did not hold back, but voiced strong disagreement with Bridges' theories of prosody, hardly surprising, since they went violently against the whole theoretical basis of his sound-of-sense ideas. A note of alarm—leading him as usual into overstatement—even a tinge of scorn, is very apparent in his report of the incident written some days later. As Frost explained it, Bridges maintained "that syllables in English have fixed quantity that cannot be disregarded in reading verse," and he also held "that with forty or fifty or sixty characters he can capture and hold for all time the sounds of speech. One theory is as bad as the other and I think owing to the same fallacy."

Refuting Bridges' attempt to limit the variety of sounds available to human speech, Frost protests that any such limitation would inevitably tend to fossilize poetic technique. As so often, he ends by carrying his thought too far:

> The living part of a poem is the intonation entangled somehow in the syntax idiom and meaning of a sentence. It is only there for those who have heard it previously in a conversation. It is not for us in any Greek or Latin poem because our ears have not been filled with the tones of Greek and Roman talk. It is the most volatile and at the same time important part of poetry. It goes and the language becomes a dead language, the poetry dead poetry. With it go the accents the stresses the delays that are not the property of vowels and syllables but that are shifted at will with the sense . . .
>
> When men no longer know the intonation on which we string our words they will fall back on what I may call the absolute length of our syllables which is the length we would give them in passages that meant nothing. The psychologist can actually measure this with a what-do-you-call-it. English poetry would then be read as Latin poetry is now read and as of course Latin poetry was never read by Romans . . . I say you can't read a single good sentence with the salt in it unless you have previously heard it spoken . . .
>
> Words exist in the mouth not in books. You can't fix them and you don't want to fix them. You want them to adapt their sounds to persons and places and times . . . Bridges wants to fix the vocables here and now because he sees signs of their deteriorating. He thinks they exist in print for people. He thinks they are of the eye. Foolish old man is all I say.

Despite the failure with Yeats and the disagreement with Bridges, there is plainly present in much that Frost wrote and remembered from this fall a definite feeling of satisfaction, an increasing sense of having found himself. "These Englishmen are very charming," he remarked to Mosher in October. "I begin to think I shall stay with them till I'm deported. If I were not so poor I should plan to stay five years anyway." One unusual document, produced by Frost at this time, nicely demonstrates how much he felt himself a part of the English literary scene. It consists of his handwritten marginal commentary in the pages of a copy of the December 1913 issue of Harold Monro's magazine, *Poetry and Drama,* which he had marked up as a Christmas gift for John Bartlett. The assured, breezy tone of his observations on his fellow writers springs from his three steady months of mingling with these same people or their friends. The remarks are written in the ample outside margins of each page next to the work of the author in question. A few pertinent examples will give the flavor:

Thomas Hardy: Hardy is almost never seen in a public place. When seen he is not heard. They say he looks like a little old stone-mason. He is an excellent poet and the greatest living novelist here . . . Elinor and I saw a terrible little curtain-raiser (hair-raiser would be better) called *The Three Travelers* that he made . . .

Rupert Brooke: This boy I have met once. He is near you now, in Calif. He affects a metaphysical sarcasm and would be a later John Donne. [Opposite a second Brooke poem, which refers in veiled terms to Phyllis Gardner, Frost jotted another comment]: We know this hardly treated girl oh very well. Her beauty is her red hair. Her cleverness is in painting. She has a picture in the New English Exhibition. Her mother has written a volume of verse in which he [Brooke] gets his. Very funny. No one will die.

John Alford: This boy has taken a dislike to me on account of a review in which he suffered in comparison with me. Here we get down to someone who just can't write poetry.

W. H. Davies: Davies is lovely. Tramped America till he lost a leg under a freight car. Came home and sold his own ballads on penny sheets until they gave him a pension to take him off the streets. He has done some good things in unconscious art. Said he to me, "I remember you were there the other night. I spoke to you didn't I? But I was awful. After you went I went out of the restaurant a minute for one more drink and I never found my way back."

Harold Monro: The gloomy spirit that edits this. No one can laugh when he is looking. His taste in literature is first for the theological and after that for anything that has the bite of sin. He got up a penny sheet of Blake to sell in the slums and you ought to have seen the risky selections he made. But dear me everybody is writing with one foot in the red-light district.

Ezra Pound: [Referring to some praise of Pound in an article on American poetry] The magazine has had a row with Ezra. This is olive branch. Monro needs him in his business."

Some other social pursuits of the waning weeks of 1913, otherwise unknown, are mentioned in a letter of Frost's to Flint, where he talks of being at the theater with Elinor and of "gadding" at a party in Kensington the day before: "But Godfrey Mighty it's sheer extravagance at my age. The thing of it is we were taken unawares one afternoon at the theater and were committed before we knew it. The Leibichs are good and they made us enjoy ourselves. I almost overtook something elusive about rhythm that I am after when Leibich played Debuyssy [*sic*]. I have to thank the day for that." His uneasy feeling that in so much untypical socializing he was squandering his time became more evident as the weeks wore on, but there was another factor, more urgent, that tended to restrict his freedom to roam, the old question of his finances. In his correspondence of the fall he does not have much to say on the topic, but once, to Bartlett, he drops his guard long enough to explain why he is hampered in taking advantage of the many invitations that reached him: "Our means forbid. Wander not from the point I keep making, that we are playing a rather desperate game with our little wealth."

At Christmas, especially, the pinch was felt. Gifts for the children were few and simple, mostly wooden toys made by Frost himself, something he had often done in the lean years on the farm. For their part, at Christmas the children presented their parents with the daily composition books each had faithfully filled up during the year. As grownups the children were to deny ever having been particularly aware of deprivation while in England, which is a fairly normal reaction for poor children in close families. But there is one passage in a Frost poem written about now (though not published until after his death) which shows that empty pockets did sometimes bring moments of sadness. While not identified as such, the lines plainly announce themselves as a portrait of Frost with his children in High Wycombe at Christmas 1913, doing the little shopping they could afford and enjoying the festive atmosphere. For purposes of the poem the four children have been changed into two lone waifs, a boy and a girl. Of course, what the little boy pointed at in the window, he did not get:

> . . . *two babes had stopped alone to look*
> *At Christmas toys behind a window pane,*
> *And play at having anything they chose.*
> *And when I lowered level with the two*
> *And asked them what they saw so much to like,*
> *One confidentially and raptly took*
> *His finger from his mouth and pointed, "Those!"*
> *A little locomotive with a train.*
> *And where he wet the window pane it froze . . .*

*   *   *

PERHAPS the single strangest development of Frost's sojourn in England was his conviction, materializing in the fall of 1913, that he might have something to learn as a poet from the thirty-four-year-old Wilfrid Gibson. Yet the evidence for this surprising if temporary enthrallment is available for all to see, confessed in Frost's own words— "I have no friend here like Wilfrid Gibson," is only one of several such comments he made, all of which identify the friendship as more literary than personal. But that Frost could ever have entertained a serious regard for Gibson's sentimental realism—obvious themes treated in undistinguished rhythms—would be little short of astonishing, and perhaps after all Gibson's poetry was not the main attraction. Two other reasons, more personal, suggest themselves, and these when taken together perhaps afford sufficient explanation. First, Gibson's career in the various stages of its development closely paralleled Frost's own, and second, Gibson had already to a large degree found that "general reader who buys books in their thousands." Gibson, so it seemed, had actually become that elusive figure mentioned by Frost, a poet "for all sorts and kinds."

Starting in his early twenties, Gibson had published volumes of poetry during some eight years with little success, all of it couched in the familiar accents of Tennysonian lyricism. He then underwent an abrupt change in his art and outlook, and from about 1906 he began writing in a style drastically simplified, of a sort he took to be a reflection of the plain speech of plain people. At the same time he concentrated his attention on events and emotions arising out of ordinary life, and this for Gibson always meant the poor, the miserable, and the downtrodden—"The life-song of humanity," he called the result. This new approach, taking advantage of the radical simplifying trends already sweeping through English poetry, rapidly succeeded with the public, and by 1912 of all the younger English poets of the day, only one, John Masefield with his *The Everlasting Mercy*, could challenge Gibson in the matter of general popularity. His reputation had also quickly crossed the Atlantic, so that even before leaving home, Frost could scarcely have missed knowing of his name and work. He must also have been abundantly aware of the restricted scope of Gibson's abilities—it is not really possible to suppose otherwise—so perhaps in the end what fascinated him was mostly Gibson's mysterious power of reaching a wide and diverse audience.

Acquaintance between the two had begun in August, just prior to the Kingsbarns interlude. As part of his initial campaign for *A Boy's Will*, Frost had asked Monro to arrange a meeting, and had promptly received an invitation from Gibson by postcard: "I'll be here at 7:30 on Wednesday evening and delighted to see you. Bring some poems." The "here," as the card indicated, was the Poetry Bookshop, where the unmarried Gibson had lately become something of a permanent resident, occupying a room in an upper story (convenient for paying court to the shop's secretary, whom he was to marry early in 1914). The meeting was later put into verse by Gibson, unfortunately in the flat style he eventually came to mistake for poetry. Alone in his room at the bookshop, occupied on some narrative verse, he was interrupted by a messenger at his door who said that an American named Frost "had turned up." The two were soon chatting away in Gibson's room, with Frost's "racy speech" and "pithy commentary" supposedly much in evidence. What was talked about remains unstated, but when Frost rose to leave,

> *I gladly took from him a sheaf*
> *of verse he diffidently handed me*
> *Saying he'd be obliged if I would bother*
> *To look it through, and let him have a word*
> *Of what I thought of it . . .*

which overlooks the fact that Frost had brought the poetry to the meeting on Gibson's invitation. That is not a point of large significance, of course, yet it may stand as still another example of all those many distortions, large and small, that have worked themselves into the Frost story. Because of Gibson's retrospective poem, it has been accepted that Frost was the initiator, imposing his "sheaf of verse" on Gibson unasked.

From that first visit a real friendship quickly sprang up between the two, though this result can be credited as much to the Englishman as to Frost—with his warm and open temperament, as was admitted by more than one contemporary, Gibson always made friends easily. Thereafter, through much of the fall and winter, there were fairly frequent meetings, and by the close of November Frost was writing a friend back home that "Gibson is my best friend. Probably you know his work. He is much talked of in America at the present time. He's just one of the plain folks with none of the marks of the literary poseur about him—none of the wrongheadedness of the professional literary man." There were also further introductions, notably to Gibson's own close friend Lascelles Abercrombie, a poet of limited popular appeal but of some critical distinction. These three, especially, found so much in common, and got on so well together that very shortly—by early October, indications say—Frost had decided to accept the suggestion of his friends that he leave Beaconsfield and move with his family to the Gloucestershire countryside, where Gibson and Abercrombie both had permanent homes.

This decision to leave Beaconsfield was not so sudden or unexpected as the absence of detail makes it appear, for an urge to find more congenial surroundings than those in the London suburb had been growing since at least the Kingsbarns holiday. A wish to be in open country once more was part of it, but for Frost himself it was the desire for sympathetic company that drew him, something for which, over the years, he had often silently yearned. Never dwelt on, then or later, in only a single instance were his feelings about artistic companionship taken down and preserved, but they are unequivocal and they refer precisely to the move to Gloucestershire: "There were the friends we had made; there was the urge to be with those who spoke our language and understood our thoughts . . . We had never lived among poets before, working poets . . . it was a new experience for us in every way. Maybe it stirred me up, roused me."

He was also becoming, as it would seem from some frank comment in another letter, more or less sated with what had now begun to strike him as the rather dandified and superficial talk of many of his London acquaintances:

I shall have to run into town, as on Tuesday, for a meeting of the younger poets. We'll eat in Soho and then talk about what it is necessary not to know to be a poet. Of course the all important thing to know nothing about is metre. There are two ways out of it for the candidate: either he must never have known or he must have forgotten. Then there is a whole line of great poets he must profess not to have read or not to have read with attention. He must say he knows they are bad without having read them. I should like these fellows in or out of motley. Their worst fault is their devotion to method. They are like so many teachers freshly graduated from a normal school. I should have thought to escape such nonsense in the capital of the world. It is not a question with them of how much native poetry there is in you or of how much you get down on paper, but of what method you have declared for. Your method must be their method or they won't accept you as a poet.

His dislike of his friends' penchant for literary politics, it should in fairness be said, did not extend to them as personalities, for he ends his comments by admitting, "they're nice fellows all the same and one wants to see something of them."

Frost biography takes it for granted that both Abercrombie and Gibson together were the attractions for the move to the country, and there is a tendency to make Abercrombie the more important of the two. That was not the case, however. Once or twice in his letters about the move Frost does mention Abercrombie, but in passing. In February 1914 he definitely gives as his reason for going that it made it possible for him "to be with Wilfrid Gibson the English poet for a year," and that admission is echoed even as the move to Gloucestershire was accomplished: "The important thing to us is that we are near Gibson."

Sadly, proximity was to bring an end to Frost's admiration for his accommodating friend. When the revulsion came, moreover—fueled also by a certain incident involving Edward Thomas in which Gibson failed to take a worthy part—it thrust Frost too far in the opposite direction. But in the fall of 1913 this outcome was wholly unguessed, and Frost continued anxiously planning his departure from Reynolds Road. As it developed, his wish was to be temporarily thwarted by the lease he had already signed for a second year. His only hope, he was told, was to find another tenant who would sublet the cottage, and for many months that goal proved elusive.

The change of residence necessarily raised anew the question of how much longer the Frosts would remain in England. Their original plan, for a single year with another year to be spent in France, had been dropped on the successful publication of the first book, perhaps also influenced by the ease with which Frost had found a place in London's literary society. Several glancing references in his letters show that by the fall of 1913 he had actually made up his mind to remain in England for another two years, in which time he hoped to publish his third and fourth volumes, one of poetry and one of plays. Four books, he reasoned, should allow him to return home buoyed by a real if moderate triumph. The plays, mostly one-acters, he counted on to widen his public appeal, as well as giving him an added source of income.

His home life during that fall also underwent a slight change, and it proved to have some temporary effect on his writing. Lesley and Irma, after attending the Beaconsfield dames' school for two terms, at last began to complain of the difficulties of adapting to English methods. Frost, already hard-pressed in money matters and now saving for the impending move to the country, gave in to his daughters' urging and withdrew them. They took their places in the daily classes conducted by Elinor at home, and the result, shortly after, was a mild case of nervous exhaustion for the overburdened mother.

Elinor's succumbing to a case of nerves at this time was nothing very new. A delicate, quiet, shy woman, given to brooding, seldom at ease with talkative strangers, she was to experience three or four such debilitating episodes while in England, depressed moods in which she felt unable to muster the energy for even simple daily chores. At these times Frost would take over care of house and children, and eventually Elinor would begin to recover her accustomed spirits. Though she was to die of a heart attack twenty-five years later, these early incidents seem not to have been connected with coronary disease. They are detectable all through her married life, as common before England as after, and they seem to have involved nothing more than the periodic exhaustion of a sensitive nature that has been overtaxed—though perhaps it is as well to note that she customarily exhibited a rather pervading strain of melancholy, mild but noticeable.

At least for the children, if not entirely for the parents, the year 1913 ended on a happy note. At some unidentified home, in Beaconsfield or London, the whole family attended a New Year's Eve party. "We had a lovely time," Irma wrote a friend back in America the next day, "we had dancing and music I danced too and then we had a big party and the children sat down and the grown-ups stood up with cups of tea and cookies. We had cakes and candies and everything. I did not eat much cake because it was too rich at night about eight o'clock we went home in a automobile."

*   *   *

FOR the early months of 1914, the last before the removal from the Bungalow, little is known about Frost's activities, though good evidence places him at various times in the homes of Hulme, Flint, Thomas, and some others, including Mrs. Mair (at Campden Hill Gardens, where he met and became friendly with the future Lord Beveridge). The manuscript of *North of Boston* had already been turned in to Mrs. Nutt, so he had no work to do on his book until he received the proofs, and indications are that he was at this time concentrating on his playwriting. This gap of two or so months in Frost's English story is relieved only by a single lengthy letter to Frost from J. C. Smith. Though not of great significance, its implications and assumptions, and the many rambling allusions, do help to evoke a sense of the poet's presence during the period. It was written from the Smith home in Edinburgh on January 31, 1914, in answer to what appears to have been a rather frank and open letter from Frost:

Dear Frost,

(Excuse the memorandum form—my wife is away and I can't come at the note paper).

I have had you on my mind for a fortnight at least. But what brought me to the mark was observing that Amy—more faithful than I—had written to Lesley. And that reminds me: you are not only a poet yourself but (unless I am mistaken) the father of one. I read Lesley's last effusion (as Wordsworth would call it) with the greatest interest. Scientifically I am afraid her theory wouldn't hold water; but her description succeeded in conveying with remarkable vividness the feeling of a water-logged valley—vegetation, everything soaked, sunless and strange. Yes, quite remarkable. Keep your eye on Lesley.

Now about yourself. My dear boy, you're in the cold fit. It's the penalty of the poetic temperament. Have confidence in your inspiration. I happened to read over a letter of Bradley's the other day in which he spoke of your poetry. 'Original' and 'sincere' were his epithets. Now Andrew Bradley is the best judge in England. Of course it's vexing that the magazines of your own country should give the cold shoulder at this juncture. But are your American magazines infallible judges? I think not. Richard Watson Gilder was a good man: is he any longer editing? Howells seems to me to be off Harper's now (I must stop to take the children to church).

Later. Well, as I was saying, trust your inspiration and your theory will look after itself. I have said my say on the question of poetic ideas, whereby I mean ideas suitable for treatment in verse. But I am interested to hear you are trying a prose tale, and I shall be glad to see it. Meanwhile I do what I can to make you known. There is in Edinburgh a branch of the English Association, of which branch I am President. This winter we meet in each other's houses to read contemporary poetry. Sarah Adamson and I have promised to give one show, the purpose of which is to introduce to the Association a new American poet, Mr. Robert Frost. Our show will consist chiefly of Sarah's reading your poems—she reads beautifully—while I will supply any patter that seems needed. Now I have your Boys Will; but I've returned all the North of Boston poems. When may we look for that volume? Can you let me have an advançe copy? If not can you send me back some of the typescripts? There's no great hurry—we don't come on till March.

But a still happier idea strikes me. I gather from my brother-in-law that he met you in London at Christmas, and that you talked of Scotland as a possible place in which you might pitch your tent for a time. Why not come to Edinburgh in March to prospect—*and read us your poems yourself*? If the latter proposal would be too great a trial yet the former stands. If you seriously think of Scotland, come to 20 Braid Avenue and have a look round. From the hill behind this house you can see large tracts of Scotland—away to Ben Lomond in the west and all the edge of the Grampians, and Fife and Berwick and the gallant Frith between them.

What about Gloucestershire? Talking of that, the first of our contemporary poets that we went into was Gibson. There's something I like about Gibson—something genuine and tender. Then we had Yeats, and next we are to have Davies—the super tramp. I know very little of his verse.

I am writing this on my knee—as you may guess—with Edie deep in *Paradise Lost* and Hope in *Punch* and Amy upstairs embowering herself in oranges. My wife is at Newport with Anne. She (my wife) hasn't been well since Christmas. She has gone off for a rest. I am full up with official work, and likely to be fuller for some months to come; with several bits of writing on hand if I could only find time for them. (One is an article on Emily Bronte!) I've just finished Thomas's Pater—not very good: but then I never cared for Pater. Thomas says there was something about Pater from which Symons shrank as from a civet-cat. I have that feeling. Perhaps one of the reasons why I like your muse is that she walks—as you say—straight up to life, instead of skulking off into a corner with a picture book.

I've been rereading your last letter. Yes, the "Death of the Farm Hand" is all right, just right. And it couldn't have been done in prose—not as well. Of course, something on the same incident could have been done, but the effect would have been different and lower. You can speak out in verse as you can't in prose.

Write whenever you want to. About metre, you might care to read Newbolt's note on prosody in his *Richard II*. I've written something similar in *Macbeth*.

Yours Sincerely,
J. C. Smith

The mention of praise from Andrew Bradley should have heartened Frost considerably, for Smith's naming him as the country's best judge of poetry was only a slight exaggeration. An Oxford don in his sixties, Bradley was the author of several highly respected critical works, among them *Shakespearean Tragedy* (1904) and the influential *Oxford Lectures on Poetry* (1909). But if Frost harbored any hopes for a review by the eminent don of his forthcoming volume, he was to be disappointed, and the omission seems to argue some letting down in Frost's publicity campaign. Mention of Bradley should have triggered a serious effort by Nutt to engage the critic's attention further, yet nothing seems to have been done.

Apparently, Smith's giving the title as "The Death of the Farm Hand" was not a slip of the pen, for the same title had been used previously by Ezra Pound in a letter to his father. It does seem probable that "Farm Hand," rather than "Hired Man," was the original phrasing, and was altered only at the last moment. The change is a decided improvement, even a crucial one, for the implications of "Hired Man" open up the thought well beyond the more restrictive "Farm Hand," which indicates a more regularly employed worker, rather than the pathetic old itinerant portrayed in the poem. The invitation to read to the Edinburgh group was not accepted, probably because the thought of such an ordeal frightened Frost—aside from classrooms, he had never read his or anyone's poems aloud before an audience.

Sometime in January 1914 a tenant was found for the Bungalow, one who it seems was willing to await Frost's convenience, and the hunt for a place in Gloucestershire was begun in earnest. Gibson and his new wife had already set up housekeeping there, in an ancient cottage in the hamlet of Greenway, some two miles from Abercrombie's thatched house in Ryton. Cheerfully, the Gibsons volunteered to find something in the area for the Frosts, only to discover that rental housing was very scarce in that corner of Gloucestershire. Mostly rolling farm country, it afforded very few houses that had not been long and continuously inhabited. "We've been thinking of you constantly," Gibson wrote in late January, "and I'm asking everyone I meet to look out for a cottage for you. The one across the way hasn't a roof on yet and the proposed rent is preposterous. The agent thinks it will probably have to be offered for less, but we must wait and see. As soon as we're settled we'll scour the countryside for a home for you."

Still without news of a house a month later, Frost began to fear losing his promised tenant, or perhaps he just became impatient. In any case, he wrote Gibson that, sight unseen, he'd take the house across the way as

soon as the roof was put on if the rent came down. The reply came from
Mrs. Gibson, who addressed her letter to Elinor. If the Frosts ever
doubted the welcome they would receive in the west country, Mrs.
Gibson's enthusiasm must have reassured them: "We have just this
moment got your husband's letter saying you are coming here—we are
absolutely rejoiced and I'm dashing off this line to tell you so. How
perfectly splendid! . . . We've been hoping and hoping you'd take the
corner house but were afraid to count on it . . . it's especially fortunate for
us, it's so near. It *will* be splendid."

For whatever reason, the corner house in Greenway was not to be the
one, and the search went patiently on. Finally, three weeks later, Gibson
found a place he thought would do—in Ledington, the next hamlet over
from Greenway. His report to Frost must have been convincing, for
within a week arrangements at the Bungalow had been closed out, and
the Frosts were free to move. Until they reached Gloucestershire they
wouldn't know exactly what their new home was to be like, though they
were already quite taken with its name: Little Iddens.

Packing and shipping of household goods was complete by the start of
April, and it was a day or two afterward that the Frosts bid farewell to
Reynolds Road. They did not go directly down to the country, however.
Some months before, on selling some poems to Monro for use in his
magazine, Frost had arranged to take his pay in the form of a week's use of
two of the bedrooms above the Poetry Bookshop. Whenever he and the
family wanted to have a good look round at London's sights the rooms at
the shop would give them a sustained holiday otherwise unaffordable.
"We mean to do the city for the youngsters," Frost wrote home, "as much
as I am capable of doing a city or anything else." Except for some picture
postcards mailed by the children to friends in Plymouth, that holiday
week has gone unrecorded, though the cards show that the Frosts "did"
the city in much the same fashion as any tourist. "We are staying in
London for a few days," wrote Lesley. " . . . we went to see Westminster
one of the days and [saw] many interesting things and the graves of kings
and queens." Irma seconded that, saying "We are having a lovely time
here in London. We have stayed three days and are going to stay three
days more. We see all sorts of pretty things."

A day or two before he took his leave of Beaconsfield, Frost wrote his
last letter from the Bungalow. Not its contents, but a lone casual phrase
jotted at its head affords the interest at this juncture. In the upper right-
hand corner of the notepaper he wrote the date, March 26, 1914. Then,
beneath the date, he scribbled the uncharacteristic words, "This being

my birthday." Of all the many Frost letters that have survived, no other takes note of this sort of personal aside, and a curious reader may be pardoned for asking what prompted it now. The clue resides in what he has left unsaid. He has neglected to say which birthday.

It was his fortieth.

LEDINGTON:
Little Iddens

THE house found for the Frosts in Ledington, in the Dymock region of rural Gloucestershire, nicely answered the two main conditions Frost had laid down: the rent was cheap, and it was not far from Gibson's place. A leisurely stroll of two miles on footpaths through wide green fields would bring him to the Old Nailshop, as Gibson's ancient brick-and-thatch house was called, at a crossroads in Greenway. And the yearly rent was $50, a fifth of what he had been paying at the Bungalow.

The cottage itself, a squarish, two-story, half-timbered structure, was a product of the sixteenth century, built while Shakespeare, forty miles to the east at Stratford on Avon, was still a schoolboy. Despite its pleasantly quaint air, though, Little Iddens had its drawbacks, beginning with the inconvenient fact that it was even more cramped than the Bungalow, and would be expensive to heat.

Downstairs there was a tiny kitchen with pantry, flanking a combination living-dining room. The rest of the ground floor, almost half the whole, was taken up by a shed, a bare-walled barn originally intended for cattle, now used for storage (from outside, the shed is not visible, so that the house appears larger than it is). The second floor, reached by a steep, narrow stairway, contained two bedrooms and a sleeping alcove. An undulating pavement of bricks, gently distorted by age, formed the downstairs floors. The hinged windows, all diminutive, carried leaded-glass panes. Ceilings throughout were low. The exterior walls were whitewashed brick, with the blackened and crumbling timbers left showing. Nearly over the entrance door, the upper front wall under the weight of centuries had begun to buckle inward, and at some time in the past had been reinforced by the insertion of a thick iron rod. A flaw noticeable only from close up, the slightly concave facade lent to the house the final touch of picturesque decrepitude.

If the house had shortcomings as a dwelling for six, they were compensated more than adequately by the gorgeous country setting. Sitting gable end to the road, its front door looked out over a panoramic view that swept for miles across rolling, varicolored fields of hay and pasture grass. Hedging each green or yellow or mottled field were tall, constantly swaying elm trees and bushes in profusion, with flocks of sheep and herds of cows dotting the scene with whites and blacks. Near the house were orchards of apple, pear, and plum, all the property of the extensive farm, well over a hundred acres, of which Little Iddens was a part. Spread at the cottage door was a large vegetable garden, which the Frosts put promptly to use, sowing it mostly in potatoes. "Think of me still as a literary person with literary interests," Frost wrote Flint a month after moving in, "though already up to my waist in peas and broadbeans, and holding up a hoe to mark the place of my disappearance."

Situated four miles from the area's commercial center, the old market town of Ledbury, the house would have been considered quite isolated had it not been for the close presence of two neighbors. Across the road and down a bit stood the large red brick house of the farm's owner, and a similar house of red brick—called Glyn Iddens, also part of the farm—lay fifty yards or so further along the road, occupied by an elderly couple. When first built, and for many decades after, Little Iddens had sheltered the family of some fairly well-off farmer or landowner. By the time of the Frosts' occupation, it had come down in the world, serving a succession of the farm's hired men (a use it still serves, after having been rented out for a while more recently as a holiday cottage).

Visitors to Little Iddens began arriving almost immediately, more coming in the first few weeks, it seems, than had been to the Bungalow in a year and a half. Gibson and Abercrombie, often with their wives and the two Abercrombie boys, at first came over nearly every day. A relative of Abercrombie's, John Haines of the town of Gloucester, also put in an early appearance, and quickly became a friend. Urged by Abercrombie to make the newcomer's acquaintance, he showed up in Ledington one day, by chance stopping Frost himself on the road to inquire about the Frost house. Not a poet, by profession a barrister, Haines was an avid reader and collector of poetry, and a follower of all the latest literary trends. Between these two there grew up a special friendship, based less on literature, however, than on both men's love of botanizing on long, leisurely rambles through the Malvern Hills. At their first meeting, Haines was able to talk knowledgeably about A Boy's Will, having just finished reading a copy sent him by Abercrombie. In a note written to Frost the day after their encounter on the road, he gives a list of his favorites from the volume, and, losing no time, adds, "I will concoct plans for a walk soon."

Haines is the only friend of those Gloucestershire days to have left a personal description of Frost, showing him as he was in the spring of 1914, so it is worth preserving. Frost, Haines thought, was "a very fine looking man indeed. He was of medium height but had a splendid physique and was especially broad-shouldered. His eyes were an attractive shade of jade blue, and extremely penetrating . . . In disposition he was happy and cheerful. He talked much and well but liked occasional long silences and especially late at night enjoyed giving long, slow soliloquies on psychological and philosophical subjects . . . His sense of humour pervaded all his talk and he could be sarcastic if he wanted to, though usually his humour was kindly and he had a great sense of fun." Haines also noted that Frost liked to talk about New England farm folk, and was "full of anecdotes."

Following Haines, Edward Thomas and his son, on the final leg of a cycling trip through Wales, showed up unexpectedly, and they lingered for a whole week. Then W. H. Davies turned up, the eccentric nature poet whom Frost had met in London, and of whom he had formed no very favorable opinion. Unlike the other guests at Little Iddens, Davies did not add to the Frosts' growing sense of contentment with country living. He was brought to the house by Gibson almost every day for a week in early May, and quickly managed to rub everyone the wrong way. "No one doubts that he is a very considerable poet," wrote Frost in a letter, "in spite of several faults and flaws everywhere. But his conceit is enough to make you misjudge him—simply asinine. We have had a good deal of him at the house for the last week and the things he has said for us to remember him by! He entirely disgusted the Gibsons with whom he was visiting." The things Davies said involved a good deal of boasting, and some nonsense about nature, even some prattle about London streetwalkers. But whether he fully deserved Frost's exasperated strictures is hard to say. Relevant is the fact that Davies was an embodiment of the artless "natural" poet—as Frost wrote pointedly, and justly, he was "absolutely uncritical untechnical untheoretical." In other words, Davies was the very thing that Frost, in that summer of 1914, feared critics might take *him* to be, and his response to the man could scarcely avoid being colored by the fact.

The only other caller to have left any account of the Frosts in their new home was Eleanor Farjeon, a friend of Edward Thomas, whose visit came in August. Her perceptive comments coincide closely with what is remembered of the Frosts by others, both before and after England (though her observations may also depend on one or two other meetings, in London and back again at Ledington in the fall). Frost personally, she recalled as easygoing and friendly, if undemonstrative: "Whatever he did he made worth doing by the reality he carried within him, in his brain and in his hands . . . he looked at you directly, his talk was shrewd and speculative, withholding nothing, and derived from nobody but himself . . . and of all the writers of worth whom I have known he spoke with the least sophistication. He was unhurried in all he said and did."

What she remembered of the Frosts' household affairs, again quite similar to what others have described in the United States, is perceptive in what she says of the children especially—unscheduled mealtimes, nondescript diet, and what appears a total absence of routine or set hours. Of course, all this must be weighed against the fact that the looser conditions of country life, particularly in summertime, tended to exaggerate such habits:

> The Frosts did not live by the clock, their clock conformed to the Frosts. There was always time for the thing in hand. Meals (bedtime too I believe) were when you felt like them. Irregular hours for children meant an extension of experience for them; it was more important for a child to go for a walk in the dark than to have an unbroken night's rest. By day, walks and talks were not shortened for the sake of things less interesting. When the children were hungry enough to be more interested in eating than in what they were doing, they came indoors and helped themselves to food that was left available in the small, pink-washed living room: bread, fruit, cold rice in a bowl . . . The centre of the Frosts' life was out-of-doors and household standards mattered very little. If they had, Elinor struck me as too delicate to cope with them, indeed none of the family seemed especially robust; but though they were pale-complexioned they were lively and active, and too resourceful to be at a loose end.

Miss Farjeon's estimate of Elinor's constitution proved accurate, for the parade of guests and callers at Little Iddens, and all the hurry and bustle of settling her family into the confined space of her new home, soon had an effect on the already tight nerves of the sensitive Elinor. This time the nervous debility threatened to be more serious, verging, as she later admitted, on "complete nervous prostration." The weather, sunny and mild, helped her recovery, but before she was sure the crisis had passed, it was mid-June.

Contributing to the ragged state of Elinor's nerves had been the tension she shared with her husband in awaiting the first reviews of *North of Boston*. The book had been issued on May 15, when the Frosts had been in Ledington about a month, and for two weeks thereafter there was only silence. Then, in the *Times Literary Supplement*, once again on a page crowded with other notices, there appeared a brief and tepid mention. Alarmingly, it came perilously close to sounding the very notion that Frost was most apprehensive of having take hold, the idea that he was little more than a simple country rhymer: there were such words as "unpretentious," and such phrases as "naive individuality," and "little pictures from ordinary life . . . unembellished." The passage of another two weeks brought nothing further.

Three of his friends—Abercrombie, Gibson, and Thomas—he knew had already written reviews on assignment from various periodicals. But he would not have seen any of these beforehand, and there was no guarantee, as he was well aware, that any of the three would actually see print. A fourth possible notice, by Ezra Pound, was also in the offing. Early in June Pound had sent a curt note complaining that "your damn-fool publisher" had not provided him with a review copy, but this expression of interest, in light of the way in which Pound had handled his first volume, may not have entirely pleased Frost. It is not unlikely, in fact, that Nutt's oversight had been deliberately arranged. Frost did have a copy sent, but he was later to say that he had acted in the matter only after getting the request from Pound—"I couldn't refuse to meet what looked like generosity halfway." As matters turned out, he was to have cause once again to regret Pound's attention to his verse.

To some extent the tension of waiting for reviews was lessened when a note arrived from Abercrombie, who had been away for several weeks staying with a friend in Surrey. Supposedly written to compliment Frost on his new volume, the note's real purpose was to alert him to an upcoming review. *North of Boston*, wrote Abercrombie, "is good stuff, the very best stuff, the stuff we want more than anything else these days. Bob Trevelyan has quite come round to it; and I got you another admirer tonight—a prim old lady who was rushed off her feet by 'A Servant to

Servants.' That's one of the finest, I think; but so are most of them. One or two still puzzle me a little; but always the art of the business surprises me . . . If you see an article in The Nation please don't read it."

The mere sight of the *Nation's* issue for June 13, page 423, must have gladdened Frost's heart. Abercrombie's essay occupied one whole large-format page and continued over for a quarter of the next. Not only was the review a lengthy one but, as Frost soon saw, it gave judgment on the poems in the light of reasoned literary principles. Always he was to remember this particular review with more than fondness. "Yours was the first praise over there," he wrote his friend later from America, "and there will never be any other just like it."

Abercrombie's review begins by distinguishing between the ever mysterious "essence" of the poetic spirit and the innumerable accidents of daily life in which that essence is caught and held. Frost's poems, he found, were of fundamental interest on both counts, though here and there the two elements were insufficiently fused and the essence "exceptionally shy and elusive." That mild caveat disposed of, Abercrombie spends the rest of his space setting forth the "unique and entirely original" nature of the volume's contents, incisively treating both matter and technique. Here, he roundly declares, was no inspired rustic at work, no simple-hearted rhymester:

> His method—we cannot quarrel with it because in its final result it nearly always accomplishes something remarkable—is to invite us to assist, first, at his careful and deliberate laying of the material for a poetic bonfire; the skill is interesting, and the stuff is evidently combustible; and suddenly, we do not quite know when, while we were intent on these structural preliminaries, we find that a match has been put to the pile. It burns out, as a rule, rather quickly; but while it is burning, substance and fire are completely at one, and at the end we are not left with embers, but with the sense of a swift and memorable experience . . .

> These specimens of New England life are not greatly different from the corresponding life of Old England; yet there is an unmistakeable difference, on which it would not be easy to lay one's finger. American democracy contributes to the difference, but it is certainly not the most important element in it. The life seems harder and lonelier, and it also seems, oddly enough, more reflective and philosophic . . . It is life that has, on the whole, a pretty hard time of it, though a queer, dry, yet cordial humour seldom fails it; but it is life that has time to look about itself. How much of this is due to Mr. Frost's interpretation of New England we, on this side of the Atlantic, can hardly say; but if internal evidence goes for

anything, life has seldom been made into literature with as little manipulation as in this book . . .

We find very little of the traditional manner of poetry in Mr. Frost's work; scarcely anything indeed, save a peculiar adaptation, as his usual form, of the pattern of blank verse. It is poetry which is not much more careful than good prose is to stress and extract the inmost values and suggestive force of words; it elaborates simile and metaphor scarcely more than good conversation does. But it is apt to treat the familiar images and acts of ordinary life much as poetry is usually inclined to treat words—to put them, that is to say, into such positions of relationship that some unexpected virtue comes out of them . . .

After a glance at Frost's spare yet effective use of simile and metaphor, Abercrombie turns to the "specialized language," a critical aspect of the verse, he says, which is not at first apparent, though it is vital to the effect. For the first time in print, Frost's sound-of-sense ideas receive a serious evaluation, a fact which gives this pioneer review an added honor all its own. (Abercrombie had not discerned all this unaided, but was making good use of his many talks with Frost on the subject.):

We have heard a good deal lately about the desirability of getting poetry back again into touch with the living vigours of speech. This usually means matters of vocabulary and idiom; and Mr. Frost certainly makes a racy use of New England vernacular. But he goes further; he seems trying to capture and hold within metrical patterns the very tones of speech—the rise and fall, the stressed pauses and little hurries, of spoken language. The kind of metrical modulations to which we are most accustomed—the modulations intended for decoration or purely aesthetic expressiveness— will scarcely be found in his verses. But, instead, we have some novel inflections of metre which can only be designed to reproduce in verse form the actual shape of the sound of whole sentences. As a matter of technique, the attempt is extraordinarily interesting.

Picking three poems for special mention—"Mending Wall," "Home Burial," and "A Hundred Collars,"—Abercrombie confesses that he finds it a peculiarly difficult matter to define Frost's distinctive quality. A comparison, he suggests, may help. Somewhat surprisingly, he then reaches back past the obvious ones, Wordsworth and Chaucer, all the way to the classical ages:

When poetry changes by development rather than by rebellion, it is likely to return on itself. Poetry in Mr. Frost exhibits the identical desires and impulses we see in the "bucolic" poems of Theocritus. Nothing so futile as a comparison of personal talents is meant by this; but for general motives, the comparison is true and very suggestive. Poetry, in this book, seems determined once more, just as it was in Alexandria, to invigorate itself by utilizing the traits and necessities of common life, the habits of common speech, the minds and hearts of common folk.

After the *Nation*, another long week of waiting ensued before the *Pall Mall Gazette* arrived, carrying some brief praise. Impressed as Abercrombie had been by the originality of the sound-of-sense technique, the anonymous writer in the *Pall Mall* managed to describe it in a fashion that had never occurred to Frost himself. To one way of thinking, it may stand as the aptest description of all: "With plain words, with the woof of familiar metres crossed constantly by the warp of instinctive cadences, without declaiming or any emphasis that hides truth by magnifying it, he creates a series of idylls in an infinite variety of greys." How curious to think that this image of warp-and-woof—also calling up as it does the notion of handmade cloth, home spun—has not since then been used in talking of Frost's unique quality.

The prestigious *Outlook* was next to arrive at Little Iddens, and it brought a notice from the pen of the prominent editor-novelist Ford Madox Ford, Conrad's friend and collaborator. Though favorable, to Frost the review must have been a distinct disappointment. A good deal of space was wasted in asking such questions as why Frost chose to avoid *vers libre*, and why America was so full of "trickery, make-believe, lying and empty loquacity." Frost's poetry, Ford at length concludes somewhat archly, is superior even to that of Whitman, "much finer, much more near the ground, and much more national, in the true sense," leaving readers to wonder what was so commendable about poetry being "near the ground" (a tricky way of saying "down to earth"?).

Of the four reviews of *North of Boston* that had appeared to the close of June, only that of Abercrombie had allowed the poems their full value as powerfully original works. But the others had at least been favorable, and all had appeared in respectable journals. Still to come were those of Gibson, Thomas, Pound, and from the first two of these Frost knew he could expect at least sympathetic treatment. From Edward Thomas, then enjoying a considerable reputation as a professional critic, he looked especially for some well-considered analysis, as well as publicity. Thomas may already have reported getting commissions for reviews of *North of Boston* from no less than three different magazines.

By happy accident it is possible to catch a glimpse of Frost just at this time, when tension over the reviews had begun to relax, displaying a renewed sense of well-being and comfort. It occurs in some nostalgic verse by Gibson, commemorating a gathering of the Dymock Poets one evening in 1914 at his home in Greenway. Present, besides Frost and Elinor, were Gibson and his wife, Abercrombie and his wife, Gibson's close friend Rupert Brooke, who had just returned from foreign travel, and Edward Thomas and his wife, down from London to make a stop of a few days at Ledington. It was a "still summer evening" late in June when the friends gathered in the cozy, gold-colored living room at the Old Nailshop, light streaming in through rose-latticed windows. The picture of a more than usually expansive Frost, oldest of the group and the most practiced talker, leading the fun with a rare mixture of homely wit and backcountry wisdom, strikes an authentic note:

> *In the lamplight*
> *We talked and laughed; but for the most part listened*
> *While Robert Frost kept on and on and on,*
> *In his slow New England fashion, for our delight,*
> *Holding us with shrewd turns and racy quips,*
> *And the rare twinkle of his grave blue eyes.*
>
> . . . . .
>
> *Now a quick flash from Abercrombie, now*
> *A murmured dry half-heard aside from Thomas;*
> *Now a clear, laughing word from Brooke; and then*
> *Again Frost's rich and ripe philosophy,*
> *That had the body and tang of good draft cider . . .*

The lines, written in 1926, are not much as poetry but they do preserve the author's fond remembrance of that long-ago evening of talk and laughter. Perhaps a good part of the reason for Gibson's nostalgia lay in a sad fact that goes unmentioned in the poem—two of the happy participants, Brooke and Thomas, both men of exceptionally bright promise, would shortly give their lives for their country. It was only three days after this evening of gaiety that there took place in Sarajevo the tragic event that would, within a month, plunge Europe into World War I, the assassination of Archduke Ferdinand.

Frost's surviving letters of this time, those he wrote during that politically troubled July, contain no reference to the assassination or the growing war crisis. It was not an unusual omission, however, for hardly anyone in England in those first hectic weeks felt that a shooting war was a serious possibility. Still concerned much more with his personal destiny, Frost continued to look anxiously for reviews, and just before the outbreak of hostilities he was rewarded with three more, including a second notice in the *Times*. The most important of the three was Gibson's, but here he would encounter an unpleasant surprise.

The *Times* faulted the poems for some monotony, and for an occasional obscurity. But the paper then put aside all caviling and offered generous praise, pointing in particular to the "stark concentration" to be seen and felt throughout the volume: "Poetry burns up out of it—as when a faint wind breathes upon smoldering embers . . . One is always conscious of the silence, the mystery, that saturates life; of that presence—call it what you will, God, Nature, Subconsciousness, Beauty, Reality—which makes miraculously significant the mere falling of one leaf in all the forest."

In the *Egoist* another London acquaintance of Frost's held forth, and perhaps not entirely to his liking. While in its way quite favorable, the *Egoist* review exuded a peculiarly uncertain air, and it managed at one swoop to express all the doubts about Frost's technique that would crop up at intervals in the following years and decades. Or, to say it better, the review demonstrates in a wonderfully pure form a reader's need, if the true power of Frost's poetry is to be felt, to adjust the mental pace, and the ear itself, to his slower, calmer, quieter world. This adjustment the review's author, Richard Aldington, had not then quite succeeded in making. Like Ford in the *Outlook*, he spent his first paragraphs lamenting American crassness ("We in England are rather apt to be scornful of American poetry—and rightly so, for there is nothing so appallingly boring as the average American cosmic poem," etc.). When he settles down to discussing the poetry, he quickly reveals his lack of appreciation for Frost's metrical originality, yet he also confesses to a grudging acceptance of much else in the book:

Mr. Frost is a better poet than Whittier. I hear it whispered that he is better than Whitman. That is going some. Perhaps he is . . . It is in cumulative effect rather than in detail that Mr. Frost gets his results. He tells you a little or a big incident in rather stumbling blank verse, places two or three characters before you, and then tells you another incident with fresh characters, making you more interested all the time, until at the end of the book you realize that in a simple, unaffected sort of way he has put before you the whole life of the people "North of Boston."

The initial plunge into Mr. Frost's book is a little difficult. Quite frankly it seems dull, devilish dull. And yet it isn't. I quite thought it was dull. I was certain of it. And yet I have gone on reading a poem here and a poem there during the last fortnight until I am positively fascinated with the book. I think the reason for this apparent dullness is due to the monotonous cadence of the verse. Line follows line with almost exactly the same rhythm and tone . . . I understand that Mr. Frost tries to use in his poetry the speech of everyday life. That is an excellent thing; but there is surely more variation of rhythm in our ordinary talk . . .

Simplicity of speech, directness of treatment, episodes of life not too obviously treated—those are qualities of Mr. Frost's poetry, and very excellent ones too . . . He has avoided most of the faults of contemporary poetry—and yet he has plenty of his own. The question of rhythm bothers me immensely; and yet it shouldn't. Mr. Frost is obviously a poet; one has no right, I suppose, to try and fit him to the measure of one's own poetic foot-rule.

Gibson's review appeared in the *Bookman* for August. Disappointingly, it was embedded once again in simultaneous reviews of three other volumes of poetry, and perhaps Frost could not have been faulted for questioning why his friend, this time, had not managed to present *North of Boston* separately. But that was not the most prominent drawback of the *Bookman* review. Rather, it was Gibson's halting and inept appraisal of the poetry itself, to the point where the review very probably marks the start of Frost's disenchantment with his friend—other evidence indicates that the change in attitude began about this time.

Gibson too at first wastes precious space in disparaging contemporary American poetry. When, finally, he settles to judgment on Frost, the result becomes a strange amalgam of measured approval and uneasy rejection. In his opening paragraph, for example, he insists on Frost's literary sophistication, but he manages at the same time to sow doubt:

In its quiet and unsensational way, Mr. Frost's *North of Boston* is the most challenging book of verse that has been published for some time. To the unsophisticated reader it may seem to be an unsophisticated production, the work of an ingenuous mind. Even the innocent reviewer may be beguiled by Mr. Frost's apparent simplicity into forgetting the reviewer's own pet tag about the art which conceals art, mistaking Mr. Frost's assured art for artlessness. Yet of the four poets now under consideration Mr. Frost is certainly the most sophisticated . . .

Faint enough praise, putting Frost above three unknowns rather than ranging him against established names. Still, a reader might legitimately expect, after that, to be shown something of Frost's sophistication at work. Yet as the review proceeds it manages in its hortatory style only to raise doubts anew:

> He is individual without being eccentric. He has become so absorbed in the characters he delineates that he has neither time nor inclination to put on frills, or in any way to attract attention to his originality. The challenge of his work lies in its starkness, in its nakedness of all poetic fripperies. The blank verse in which the tales are written is entirely made up of ordinary speech-phrases, through the medium of which Mr. Frost manages to convey not only the sense of the speakers, but the very tones of their voices . . .

Surprisingly for one who had the advantage of many leisurely talks with Frost, those last sentences somehow seem to deny any real or deliberate art in prosodic innovation, so much finer an accomplishment than that of the contemporary Imagists. Gibson, it may fairly be said, despite referring to Frost's "careful and deliberate art," at last makes it appear as if this compelling new voice was no more than a lucky accident. To make matters worse, and still more unexpectedly, an expression of outright dissent promptly follows: "I am inclined to wonder at times if, in his determination to avoid artifice, Mr. Frost has not discarded too much. There are legitimate excitements, as well as illegitimate, in the enjoyment of verse; and in reading some of these poems I have missed the exhilaration of an impelling and controlling rhythm."

Carefully phrasing his closing remarks, Gibson combines approval with a palpable measure of restraint, especially noticeable in the reason he assigns for the way the poems achieve significance: "Tales that might be mere anecdotes in the hands of another poet take on a universal significance because of their native veracity and truth to local character." The psychological penetration, the unerring eye for the selection of detail, the profound sympathy, so well concealed, are all ignored. Instead, everything is explained by "native veracity," as if it were some sort of trick, a matter of a photographic eye, and all that Frost's art contributed were angle and lighting.

Why Gibson should have discerned less of Frost's accomplishment than Abercrombie is hard to say. The two certainly must have talked at some length, and repeatedly, about Frost and his book. Beyond mere obtuseness, one reason for his blindness may have been a burdensome tinge of jealousy, aroused by his recognition that while Frost and he were in pursuit of much the same goals, the American had reached heights of art beyond anything in Gibson's prolific output, perhaps beyond anything imagined by him as possible. At any rate it is a fact that in talking with Frost about *North of Boston*, Gibson's manner at some point betrayed something disturbingly like envy. In a letter to Haines written soon after his return to the United States Frost mentions Gibson and says pointedly, "I saw enough of his hypocritical joy over my good reviews last summer." Another letter, of February 1916, more than a year after Frost had seen the last of his Gloucestershire friend, is even more outspoken. The recipient of the letter, Frank Flint, was also well acquainted with Gibson: "Poor dear Gibson! Whatever else has been corrupting me since last I saw you bareheaded in Oxford St. it hasn't been Gibson. No sooner had I got down into the country near him than I began defining my position with regard to him—and you know what that means. It means sheering off from him."

As Frost saw it, Gibson had two insuperable defects as an artist: a serious lack of real knowledge about the sort of common-life situations that formed the staples of his writing, leading to artificiality, and a truly startling deficiency in prosodic skill and understanding, a lack of which Gibson was actually inclined to boast. What emerges from these and other stray mentions by Frost is unmistakable—a settled conviction that the Englishman's real offense lay not so much in his artistic ineptitude as in his inflated opinion of himself, and in his way of making artistic ignorance seem commendable. With this beginning, what happened later in the fall merely hastened the souring of the friendship.

And yet, it can also be said that Frost's disenchantment with Gibson needs to be judged in a still larger framework, for in the end it can be seen as part of his strong revulsion against the whole concept of literary groups and coteries. Frost's supposed idyllic country interlude, contrary to what is usually thought, was of fairly short duration. Its most immediate result, quite unlooked for, was to stir in him the beginnings not only of discomfort with, but a deep distrust of any too close link with literary circles of any sort. It is true that he went down into Gloucestershire roused by the thought of living among kindred spirits, but by late June, three short months after his arrival, he had begun to change his mind, and both he and Elinor talked of moving nearer London again. The most direct proof of his change of heart toward what he eventually came to deride as literary "gangs" is sufficiently seen in the facts and opinions of his later life, starting on his return to America. While he enjoyed epistolary friendships with many writers, and knew some in person, he was never to have even one close personal friend—real friend rather than intimate colleague—among the literary (Louis Untermeyer notwithstanding). To a college friend he later confessed, "I keep far enough away from the crowd [of fellow writers] so that I don't have to get mixed up with that sort of insincerity." And Sidney Cox adds a similar note when he describes Frost in about 1938: "He's always differentiated himself, though not so much by assertion as by behavior, from the prim and the ladylike and the hyperaesthetic."

Frost himself toward the end of his life can be found still making gratuitous references to just this attitude, in explaining why he had not mixed more with his peers. In a rambling interview of 1956, without being asked he contrasted himself with most other poets he had known or heard about, aptly summing up his manner of life after England. "You see, I haven't led a literary life," he volunteered. "These fellows, they really work away with their prose trying to describe themselves and so on. I don't do that. I don't want to know too much about myself . . . I don't have hours, I don't work at it, you know. I'm not a farmer, that's no pose of mine. But I have farmed some and I putter around. And I walk, and I live with other people. Like to talk a lot. But I haven't had a very literary life."

In sharing his days with the practicing poets of Dymock Frost discovered that the stimulus of literary companionship, professional encouragement, was not what he needed or wanted. No doubt it was partly his age, relatively advanced, that led him to favor artistic separateness. But whatever the reason, his instincts were right. Few poets have depended as much for inspiration on an immediate, undistorted contact with the apparently ordinary things of life.

ELEVEN

THE ONLY BEGETTER

REACTING speedily to the invasion of Belgium by Germany, England announced its entry into the Great War on August 4, 1914, and the next day throughout the country full mobilization began. Frost, taken by surprise as were most others, suffered some initial confusion over his best course, and at first thought only of getting his wife and children safely back to the United States. Then, failing to grasp all the implications—and no doubt lulled by the widely voiced sentiment that hostilities would be "over by Christmas!"—he decided to stay. His whole future, he concluded, depended on firming his reputation with just one more successful London book. But that attitude did not last long either, especially when he found that Abercrombie and Gibson, and some others of his acquaintance, had been notified by the various magazines and newspapers that strictly literary matter, including book reviews, was to be sharply curtailed for the duration. Book publishers also announced drastic cutbacks in their lists, particularly poetry. With that, Frost awoke to the reality. "The war is an ill wind to me," he wrote Cox on August 20. "It ends for the time being the thought of publishing any more books. Our game is up . . . so we may be coming home if we can find the fare or a job to pay the fare after we get there."

From that point on, as his letters show, Frost's mind seldom rested from the twin problems of how to get his family home, and exactly what he might do to earn a living when he got there. His dream of using a farm as his base and devoting himself to poetry was still very much alive, but by now he was less sure that it could be made to work, and his choice of livelihood remained what it had always been: teaching or farming, with the latter the more problematic. A related difficulty concerned the transference to America of the reputation he had begun to earn in England, a necessity if he was to build on what he had already accomplished. None of these questions was easy of solution, and Frost's state of mind during the fall of 1914 is perhaps best summed up in a remark he made about that time to John Haines. "Life," he wrote, "is once more one grand uncertainty."

If he had possessed the means, it is virtually certain that Frost would have left England for America a good many months before the date of his actual departure in February 1915. If he had, then it is likely that one of the most fascinating and fateful results of his English sojourn never would have occurred. This was the dramatic development, under Frost's direct influence, of Edward Thomas as a poet—and, as it increasingly proves, a poet of considerable stature, as well as popularity. It was during some eight or nine months, from spring to fall of 1914, that Thomas's belated transformation from prose writer to poet progressed steadily to its surprising culmination. Thomas's wife Helen, years afterward, was to record Frost's part in it, the striking effect, artistically and personally, that he had exerted on Thomas, which she described as "wonderful." Her husband, she admitted, was a man of "strange, complex temperament," something that Frost had understood "as no other man had ever understood . . . the influence of this man on [Edward's] intellectual life was profound, and to it alone of outside influences is to be attributed that finest and fullest expression of himself which [Edward] now found in writing poetry."

Here, certainly, was one of history's most extraordinary literary pairings, vividly recalling, as does no other, the bond between Wordsworth and Coleridge, for the response of spirit was not all on the Englishman's side. As Frost was later to recall, he found in Thomas's intellectual temperament, and in his feeling for the life of the country, a powerful attraction. "The closest I ever came in friendship," he said afterward, was with Thomas, and elsewhere he referred to the Englishman as "the only brother I ever had." In 1917, on hearing of Thomas's death, and remembering all the plans he and his friend had made for the future—which included Thomas immigrating with his family to the United States and joining in a proposed summer school as a lecturer—he said that "he more than anyone else was accessory to what I had done and was doing. We were together to the exclusion of every other person and interest all through 1914—1914 was our year. I never had, never shall have another year of such friendship." Making even stronger the bond between the two was Elinor's nonliterary response to Thomas, helping to explain the attraction he had for so many: "He is quite the most admirable and lovable man we have ever known."

Generally similar in personal traits and background, each of the two had independently achieved precisely the same sensitive relation to his subject—nature and the rural life—and each went on to earn about the same standing in his own country (in kind, though not yet with Thomas in degree). The popular appeal of each today is much the same, a minute focus on the land, and its people and customs, often seen through a darkening haze of actual or impending loss and decline. But Thomas, though employing a spare, dry, often nervous style which he built directly on Frost's theory and example, was still able to free himself, to wholly disengage his voice from that of his master and friend. As is Frost's, Thomas's sound is distinctive, as essentially English as Frost's is American—which perhaps explains why neither has yet been able to make much headway in the other's country.

It was a rare and certainly an unpredictable outcome of an unusual friendship. How it all happened is worth a closer look than it has so far been given.

*   *   *

THE London restaurant at which Frost first met Thomas, the St. George in busy St. Martin's Lane, was a favorite lunchtime haunt of writers, those at least who favored vegetarianism ("through the little door at the right, up two flights of brass-bound steps, through the door with Smoking on it, to the Chess Room"). Apparently it was at Thomas's own request that the two were brought together, Thomas having recently read in manuscript "The Death of the Hired Man," with the introductions being arranged by Thomas's close friend Ralph Hodgson. The date of the meeting was October 6, 1913.

At thirty-six, Thomas, an Oxford graduate, had been married a dozen years and was the father of three. For over a decade, starting on his graduation from college, he had earned his living as a writer, turning his hand to a wide range of assignments given him by book publishers and periodicals. Though he was capable of considerable descriptive charm, especially when handling rural themes and the outdoor life, in general as a prose writer he can be counted as little more than competent, and he enjoyed no very great reputation with the public. As a book reviewer,

however, especially when treating poetry, he had gained a definite standing, and it was not unusual for him to be spoken of as ranking among
England's leading critics of the day. No doubt it was this fact, with
publication of *North of Boston* imminent, that caught Frost's attention
when Hodgson suggested a meeting.

In his composed manner and quiet demeanor, Thomas gave the impression of being a well-contented man, in control of himself and his life. In
reality he was not at all happy. A settled tendency toward endless brooding had produced in him a severe melancholy, which frequently degener-
ated into dark moods of despair. As he was always first to admit, his
frequent moody discontent was often the cause of serious discord in his
home—a small workman's cottage in the village of Steep, about an hour
southwest of London by train. Noisy children, a clinging wife who, while
conscientious and loving, had only a loose grasp of household affairs, and
the lack of a separate study, all made it necessary for him to be away much
of the time in order to get his work done. Often he stayed for days or
weeks with one or another of his many friends in and around London, or
simply took temporary lodgings. When he and Frost first met he was a
guest at the home of a friend in the suburb of East Grinstead, doggedly
giving many hours a day to a short, commissioned biography of Keats, and
visiting his family at Steep weekly.

Methodical in his writing habits, he spent a fixed number of hours
daily on his work, seldom missing even when away from home. But the
great bulk of his writing was undertaken for the pay alone, and most of it
was thoroughly at odds with his temperament and aspirations. More and
more he had come to resent the unceasing demands of a way of life that he
had taken up in the earnest hope of winning a literary name, but which
now seemed to be leading nowhere.

While Thomas's most ardent admirers readily concede that he was
afflicted with a genuine case of neurasthenia, it seems more probable
that, as a man of delicate organization to start with, he was mainly
suffering from a burden of overwork long continued, complicated by
worry over the uncertain income of the writer's trade. The sheer quantity
of his writing in itself would suggest the likelihood of mental and emotional fatigue. In the space of a dozen years he had churned out an
astonishing amount of finished composition, no less than twenty-four
books (six biographies, nine volumes of nature and travel writing, eight
volumes of essays and stories, and a novel), all in addition to many
hundreds of book reviews and articles. Though he was a ready, rapid
writer able to draw on a large store of personal knowledge for all his

subjects, such a fierce pace, offering no respite or escape if he was to earn his family's living, would have inevitably worn down a far more robust spirit. At one point, indeed, several years before he met Frost, his headlong efforts did, as it appears, bring him to a crisis of frustration and to thoughts of suicide. Taking an old revolver he kept in a drawer, he left his house and went alone to some nearby hills. Several hours later he came back unharmed—and proceeded to turn the experience into a short story.

During their first months together it was Thomas who actively pursued the friendship—at this time and for months afterward, Frost considered Gibson, not Thomas, to be his "best friend." He read and commented on several Frost poems, and once he asked about the possibility of finding temporary lodgings in the Beaconsfield area. From Steep in mid-February, while wrestling with his usual overload of writing assignments, he confessed in a note to Frost, "I wish you were nearer so that we could see one another easily and our children." Frost's response may have been slower, but that he took an immediate interest in the personal trials of his new acquaintance is evident in a remark he made later to Helen Thomas: "I knew from the moment when I first met him that he would someday clear his mind and save himself." In fact he soon went further, at an early date suggesting that Thomas should throw off the burden of his unrecognized writing and make a new start with his family in America by joining the Frosts when they returned to New Hampshire. Doubtful of the idea when first broached, as time went on Thomas came to think well of it, especially after he began writing poetry. Only the war prevented his career from having an American phase.

Artistically, the crucial period in the relationship occurred during a period of five or six weeks in late spring 1914, beginning with Thomas's April visit to Ledington. He and his son had been on a bicycle trip through Wales and their return route took them by way of Dymock. At the Frosts' they were persuaded to remain for a week, finding lodgings at some farmhouse. Of this first extended visit between the two, only a later remark of Thomas's is recorded, a remark which shows that Frost's calm strength had a peculiarly soothing effect on him (so like Wordsworth's on Coleridge). "I tell you," he wrote Frost the following spring, "I should like another April week in Gloucestershire with you like that one last year. You are the only person I can be idle with." On this same April trip, Thomas left with Frost a copy of his latest book, published that month, *In Pursuit of Spring*. It was to prove a fateful gift.

Several weeks after that visit, Thomas wrote Frost his first letter of any length. A meandering mixture of comment, its real purpose lay concealed in the seemingly casual question dropped gingerly into the text at the start of the third paragraph. The full significance of that question—for those who know the questioner—can be judged by the fact that, once posed, it is promptly veiled in banter:

My Dear Frost

    I wish I could write a letter. But every day I write a short Welsh sketch & a review. I read a bit & weed a bit & every evening type something, not to speak of touching the fiction still sporadically. And then there is the weather to enjoy or (here comes the laugh) to imagine how it should be enjoyed . . . Don't get at me about my T.P. article, which wasn't all that even I could do, but a series of extracts from an essay I shan't do. You could do one now. And you really should start doing a book on speech and literature, or you will find me mistaking your ideas for mine & doing it myself. You can't prevent me from making use of them: I do so daily & want to begin over again with them and wring all the necks of my rhetoric—the geese. However, my "Pater" would show you I had got unto the scent already . . .

    Your second note pleased me. I shall perhaps come soon. My wife & I are to have a week or so very probably early in July. We have to get in several calls. If we can we will come to Ledington . . . Now about August, could we *all* get into Chandler's for a month & would they have us & at what price? The only difficulty would be a room for me to work in, for work I must . . . I don't hear when your book is coming. I tried to get T.P. to let me write on it but they wont.

    I wonder whether you can imagine me taking to verse. If you can I might get over the feeling that it is impossible—which at once obliges your good nature to say 'I can.' In any case I must have my 'writer's melancholy,' though I quite agree with you that I might spare some of it to the deficient . . . I am pleased with myself for hitting on 'Mowing' & 'The Tuft of Flowers'. For I forgot the names of those you meant me particularly to read, these I suppose being amongst them. You see that conceit consorts with a writer's melancholy.

    I go on writing something every day, sometimes brief, unrestrained impressions of things lately seen, like a drover with 6 newly shorn sheep in a line across a cool woody road on market morning & me looking back to envy him & him looking back at me for some reason which I can't speculate on. Is this North of Bostonism?

In tracing Thomas's development as a poet, that rather wanly expressed query about "taking to verse" comprises perhaps the most important words he ever wrote. It establishes beyond any doubt that the initial impulse to turn to poetry came from his own heart and mind, and was not, as is often said, simply a result of repeated urging by Frost—an idea which is wonderfully naive to start with. Could a poet of stature ever come to his vocation in such accidental fashion?

Together in Ledington in April the two must have talked of poetry, both in general and of Frost's own. But the phrasing of Thomas's question of May 19 shows that up to then, some three weeks after the April visit, there had been no talk of his writing verse. It also shows that during that brief April week in the country Frost had somehow been able to reach past Thomas's reticent ways, in some manner drawing to the surface the final confidence needed to make him a poet. That Thomas had nurtured such a hope in silence for some unknown length of time is further shown by a study of his prose of the whole previous decade, and of his many incisive reviews, not to mention the actual prose-poetry scattered through his otherwise rather pedestrian books.

Others of Thomas's friends, well before this, had glimpsed the frustrated poet behind the busy journalist. One of them, W. H. Hudson, in the spring of 1913 said as much in a letter to another Frost acquaintance, Edward Garnett: "I believe he has taken the wrong path and is wandering lost in the vast wilderness. He is essentially a poet." It has also been claimed that some of his friends had actually urged him to make the attempt, and the second half of Thomas's May 19 question supports this. If Frost can imagine him writing poetry, he says, then "I might get over the feeling that it is impossible." Clearly, he has been engaged in a running debate with himself over the writing of verse, but has been unable to find the necessary confidence. Frost, happening to be on the spot at the right moment, possessed the ability to offer sympathy and encouragement in just the right blend. As will be seen, he also provided some help of a very practical sort.

As nearly as it can be traced now, the final stage in the process began late in June 1914, when Thomas and his wife Helen spent three days as guests of the Frosts. It was a quick visit, without their children, prior to the longer holiday they planned for August (on one of these three days there occurred the memorable gathering of poets in the Gibson home at Greenway). During this visit two distinct ideas emerged that were to become the controlling factors in Thomas's three remaining years of life: his first slightly hesitant, unvoiced acceptance of himself as a practicing poet, and a related decision that he would leave England with his family and settle near the Frosts in New Hampshire. The first of these ideas, it is likely, fostered the second, which Frost had been urging on him for weeks or months.

Frost's reply to Thomas's May 19 question about taking to verse remains undiscovered, perhaps no longer exists, but it could scarcely have offered anything other than enthusiastic approval. Then, a month later, when the two met again in Ledington, Frost performed his most crucial service for his friend. What this was can best be described by Frost himself, in extracts from two of his letters, the first written within four years of Thomas's death, the second five years after that. Neither statement is a formal or deliberate attempt to describe what happened, so some little effort is required to see past the loose and hurried expression.

The first was written in June 1921 to a friend in Chicago who had inquired about the dead Thomas's career. Frost assures his correspondent that much of what he and Thomas had had in common—a sensitive response to nature and the life of the country, and a liking for unrhetorical verse—they had before they ever met: "The most our congeniality could do was confirm us both in what we were." That said, he quickly sketches in his own contribution:

> I dragged him out from under the heap of his own work in prose he was buried alive under. He was throwing into his big perfunctory histories of Marlborough and the like, written to order, such poetry as would make him a name if he were but given credit for it. I made him see that he owed it to himself and to poetry to have it out by itself in poetic form where it must suffer itself to be admired. It took me some time. I bantered, teased and bullied all the summer we were together at Ledington and Ryton. All he had to do was put his poetry in a form that declared itself. The theme must be the same, the accent exactly the same. He saw it and was tempted. It was plain that he had wanted to be a poet all the years he had been writing about poets not worth his little finger . . . His timidity was funny and fascinating. I had about given him up, he had turned his thoughts to enlistment and I mine to sailing for home, when he wrote his first poem.

Allowing for Frost's habit of overstatement, the teasing and bullying he mentions may well have taken place, in some small and friendly degree, in person and by mail. The timidity and hesitation on Thomas's part seem also to have been real, for he delayed making any sustained trial of his powers until late November, fully six months after that question of May 19 about taking to verse. But missing from Frost's description is a certain highly practical suggestion he made, and which he did take the trouble to set down in the second letter. Thomas, he explains, "had about lost patience with the minor poetry it was his business to review. He was suffering from a life of subordination to his inferiors. Right at that moment he was writing as good poetry as anyone alive, but in prose form where it did not declare itself and gain him recognition. I referred him to paragraphs in his book *In Pursuit of Spring* and told him to write it in verse form in exactly the same cadence. That's all there was to it."

With such offhand statements as these—and no doubt the same information conveyed in talk—there began the unintended distortion of Frost's part in the artistic maturing of Edward Thomas. What Frost has inadvertently left out of his two accounts is the fact that he was not in any way initiating the idea of Thomas becoming a poet—rather, he was generously responding to a desire, and perhaps a request for advice, previously expressed by his friend. In saying "I referred him to paragraphs in his book," Frost was not claiming that he did so without invitation, and nowhere does he even hint that he was first to suggest that Thomas try his hand at poetry. What actually did happen is not hard to reconstruct.

As the two went rambling round the Dymock countryside, Thomas's warm if hesitant expressions of desire to become a poet led the sympathetic Frost to urge his friend to make a start. When Thomas continued to hold back, Frost suggested he might begin by recasting passages from his own book, "in verse form in exactly the same cadence." In this, Frost was doing no more than passing on to Thomas a method he himself had repeatedly employed, and would employ in the future, reworking in his mature manner the ideas and sentiments he had years earlier composed in more traditional style. (It was to this fact that he referred in his ever-fascinating letter to Untermeyer in 1916, in which he says, cryptically and with more than a tinge of his usual hyperbole, "The calf I was in the nineties I merely take to market . . . I have myself all in a strong box where I can unfold as a personality at discretion.") He then went a step further, hunting through the pages of Thomas's book for passages that might lend themselves readily to metrical development. He chose *In Pursuit of Spring* because it was handy, and because he had found it, as he said earlier, "the loveliest book on spring in England." Sufficient proof that Frost was here telling the strict truth is available in a fact now well understood, that a great many of Thomas's poems, especially those first written, are taken directly from specific passages in one or another of his many books. At least four have been traced to *In Pursuit of Spring*.

How soon after that hasty but pivotal June visit Thomas may have begun at least experimenting with verse, it would be interesting to know. The only clue turned up so far consists of a single ambiguous remark he made in a letter of early August. From his home at Steep he wrote Eleanor Farjeon that, since he had completed his latest writing assignment and was at loose ends, "I may as well write poetry. Did anyone ever begin at 36 in the shade?"

*   *   *

WELL within sight of Little Iddens, across several hedges and open fields, there stood (and still stands) the Chandler farmhouse, called Oldfields. Here Thomas had arranged to take rooms for himself and his family for their extended August holiday. Originally he had planned on a whole month, but the war, beginning just as he and his family arrived in Ledington, cut that down to little more than half when he was forced to depart on a hurried writing assignment, a war article for the *English Review*.

Nor, despite a succession of bright, warm days, did the holiday start well. All too quickly the three Thomas children became bored with the solitude, and Helen Thomas grew listless when the living arrangements at the Chandler's proved much too confining. Then, only a few days after arriving, Thomas received word from a London publisher that a manuscript he had just turned in was short a few thousand words. Finally, the youngest Thomas daughter, Myfanwy, caused some real concern by taking an ugly tumble off a swing. "One thing and another," Thomas complained not unreasonably in a letter, "leaves me very irritable indeed," and he began to think of getting away from Ledington with Frost on a bicycle tour through Wales. Further turmoil arose when Mr. Chandler, a farmer in his forties but an army reservist, was called to the colors, and it appeared that Frost and Thomas might be expected to finish up the farm work he would leave undone.

On the day Chandler left, Thomas sat writing a rather downcast letter to Eleanor Farjeon, who was to join the party later that month. "The Frosts are all over the house seeing Mr. Chandler off," he wrote. "Peter's chair creeks as he reads the Baroness Orczy and Merfyn sounds incompletely satisfied with the old Strand magazines. But it is a very fine hot day. God is in *His* heaven all right, obviously and ostentatiously. Mr. Chandler will be in *his* in Hereford. Goodbye. I am sorry this letter turns out so." Eventually things settled down, the Wales escape was postponed, and for the two families life at Ledington resolved itself into a succession of shared picnics, leisurely meals at home, visits to the homes of Gibson and Abercrombie, and deliciously lazy days of "talk and strolling and odd games of cricket."

For Frost during these leisurely weeks there were additional sources of pleasure, even excitement, for Thomas had brought with him at least two of his three reviews of *North of Boston*. With the earlier reviews by Abercrombie and Ford, it was these three notices by Thomas that firmly established Frost's critical reputation in England. But of equal interest in this regard is another fact, so far overlooked, having to do directly with Thomas himself—these reviews were written at a time when his own poetic aspirations, and perhaps his poetry, were just starting into vivid life under Frost's potent spell. Thus, in a real sense they afford a kind of running record, even if veiled, of the awakening of Thomas's own rapidly ripening sensibilities. The reviews, in other words, may be read as much for what they reveal about Thomas, as about his subject.

The bold opening sentence of the first review, from the London *Daily News*, immediately sets the tone, hailing the advent of something new in literature and in Thomas's own experience: "This is one of the most revolutionary books of modern times, but one of the quietest and least aggressive." (Quiet and unaggressive are words eminently well fitted to characterize Thomas's own poetry.) After detailing the volume's entire contents, he returns to expand his opening thrust:

> These poems are revolutionary because they lack the exaggeration of rhetoric, and even at first sight appear to lack the poetic intensity of which rhetoric is an imitation. Their language is free from the poetical words and forms that are the chief material of secondary poets. The metre avoids not only the old-fashioned pomp and sweetness, but the later fashion also of discord and fuss. In fact, the medium is common speech and common decasyllables, and Mr. Frost is at no pains to exclude blank verse lines resembling those employed, I think, by Andrew Lang in a leading article printed as prose. Yet almost all these poems are beautiful. They depend not at all on objects commonly admitted to be beautiful; neither have they a merely homely beauty, but are often grand, sometimes magical. Many, if not most, of the separate lines and separate sentences are plain and, in themselves, nothing. But they are bound together and made elements of beauty by a calm eagerness of emotion.

The book is not without failures, Thomas next observes, notably in an occasional obscurity which asks too much of the reader. But he insists that the volume's finest poems leave no doubt whatever that Frost must be accepted as standing well above all other living American poets, an assertion which consciously places Frost high among the poets of America's past. His concluding remarks offer an observation peculiarly personal when read in the light of his own verse. Frost, he says, "will be accused of keeping monotonously at a low level, because his characters are quiet people, and he has chosen the unresisting medium of blank verse. I will only remark that he would lose far less than most modern writers by being printed as prose. If his work were so printed, it would have little in common with the kind of prose that runs to blank verse . . . It is poetry because it is better than prose."

Quite aside from what the remark says in an original way about Frost, it reveals Thomas in the very act of gauging his personal response to this disturbing new form of poetry. It even hints at what seems to have been the truth: when Thomas began writing poetry, he did not view the change from prose as a radical or even marked departure. Intimately familiar with the written word in all its many guises, he saw poetry not as something rare and remote, but only as a different form of expression, it might even be said as another tool of the writer's trade, even if higher and more demanding than prose. Finally, this can be said: The impact of Frost's poetry on Thomas's sensitive soul—as he met it in the fifteen poems of *North of Boston*—must be recognized as powerful beyond anything the American could have said or suggested in their rambling discussions that summer. By itself, Frost's idiom and the arrestingly original manner in which it illuminated his rural settings, as well as the endless subtleties it evoked, was the strong, insistent whisper that fully awakened Thomas's dormant inspiration.

The dual revelation—of his own feelings as well as Frost's poetry—observable in Thomas's dexterous handling of *North of Boston* proves even more traceable in the other two reviews. Also quite evident is Thomas's professionalism, in the deft way he is able to vary his comment while saying essentially the same things in each review, at the same time adding something new. In the *New Weekly* his opening carried the "revolutionary" concept of the first notice a step further: "This is an original book which will raise the thrilling question, What is poetry?" After again supplying lengthy selections, he proceeds to invoke the names of both Whitman and Wordsworth, and his rapid, indeed nearly breathless analysis of Frost's technique shows how deeply it had impressed him:

> At first sight some will pronounce simply that anyone can write this kind of blank verse, with all its tame common words, straightforward construc-

tions, and innumerable perfectly normal lines. Few that read [the book] through will have been as much astonished by any American since Whitman . . . I have not met a living poet with a less obvious or more complicated ancestry . . . Mr. Frost has in fact gone back, as Whitman and Wordsworth went back, through the paraphernalia of poetry into poetry again. With a confidence like genius, he has trusted his conviction that a man will not easily write better than he speaks when some matter has touched him deeply, and he has turned it over until he has no doubt what it means to him, when he has no purpose to serve beyond expressing it, when he has no audience to be bullied or flattered, when he is free, and speech takes one form and no other. Whatever discipline further was necessary he has got from the good old medium of blank verse.

Mr. Frost . . . writes of what he or some country neighbor in New Hampshire has said or done. Extraordinary things have not been sought for . . . yet it might be said that Mr. Frost sometimes combines an effect resembling Wordsworth's, while he shows us directly less of his own feelings, and more of other people's than Wordsworth did . . .

The effect of each poem is one and indivisible. You can hardly pick out a single line more than a single word. There are no show words or lines. The concentration has been upon the whole, not the parts. Decoration has been forgotten, perhaps for lack of the right kind of vanity or obsession . . . The main result is a richly homely thing beyond the grasp of any power except poetry. It is beautiful achievement, and I think a unique one, as perfectly Mr. Frost's own as his vocabulary, the ordinary English speech of a man accustomed to poetry and philosophy, more colloquial and idiomatic than the ordinary man dares to use in a letter . . . possessing a kind of healthy natural delicacy like Wordsworth's, or at least Shelley's, rather than that of Keats.

The phrase, "anyone can write this kind of blank verse," may reflect a thought that passed through Thomas's own mind, before he saw how deceptive was the simplicity. Another of his comments certainly holds an even more personal application: "When he has no purpose to serve beyond expressing it, when he has no audience to be bullied or flattered." Here speaks Thomas's own resentment of the burdensome position he held as a writer, his constant need to grind out assigned prose.

The last of Thomas's three reviews, in the prestigious *English Review*, was the shortest, but there was something in it which led Frost to say that, of the ten notices of his book seen till then, it was "almost the best I have had." What pleased him so much is left unsaid, but it may well have been another and more favorable comparison with Wordsworth, with an added twist that seemed in one aspect to elevate his book even above the

Lyrical Ballads of the Englishman. *North of Boston*, Thomas asserts, "marks more than the beginning of an experiment like Wordsworth's, but with this difference, that Mr. Frost knows the life of which he writes rather as Dorothy Wordsworth did. That is to say, he sympathizes where Wordsworth contemplates. The result is a unique type of eclogue, homely, racy, and touched by a spirit that might, under other circumstances, have made pure lyric on the one hand, or drama on the other."

Another observation, anticipating a judgment now common in Frost criticism, points to Frost's ability to achieve a wider and more inclusive setting or atmosphere in his poems than is afforded by the words themselves, a self-propagating or reverberating quality—though perhaps it would be truer to say that Thomas identifies this result without explaining it. "Within the space of a hundred lines or so of blank verse," he wrote, "it would be hard to compress more rural character and relevant scenery; impossible, perhaps, to do so with less sense of compression and more lightness, unity and breadth." It may, on the other hand, have been the penetrating sentence of praise with which Thomas concludes that made Frost so fondly recall this review: "Only at the end of the best pieces, such as 'The Death of the Hired Man,' 'Home Burial,' 'The Black Cottage,' and 'The Woodpile,' do we realize that they are masterpieces of deep and mysterious tenderness."

While Frost was reading Thomas's reviews that August he also received word that he had won his first popular attention back home, a reprinting by a Boston newspaper, the *Transcript*, of Abercrombie's *Nation* notice. So delighted was he, especially when he stopped to think how close a race his book had run with the outbreak of war, that as he later admitted, he actually felt "dazed" at the way it had all turned out. Considering not only the quantity of the reviews ("no book of verse has had as much space given to it for a good while," Frost wrote, a claim which was probably true) but their quality, he can hardly be blamed for feeling a bit overwhelmed. Further, from all that had been written about the masterful skills evident in *North of Boston* it was now clear that he need no longer fear being mistaken for an artless farmer-poet. The sinuous and sophisticated intelligence behind the poems had been recognized.

*   *   *

THOUGH it would have been natural in the circumstances, there is no sign that Frost and Thomas ever discussed any of the reviews of *North of Boston*. What the two certainly did talk about, and at considerable length, was Frost's sound-of-sense theories of versification, an all-important fact that might legitimately be inferred from Thomas's reviews, but which is also established by a fleeting incident that occurred on one of their many walks round the Gloucestershire countryside.

Accompanied by Eleanor Farjeon, Frost and Thomas were strolling along a lane when Frost spotted, two hedgerows away, a local farmer he knew. Pitchfork in hand, the man was standing atop a cart, his figure outlined against the sky as piece by piece he stacked some load being thrown up to him. On the spur of the moment Frost decided to give a demonstration of what he meant by the sound of sense. Between Frost and the farmer the distance was too great to allow for an easy spoken exchange, but Frost stopped, cupped his hands to his mouth and shouted something. "Whatever the words, the man on the cart could not have heard them," recalled Eleanor Farjeon. Still, wishing to be neighborly, the man "shouted some answer that rang through the air, and it was impossible for us to distinguish what was said. But the cadence of the answer was as clear as that of the question." Frost, satisfied that he had found another way to demonstrate his voice-behind-the-door idea, looked at Thomas and commented, "That's what I mean." (Of course, some idea of the man's reply must have been evident in his tone and inflection, otherwise the impromptu experiment could not have been judged quite successful.)

It was also Farjeon who recorded some of the non-literary doings of that summer, such as both families joining in the harvest of the Frosts' potato garden. In the broiling sun, as she recalled the scene, while his guests bent to their tasks, Frost strolled up and down, "a self-appointed overseer of cheap labor; while with sleeves rolled up and sweat pouring down we forked our allotted rows." In this work a heavily perspiring Thomas took a part with much quiet gusto and good humor. There was also a grand banquet in honor of the poets, given by the landlady of Glyn Iddens, the farmhouse just down the road in which Farjeon had taken a room. Included were Gibson and Abercrombie, with their wives, and all spent an evening at a groaning board, with much hard cider, a product of the Dymock countryside, passed freely around. The festivities ended with the four distinguished poets, none of whom were heavy drinkers, having to steady each other along the road on the walk home.

As it happens, Edward Thomas, too, left a written record of those days of August 1914. It is an unintended record that mainly depicts his earliest wrestling with the vexing problem created for him by the war, whether he should, despite his age and responsibilities, respond to the military's call for volunteers. The clear record of his anguish exists in the

form of a personal essay he wrote immediately after his return to Steep
from Ledington, and which was published soon after in the *Nation*. In his
usual fashion of making use of personal experience, he draws on his
recent stay with the Frosts, and tries to explain how an unexpected rush
of love for his country—full-blown patriotism, though never called by
that name—was born into the heart of a man not given to admitting such
sentiments. Though written in the loose, hurried style of too much of his
periodical work, it provides a portrait, purposely veiled, of himself and
Frost in Dymock as they shared ideas on poetry and life. Describing the
August countryside, with its open fields and crowded orchards, its flocks
of singing birds, its harvested wheat standing in tall ricks in the warm
sun, he goes on to picture the pathway leading from Chandler's farm to
Little Iddens:

> Three meadows away lived a friend, and once or twice or three times a day
> I used to cross the meadows, the gate and the two stiles . . . The path,
> having gradually approached a hedge on the left, went alongside it under
> the horse chestnut tree leaning out of it, and in sight of the house, until it
> reached the far hedge and the road. There, at another stile, the path
> ceased. The little house of whitened bricks and black timbers lay a few
> yards up the road, a vegetable garden in front with a weeping ash and a bay
> tree . . . How easy it was to spend a morning or an afternoon in walking
> over to this house, stopping to talk to whoever was about for a few minutes,
> and then strolling with my friend, nearly regardless of footpaths, in a long
> loop, so as to end either at his house or my lodging . . .
>
> If talk dwindled in the traversing of a big field, the pause at gate or stile
> braced it again. Often we prolonged the pause whether we actually sat or
> not, and we talked—of flowers, childhood, Shakespeare, women,
> England, the war—or we looked at a far horizon, which some dip or gap
> occasionally disclosed.

Shifting to a more personal key, with his usual calm he captures the
moment in which he was reminded that Englishmen were dying in battle
not far from where he and his friend were strolling. The thought gave a
sudden, violent wrench to his former detachment, teaching him what it
meant to be an Englishman at that time of danger. It happened in the
dusk of evening on August 26 as he and Frost were returning from a long
walk, and with a new moon, "a stout orange crescent" hanging just above
the horizon, bright in the gloom:

> At one stroke, I thought, like many other people, what things that same
> new moon sees eastward about the Meuse in France. Of those who could

see it there, not blinded by smoke, pain, or excitement, how many saw it and heeded? I was deluged in a second stroke by another thought, or something that overpowered thought. All I can tell is, it seemed to me that either I had never loved England, or I had loved it foolishly, aesthetically, like a slave, not having realized it was not mine, unless I were willing and prepared to die rather than leave it, as Belgian women and old men and children had left their country. Something I had omitted. Something, I felt, had to be done before I could look again composedly at English landscape.

As his letters show, from that day Thomas was plagued and harried by the thought that, in spite of everything, he should go off to fight for his country. The idea of joining Frost in New Hampshire, by then a serious consideration, began to seem like abject desertion, and that feeling was radically enforced by the research he did in September for the *English Review* war article: he was to sample the mood of the country by traveling from town to town through the midlands and listening to the talk of all sorts of people. Soon after he finished the article, and on several occasions that fall, he came close to enlisting. At the end of October he told Frost by letter that he had just made himself "ill with thinking" about the move and had determined to enlist the very next day. For whatever reason, that resolve was not carried through, and in the end his enlistment (in the Artists' Rifles, with a later transfer to the Royal Artillery), did not take place until the following July, four months after Frost had departed for home.

It may well have been on that same day of the new moon in Ledington that there occurred the remarkable incident pictured by Frost in "Iris By Night," a rare encounter of himself and Thomas with a moon-made rainbow. He describes "a misty evening" after a very wet day (a condition also specified in Thomas's article) as they returned from a ramble through the Malvern hills. Walking in the moisture-laden air the two saw, just ahead, "a small rainbow like a trellis gate." Continuing toward it, they were rewarded with the sight of a phenomenon not often met:

> . . . *Bow and rainbow as it bent,*
> *Instead of moving with us as we went*
> *(To keep the pots of gold from being found),*
> *It lifted from its dewy pediment*
> *Its two mote-swimming many-colored ends*
> *And gathered them together in a ring.*
> *And we stood in it softly circled round*

From all division time or foe can bring
In a relation of elected friends.

In addition to recalling the magic of that unusual moment, the sentiment in the concluding lines enshrines Frost's long-felt grief over his friend's early death. The poem, probably written soon after Thomas's death in 1917, did not see publication until 1936.

Thomas's August stay at Ledington was to prove eventful for him both as man and poet. But it would be overdramatizing to claim that it was one unbroken idyl, or that mundane concerns did not intrude. Only three days after leaving Ledington on the start of his research trip for the war article, he expressed to his friend Gordon Bottomley an opinion about the just completed vacation which carries perhaps a truer feel of the everyday reality of the visit. "I saw too little of Abercrombie," he said in plain language, "too much of Gibson and Frost daily—our families interwove all day long & we enjoyed many days but with all sorts of mixed feelings." Poets and their families, it is good to be reminded, are not always and in every way so different from the usual run of men.

*   *   *

HOW active a role Frost played in his friend's development as a poet after the Ledington holiday is a question yet to be decided. The one source that might have yielded something like a complete answer is fragmentary: Frost's letters to Thomas between September 1914 and April 1917 (only nine are presently known). Somewhat the same situation obtains for Thomas's letters to Frost: for the fall of 1914 there exist only four, certainly less than half of those written, and for the first three months of 1915, the most critical period, there are none. The gap becomes noticeable because afterwards, from May 1915 to Thomas's death two years later, there is available an unbroken run of forty-seven Thomas-to-Frost letters.

In three of his letters to Frost in the fall of 1914 Thomas has nothing to say on the subject of poetry. It is with the fourth, written on December 15, that he makes his undoubted debut as a practicing poet, for he enclosed a batch of at least nine completed poems, and confessed, "I am in it & no mistake." With that declaration he launches into some revealing personal comment not typical of his manner in correspondence: "My bad habits and customs and duties of writing will make it rather easy to write when I've no business to. At the same time I find myself engrossed and conscious of a possible perfection as I never was in prose. Also I'm very impatient of my prose, and of reviews & of review books. And yet I have been uncommonly cheerful mostly. I have been rather pleased with some of the pieces, of course, but it's not wholly that." In the next sentence he makes the clearest and most positive statement he ever made of his debt to Frost: "Still, I won't begin thanking you just yet, tho if you like I will put it down now that you are the only begetter right enough." Interesting as the remark is, it affords some amusement, worth at least a wry smile, to note that Thomas's use of the famous phrase tells no more about *his* literary debt than it did in its original position about Shakespeare's. In both cases it remains tantalizing.

The only reference Thomas made to the poems sent with the letter— all of which would appear in print nearly unchanged—occurs halfway down the second page. It is made almost diffidently, and seems to show that these were not the first Thomas verses seen by Frost: "My works come pouring in on you now. Tell me all you dare about them." Frost's response, apparently not extant, was delayed, keeping Thomas in suspense, and some two weeks later he can be heard complaining to Eleanor Farjeon that "Frost hasn't said anything about my verses since. I think I have got him in one of his raw places." What meaning, exactly, those last words may have carried is now lost.

For six months after he had made a start, Thomas's writing of poetry became almost a daily exercise, even accelerating when he was laid up over New Year's and into January with a badly twisted ankle. In that time nearly a hundred poems were produced, most fairly short, with the longest running to some 150 lines, and many of these were promptly posted to Frost, even after he had left England. Of the many comments Frost must have supplied in answer, only two survive (both in letters which Helen Thomas at an early period sold to an American collector). The first occurs in April 1915, and offers a brief opinion of a single poem, but it is a poem that would take its place among its author's best known and best loved. "The goodness is in 'Lob,' Frost wrote encouragingly. "You are a poet or you are nothing . . . I like the first half of 'Lob' best: it offers something more like action with the different people coming in and giving the tones of speech. But the long paragraph is a feat. I never saw anything like you for English." Thomas's reaction to that judgment was grateful, though not at all effusive: "I got a letter from you on Friday, the one I have been gladdest to get, and not only because you said you liked 'Lob.' "

The second of the two Frost comments occurs in a letter responding to

Thomas's final decision to join the army (Frost says he is both sorry and glad at the move). While brief, reference to the poetry is highly admiring: "Your last poem 'Aspens' seems the loveliest of all. You must have a volume of poetry ready for when you come marching home." Quite soon, in fact even before he had published a single poem, Thomas did begin thinking of gathering his work into a volume, a move no doubt suggested by his well-honed professional instincts. The poem "Aspens," which so appealed to Frost, may actually have been suggested by Frost's own "The Sound of Trees," which had appeared in Monro's magazine *Poetry and Drama* for December 1914—and "Aspens" in its turn may well have suggested to Frost his own much later "Tree At My Window." In this exchange of inspiration, for one observer at least, there is something eminently proper and satisfying.

Two further Frost comments are found in Thomas's own letters. In late March 1916 Thomas takes up some admonition of Frost's against a tendency toward introspection, in which he was tending to ignore the cultivation of human tones. Thomas writes in reply: "Your talking of epic and play rather stirred me. I shall be careful not to indulge in a spring run of lyrics. I had better try again to make other people speak." It was such urging by Frost, perhaps repeatedly, that helped hold Thomas to an earnest pursuit of "speaking tones," out of which came such fine verses as "Man and Dog," "The Gypsy," and "Wind and Mist."

Almost by accident, the second indirect reference offers a flash of insight into the way Frost tried to handle his friend's apparently still-marked inclination to serious melancholy. This happened because in his own letter Thomas quotes a Frost sentence. "Your letter of February 24 only reached me yesterday," Thomas wrote. "It referred to some verses I had sent—dismal ones, I gather. Perhaps one was called 'Rain.' A form of excrement you hoped it was when you said 'Work all that off in poetry and I shan't complain.' Well I never know." The poem in question had been written in January 1916, six months after Thomas joined the army but before he went to France, and the sentiment expressed in it might well have disturbed, even alarmed Frost. Openly and frankly the lines announce a strong death wish, even hinting at suicide. "Blessed are the dead that the rain rains upon," announced one of the lines, and the morbid strain is further enforced:

> *Rain, midnight rain, nothing but the wild rain*
> *On this bleak hut, and solitude, and me*
> *Remembering again that I shall die,*

And neither hear the rain nor give thanks
For washing me cleaner than I have been
Since I was born into this solitude.

.   .   .   .   .

Me who have no love which this wild rain
Has not dissolved except the love of death.

However, Frost need not have worried. What Thomas did not take the trouble to explain was that "Rain" had not been prompted by mental depression made deeper by a soldier's gloomy foreboding. It was simply a reworking of a passage from one of his books, *The Icknield Way*, published in 1911.

If Frost ever fully understood the extent to which Thomas had followed his advice about drawing on his own voluminous prose for poetic inspiration he never mentioned it. Of course, it would have made no difference if he had, for the poems are no less authentic and moving, no less deserving of their high place in the literature of England, because of their unique double birth. In the end, it was nothing so technical as the pointing out of source material that Frost identified as his most important contribution to Thomas's poetic career. As he was later to recall it in a letter to Haines of 1921, that contribution consisted of the oldest and most effective form of help that one artist can give another, "admiration for the poet in him before he had written a line of poetry."

*   *   *

THE story of Edward Thomas and Robert Frost does not end with a tracing out of literary influences. Something of equal importance, though in a more personal way, waits to be considered, a certain small incident and its large aftermath, centering on the peevish actions of an ill-tempered gamekeeper. Noticed only in passing in Frost and Thomas biography, and though it was several times later mentioned in conversation by Frost, the incident as a whole remains obscure. What gives it importance is Frost's conviction, expressed to Robert Newdick, that it supplied the final push that propelled Thomas as a volunteer into the army (thus, by implication, becoming in a way responsible for his death). Even so, that curious belief might not in itself be worth pursuing seriously, except that Thomas's own letters appear to lend it support. Exactly what happened, though elusive, can be reconstructed from scattered bits of information found in several sources.

Early in September 1914 the Frosts gave up living in Little Iddens and moved to the rambling, thatched house of Lascelles Abercrombie in Ryton, known locally as the Gallows. Several reasons have been given for this move (a wish to save on fuel bills by both parties in the winter, a demand by the owner of Little Iddens that the cottage was needed, realizing Elinor's wish to live under thatch, etc.). In any case the Gallows was standing empty for much of the fall while the Abercrombies traveled, and the Frosts quickly accepted the generous invitation to make use of it. When the Abercrombies returned at the beginning of winter the two families comfortably shared the ramshackle house during the ten weeks or so before the Frosts left for their return to the United States.

The trouble with the gamekeeper happened while Abercrombie was absent from Ryton, and while Edward Thomas was paying another short visit to the Frosts, again stopping off on his way from Wales to London. The large game preserve of over a thousand heavily wooded acres belonging to the Lord of the Manor in Ryton (William, seventh Earl Beauchamp), spread itself around much of the country adjacent to the Gallows, which was rented by Abercrombie from Lord Beauchamp's estate. By virtue of his tenancy, Abercrombie and his family enjoyed access to the preserve for walks, picnics, berrying expeditions, and the like, as did Wilfrid Gibson and other favored locals. For most, however, unaccompanied children in particular, entry into the preserve was prohibited. A stern head game-keeper—local report gives his name as Bott—strictly enforced the rule, a man whose disposition led him when childish offenders were intercepted to teach them a lesson by dumping their pails and trodding on the fruit. Customarily carrying a shotgun, he never hesitated to wave it threat-eningly at adult trespassers, real or suspected. It was this annoying habit that led to the unfortunate incident involving Thomas.

One day Frost and Thomas were returning from a long walk through the preserve—as a temporary resident of the Gallows Frost understood that he was entitled to enter the place as he wished. When the two emerged into the main road, according to a Newdick note, the keeper was "snooping in the hedge, glowering at F. and E. T." Some sharp remarks were passed—it is not known who began the exchange—and the keeper ended by calling Frost to his face "a damned cottager," an attempted insult, of more force then than now, which seems to show that the keeper knew of Frost's residence in the old cottage at Ledington. Thoroughly incensed, the keeper raised his shotgun in a blatantly threatening man-ner. Frost, his temper flaring, was on the point of doing something foolish, but was held back when Thomas, showing fright, backed off.

Talking excitedly of the keeper's behavior, the two poets walked on. Soon Frost's anger rekindled—there may have been an earlier incident between the keeper and the Frost children—and, ignoring Thomas's demur, he decided to go back. The keeper had disappeared, so Frost insisted on tracking the man to his house. Eventually it was found, and Frost went up to the door and banged loudly. The surprised keeper opened the door, then listened as Frost angrily warned him never again to make such threatening gestures, or try to regulate his or his childrens' coming and going in the preserve. The language used by the furious Frost left no doubt what would happen to the keeper if there was any recurrence—Frost would beat the hell out of him.

The next few seconds were to become the crux of the incident. As Frost turned away and was stalking off, the keeper reached back inside for his shotgun, then came out and made straight for Thomas, who had been standing slightly apart. Once more Thomas was unable to mask his fright, hastily backing off as the blustering keeper came at him. Newdick's notes on the point—the only source for Thomas's reaction—were made on the day that Frost told him the story in July 1936, and are explicit even if a bit vague: "T. coming up, the g. going for him, T's cowardice (or so it always seemed to T.: 'That's why he went to war,' said F.)." Whatever happened exactly that evening, there was no further excitement at the keeper's cottage, and the affair seemed at an end.

Next morning early, however, the Ryton constable arrived at the Gallows to inform Frost that a complaint had been lodged against him, a charge of threatening with bodily harm, and he handed Frost a summons. Since Abercrombie was away, Frost confidently turned for advice and help to Gibson—and received a shock when the staunch poet of the people declined to risk his standing with the local gentry by interfering. Frost's own words, written less than six months later, document the refusal. "You mustn't tell me a single thing about Gibson," he wrote Haines in April 1915, "if you don't want to detract from the pleasure of your letters . . . I can't help looking on him as the worst snob I met in England and I can't help blaming the snob he is for the most unpleasant memory I carried away from England: I mean my humiliating fight with the gamekeeper. Gibson is a coward and a snob not to have saved me from all that."

Frost may or may not have made an appearance in court. In any case, with the return of Abercrombie some days later the situation was resolved. Presenting Lord Beauchamp with the facts, Abercrombie managed to get the charges dropped, and Lord Beauchamp sent his personal apology to Frost by note (the belligerent keeper was told that "if he wanted so much to fight he had better enlist"). Once over their initial anger, both Thomas and Frost tried to make light of the incident—being called a "damned cottager," said Thomas, gave Frost clear title to the position of People's Poet, and he should get the gamekeeper to endorse *North of Boston* in the ads. Yet in his heart, as subsequent events plainly show, Thomas did not really see the annoying interlude as in any way funny.

Leaving Ledington, Thomas had returned to Steep by October 20, and some ten days later he answered a letter from Frost, making one remark that gives off echoes, though dim, of the recent unpleasantness: "I only hope that you wrote immediately after Gibson's call & in the worst pangs of it . . . did you want or expect a letter sooner? I should only have told you I was surprised to find you again like me." He ends with a confession that the idea of joining the army has been pressing on him to the point of discomfort: "I have just made myself almost ill with thinking hard for an hour—going up to my study and sitting there—that I ought to enlist next week in town." As it happens, his enlistment did not come until eight months later, and he spent the intervening time in an agony of indecision. When he did join up, it was in a rather abrupt fashion. Going up to London, telling no one of his plans, he returned home to his family several days afterward in uniform.

Apart from what appears a glancing mention in a letter of May 1915 (speaking of editors, Thomas says "I dread them as much as that keeper"), nothing further is heard of the gamekeeper for over two years. Then in January 1917, with Thomas a second lieutenant in the Field Artillery and about to join his battery in France, memories of the old incident unexpectedly well up once more. In a letter to Frost from camp, in which he talks of the war and of army life, he suddenly goes off at a tangent, or so it seems: "I can ride a motorcycle now (reporting progress is about all I can do towards a letter). But I daresay such things don't make a difference. You hear girls on trains saying that 'facing realities will change So-and-so' (& of course improve him): as if 'realities' hadn't always been common as mud. So-and-so can't face any more than he was born to face, I suspect; nor I. So that I worry less and less about that gamekeeper."

By month's end Thomas was with his battery near the town of Arras, and he was soon under heavy fire from German guns. Again the gamekeeper appears, in what proved to be Thomas's final letter to Frost,

written from the battlefield. But this time the gamekeeper shows up in
the context of a signal act of bravery by Thomas.

With his unit taking a heavy battering from enemy artillery less than a
mile distant across No Man's Land, Thomas decided he could improve
the direction of his own fire by making his observations from atop a tall
factory chimney that rose nearby among a mass of rubble. Recklessly
exposing himself to the German shelling, he ran and dodged his way to
the chimney, at least twice on the way being shaken by explosions.
Reaching the chimney, he began climbing the iron rungs set into its wide
interior. But he had barely begun the dangerous ascent when he changed
his mind. His own account of the incident, written to Frost in that final
letter, begins by explaining that artillery officers were sometimes
assigned so far forward that they mingled with the frontline infantry in
the trenches:

> We spend nights without shelter in the mud, chiefly in waiting for the
> morning & the arrival of the relief. It is a 24 hours job & later more to
> recover from. But it is far as yet from being unendurable. The unendur-
> able thing was having to climb up the inside of a chimney that was being
> shelled. I gave up. It was impossible & I knew it yet I went up to the beastly
> place & had 4 shells burst very close & decided that I would go back. As a
> matter of fact I had no light and no information about the method of getting
> up so that all the screwing up I had given myself would in any case have
> been futile. It was just another experience like the gamekeeper—but it lies
> far less on my mind, because the practical result of my failure was nil, & I
> now see far more from the ground level than I could have seen from 200
> feet up the factory chimney.

A week after writing those words, early on the morning of Easter Monday, while he was on duty at a forward observation post, Thomas was
killed by the bursting of an enemy shell.

The news of Thomas's death, relayed by both his wife and a friend,
reached Frost in New Hampshire sometime in the week of April 20. At
about this same time Thomas's own last letter arrived, with its poignant
reference to the gamekeeper. Partly, at least, this coincidence may
account for Frost's opinion that his friend had gone to war in order to
prove his bravery, to live down what he remembered as a momentary act of
cowardice in the Ryton countryside. Frost was wrong, of course, or
better, was exaggerating. Given all the facts, nothing is more certain than
that Thomas responded to his country's call out of sheer, high-hearted

patriotism. His decision to enlist had been reached many weeks prior to the gamekeeper incident. It had happened on a muggy August evening when, as he walked with Frost over the green fields at Ledington, Thomas looked up at the bright new moon and thought of the bloody fighting then in progress on the Meuse. It was then he told himself that the beauty of his homeland could not really be his "unless I were willing and prepared to die rather than leave it."

Yet it seems beyond question that Frost through the rest of his life believed otherwise, and in some measure blamed himself for having needlessly precipitated the trouble with the gamekeeper. Forty years later, at the Bread Loaf School in Vermont in the summer of 1954, he can be heard still harboring a lingering shade of guilt. In the course of a rambling talk on poetry he wandered into the subject of "glory, bravery, honor." Suddenly he was recalling his companion of long ago, and the tragic sacrifice he had made. But in what he said the emphasis was not on glory and honor. It was on the simple, personal things that Thomas had left behind:

I had a friend who died in the First World War—a poet, he went out to die—left his family and all that, children and all, and went out to die.

TWELVE

TELLING IT WITH A SIGH

A MONG the letters arriving at the Nutt office in London in September 1914 there was one from a leading New York City publisher, Henry Holt. Prompted by the personal interest of Mrs. Holt, a native Vermonter who had somehow acquired a copy of *North of Boston*, the letter brought an inquiry about American rights not only to that book, but for Frost's future work as well. Slowed by the war at sea, the transatlantic discussion dragged into October, however, and was not helped by Mrs. Nutt's acerbic notions of doing business. "Under present political circumstances," she responded when Holt hesitated over some point, "American publishers ought to show some willingness to help English publishers who have sufficient daring and intelligence to recognize the talent of one of their own countrymen." When an agreement was reached it was something of a disappointment: Nutt would ship Holt unbound sheets of *North of Boston*, enough for a trial edition of 150 copies, very small even for poetry.

The size of the order did not trouble Frost when, about the start of November, he was told of his American contract. "Now we can go home," he said contentedly to Elinor, "the book has gone home." With that, as his letters show, he began making active plans for departure. Though unmentioned, probably of equal force in accelerating the move toward home was the rapidly spreading rumor that Germany, with her submarines, was about to impose a naval blockade of British ports.

Money, as usual, was the immediate problem, and there was the further difficulty as to how his future would be affected by all the expenses, those of steamer passage, much dearer now than in 1912, and whatever it would take to get the family settled in the States. His only recourse was to ask his grandfather's trustee for an advance on his annuity, but this would leave little or nothing for his family's support up through the summer of 1916. At that point it seemed unavoidable that he would have to take a job once at home, instead of retiring to a farm to continue writing full time as he had planned. Wistfully, he began dreaming of the sort of teaching post that would be least burdensome, and he settled on "a quiet job in a small college where I would be allowed to teach something a little new on the technique of writing and where I should have some honor for what I suppose myself to have done in poetry."

That uncharacteristic wish for "some honor" is revealing, for in it there resides an uneasy premonition about his future, that a return to full-time teaching, particularly at age forty-one, could drastically slow, even bring a virtual end to his active career as a poet—already he was tending to look back on what he had accomplished, rather than forward to what he still might do. (The wish for honor was somewhat softened, though by no means canceled, when he footnoted to it the shyly apologetic phrase, "just a little bit.") This somber resignation did not last long, however. By Christmas his old strong desire had reasserted itself, and at length he changed his mind: he would borrow the money needed and not touch the annuity at all.

Perhaps a half dozen of Frost's English friends were approachable for a loan, but apparently he shrank from asking the whole sum from any one man. At last he settled on three: the two who were closest to him at the moment, Abercrombie and Haines (Gibson's absence here is conspicuous), and one who, though at a distance, had become equally warm as friend and admirer, J. C. Smith. All three seem to have responded readily, and to each Frost gave a promissory note (his offer to pay interest was declined by Smith, no doubt by the others as well). In choosing a ship he was at first undecided whether to go by British or American line—a British boat would set him down in Boston, which he preferred—but then for safety reasons he booked aboard the American liner St. Paul. Departure was scheduled from Liverpool on February 13.

Beyond finances, there was the question of what reception he might expect from America's literary circles, and here he seemed unusually confident. "I believe I have made place enough for myself," he stated to Cox in January, "to be sure of a hearing for anything else I do. I ask no more." In another letter to Cox a month later he grew even bolder—

talking of *North of Boston* he suddenly makes the most open and heartfelt affirmation of his new status he was ever to make, almost blurting it out: "The book is epoch-making. I don't ask anyone to say so. All I ask now is to be allowed to live." In all of this he was anticipating that the sparkling reception given him by English reviewers would transfer itself, more or less intact, across the water, something which, barring untoward developments, was quite likely. Unfortunately, something untoward did develop, in Frost's estimate looming as an instant threat to his American reception. The cause was Ezra Pound's belated review of *North of Boston* in the Chicago *Poetry*.

Reading the review in about mid-December, Frost felt immediate alarm. Mixed with the praise (restrained, and again missing Frost's true quality), there was outright condemnation of American editors, and in language more abrasive than usual. Anxiously Frost wrote Cox: "I fear I am going to suffer a good deal at home by the support of Pound . . . You will see the blow he has dealt me in Poetry . . . The harm he does lies in this: he made up his mind in the short time I was friends with him (we quarreled in six weeks) to add me to his party of American literary refugees in London. Nothing could be more unfair, nothing better calculated to make me an exile for life. Another such review as the one in Poetry and I shan't be admitted at Ellis Island. This is no joke."

Frost's concern was by no means groundless, as may be seen in his next sentence, where he gives the tangible cause for his worry, though without offering specifics or naming names: "Since the article was published I have been insulted and snubbed by two American editors I counted on as good friends." That could refer to any of the four or five American periodicals in which he had been published before going to England, and the snubs must have reached him in the form of letters written soon after the late-November appearance of the December *Poetry*. Two such complaining letters from home, descending on him even before he had had a chance to read Pound's remarks for himself, would have jarred him considerably.

Pound's "blow"—in itself not quite the massive stroke Frost imagined—was contained in a few caviling sentences. "It is a sinister thing," Pound wrote, "that so American, I might even say so parochial a talent as that of Robert Frost should have to be exported before it can find due encouragement and recognition . . . The typical American editor of the last twenty years has resolutely shut his mind against serious American writing . . . why, in heaven's name, is this book of New England eclogues given us under a foreign imprint?"

As Frost would have realized, by the time he had been able to read the review the damage back home had already been done. Still, he could not help trying to lessen its impact. "I don't see that it is possible," he wrote Cox, "to do anything publicly to dissociate myself from Pound, but do you think it would be a discreet thing for you to say a word to Sherman [a teacher at Cox's college and a literary critic] or perhaps (what do you think) even write a short letter to the Sun or the Times or both saying that you have reason to know that I would have no pleasure in that part of Pound's article in Poetry that represented me as an American literary refugee in London with a grievance against American editors." In the end, he left it to Cox's discretion whether to take any action, and he consoled himself with the thought that Pound's opinions might not, after all, gain much of a hearing.

It is a measure of Frost's continuing naïveté when it came to the practical side of his trade that he discussed all this with his young friend Cox, an unknown English instructor and graduate student at the University of Illinois, and never thought of supplying the same information to his publisher in New York.

*   *   *

DURING his final three or so months in England Frost's physical energy was often at a low ebb, sapped by continuing or recurring bouts of a flu-like illness (apparently a touch of what was then popularly known as "walking pneumonia"). It took hold of him first in early October during a two-week visit he paid, with Lesley, to the Smith home in Edinburgh where he was sick enough to be attended by a doctor. "Half heated English houses are the trouble," he complained in reporting his condition to Haines. Still weak, he had been summoned hastily back to Ryton by an exhausted Elinor, who had written him that she and the other children were also ailing. Though he seems not to have taken to his bed for any length of time, it was early January before he began to feel himself again. Even then he said he would have less worry over the trip back to the United States, "if I was sure I was well."

In mid-November the Abercrombies returned to the Gallows from their travels, and from that time until the departure of the Frosts for home, the house was full. Concerning these weeks in which the two families lived in unusual intimacy, only Abercrombie's wife, Catharine, had anything to say, and her memories are brief and of no special import. She did, however, encounter a side of Elinor not noted by her other English friends: "I admired Elinor so much for her charming imperturbability—nothing seemed to daunt her—she kept her precious metal coffee pot going all day on the stove, and imbibed more coffee in a day than I did in a month." Mrs. Abercrombie was also the only one to state that the Frost children "did not get on with the natives," in this case meaning the English children in the Ryton area. Of course, that may only indicate a preoccupation with thoughts of the fast-approaching return home, for Mrs. Abercrombie added that all the Frosts talked a good deal about their recollections of America. This is corroborated by Frost himself who, as the day drew near for departure, admitted "We think of home all the time."

The anxious waiting and the unsettled conditions of wartime, it appears, precluded much attention to poetry by Frost, hardly surprising for one who needed serenity and even isolation to write. Very real fears of a German invasion were on everyone's mind, as well as apprehension over the threatened naval blockade, a possibility that raised disturbing visions of serious food shortages and starvation diets. Even in peaceful, supposedly remote Gloucestershire people were regularly reminded of the hardships of war and the battles then raging in Belgium and France. Though Frost's talk of the military situation in his letters shows no more than an ordinary interest in the war's progress, his assurances to an American friend as early as October couldn't hide his uneasiness: "We are very quiet in spite of the war. An occasional hobnailed boot on the metaled lane [the local police patrols] is all that disturbs us—that and a certain fear we don't know what of. It won't be Zeppelins at this distance from big towns and it won't be of invading armies—yet. I doubt if we are going to be invaded at all."

More and more as the weeks went by the peaceful air of the whole Dymock region was disrupted, and by Christmas 1914 the little village of Ryton was almost permanently astir. Several times Frost looked on as truckloads of youthful volunteers pulled out of the village, headed for Army headquarters in Ledbury where they would take the oath. "There are soldiers swarming over everything," he wrote Silver in late December. "I have seen them by the thousands in all stages of development—some of them veterans already wounded, recovered and on their way to the front again. These last are the ones to pity . . . A Colonel Gordon home with a paralyzed arm, showed a photograph of the officers of his regiment taken before the war and he said every one of them was wounded, dead, or in the madhouse."

Even Mrs. Nutt, who was French born, managed in rather unexpected fashion to bring the war home to him. When sending for correction the proofs of an advertising leaflet for *North of Boston,* her covering note quickly strayed into more personal matters: "Today I feel a terrible grief about the murders and destruction at Seuchlis. Nothing can ever wipe that out. How would you feel if it had happened in America— MAD!!! and I feel like that. I can hardly bear the necessity of remaining here in business and not do something, however small, for my own land and country. If you wish to recognize in any way the fact that I divined your great talent, use some of it now to stir up the world in defense of France." Never a poet who could produce on demand, even if so inclined, Frost made no effort so far as is known to honor this request. He did, however, somewhat later produce a sonnet on the war, his only such effort. In it he attempts to stir up, not the world in defense of France, but France itself to keep on fighting at a time when there was early talk of an armistice:

> *France, France, I know not what is in my heart.*
> *But God forbid that I should be more brave*
> *As a watcher from a quiet place apart*
> *Than you are fighting in an open grave.*
>
> *I will not ask more of you than you ask,*
> *O Bravest, of yourself. But shall I less?*
> *You know the extent of your appointed task,*
> *Whether you still can face its bloodiness.*
>
> *Not mine to say you shall not think of peace.*
> *Not mine, not mine. I almost know your pain.*
> *But I will not believe that you will cease,*
> *I will not bid you cease, from being slain*
>
> *And slaying till what might have been distorted*
> *Is saved to be the Truth and Hell is thwarted.*

The poem demonstrates, at any rate, that Frost's talents did not include a knack for propaganda, and it may have been seen by no one beyond Edward Thomas, to whom Frost sent it in December 1916. (Thomas's unit had just been ordered to France, which must have put him in a receptive mood, for he wrote back that he liked the poem "very much, because it betrays exactly what you *would* say & what you feel about saying that much").

In the midst of all the turmoil of that fall of 1914, Frost did somehow manage to compose two poems that have since taken their place among his best-known work. "The Sound of Trees"—one of only two poems he wrote in England which have an avowedly English setting and subject—was inspired by a prominent feature of the Ryton landscape, a majestic stand of tall, old elm trees, called by the locals the Seven Sisters, that towered behind the Gallows ("at the bottom of our garden," Catharine Abercrombie explained proudly). Though it may be taken as a veiled projection of his impatience for the journey home to begin, the poem's close manages to hint at something else, a reluctance, or at least regret, at the thought that he was deserting in its hour of need the country that had given him his life's desire:

> *I shall set forth for somewhere,*
> *I shall make the reckless choice*
> *Some day when they are in voice*
> *And tossing so as to scare*
> *The white clouds over them on.*
> *I shall have less to say,*
> *But I shall be gone.*

The second poem of that fall, drafted at the Gallows but not given its final form until some months later in America, was "The Road Not Taken," in popular esteem perhaps second only to "Stopping By Woods." Beyond its powerful surface appeal, this poem from the first has carried an added interest, particularly for critics, for it is not the simple retrospective statement it appears to be. In reality, as Frost repeatedly explained, it was never intended as a serious effort at all, but was composed as a mild satire on the chronic vacillating habits of Edward Thomas, his endless fine distinctions when faced with a choice. Supposedly, in the writing the poem got away from Frost, simply went out of control, as poems will do, and took on a serious cast. That is perhaps true to an extent, but still it must be seen as passing strange that no hint of the original parodic intention is detectable in the fluent lines, so that some further explanation seems in order.

That Frost, by inadvertence or mere clumsy execution, could have so badly missed his aim is improbable. Control of *tone* was precisely the element of technique on which he had begun to pride himself—it had come to form, in fact, the very basis of his success as a poet. Some additional obscure impulse must have been operating in those cloudy moments when his gathering inspiration went groping for words, and a little reflection will show what that impulse must have been: a powerful surge of self-analysis, brushing aside the original intent.

Just at that time, the fall of 1914, Frost could hardly have avoided more than once taking a long, backward look at his career. Nor in so doing could he have missed the stark contrast between the customary drift and indecision of his friend Thomas, and his own straight and steady progress toward artistic fulfillment (achingly slow that progress had been, but never had its goal been in doubt). No single step or choice had made the difference. Behind him stretched a lengthy series of choices, large and small, starting long years before, most markedly with his walking out of college in 1892. Each of those decisions, arrived at through little except instinct, had taken him down an unfrequented road. Each had involved the lives of others, wife and children especially, so that behind all there persisted the question as to whether, and how, and how much, his personal choices might have marked those other lives. During more than twenty years he had repeatedly faced such diverging roads. Often he must have yearned, illogically if humanly, to avoid the necessity of choosing. But choose he did, time after time, and in so doing learned that the ability to choose—especially where the choices are not clearly marked, the usual condition in real life—was in itself a kind of mastery over circumstance:

> Two roads diverged in a yellow wood,
> And sorry I could not travel both
> And be one traveler, long I stood
> And looked down one as far as I could
> To where it bent in the undergrowth;
>
> Then took the other, as just as fair,
> And having perhaps the better claim,
> Because it was grassy and wanted wear;
> Though as for that, the passing there
> Had worn them really about the same,
>
> And both that morning equally lay
> In leaves no step had trodden black.
> Oh, I kept the first for another day!

Yet knowing how way leads on to way,
I doubted if I should ever come back.

I shall be telling this with a sigh
Somewhere ages and ages hence:
Two roads diverged in a wood, and I—
I took the one less traveled by,
And that has made all the difference.

A copy of the poem, in an early version, was sent to Thomas, probably in April 1915, and was first made public, in its now familiar form, at a college reading by Frost in Boston early that May. It was at this reading that he learned conclusively, from the sober reaction of his audience, what he must have already suspected, that his little poem had missed fire. Somewhat shamefacedly he commented to Thomas in a subsequent letter: "I suppose my little jest in the poem is too much between me and myself. I read it aloud before the Phi Beta Kappa at Tufts College and while I did my best to make it obvious by my manner that I was fooling, I doubt if I wasn't taken pretty seriously. Mea culpa." Thomas, it might be noted, had previously confirmed the failure by letter, in his remarks on the poem assuming that Frost was portraying his own very personal history. (Among Thomas's comments was this rather curious one, which he leaves unexplained: "It is all very well for you poets in a wood to say you choose, but you don't. If you do, ergo I am no poet.")

From a critical point of view, the interesting thing about this poem is not its peculiar misdirection. It is the fact that the mechanism by which it succeeds, in spite of the failure, is really very little different from that which underlies all the other poems inspired by those lonely years at the start in Derry. The veiled invocation of Thomas's indecisive nature, filtered through the medium of Frost's own very different attitude, insinuates itself subtly into the lines, and the result is that two presences are heard, or felt, not just the single voice of the speaker. One of the two is muted, made tangible only by indirection, as an echo, heard only in the distant reverberations of such equivocating phrases as "just as fair," "about the same," and "equally lay." These suggest a dissenting voice, opposing the speaker and gently raveling the basis on which the final distinction of "less traveled" is made. The slightly out-of-focus aura is completed by the poem's title: where the stanzas on the surface speak of the fortunate "difference" that was made by choosing the right road, the title calls up for further pondering that other road, the one that bent in the undergrowth and that was left untrod.

Rather than the "mock sigh" Frost confessed to Thomas that he had intended, the sigh in the last stanza now appears very real indeed, expressing, as he prepared to leave England, his own profound satisfaction—mixed certainly with some portion of disbelief and amazement—at the way it had all turned out.

*   *   *

TOWARD the end of January the Frosts left the Gallows and returned to Ledington to start their packing. Little Iddens being still occupied, they stayed at the Chandler farm, as payment for room and board giving the Chandlers their furniture. At this time arrangements were also completed for the Thomas's fifteen-year-old son, Merfyn, to accompany the Frosts to the United States on his way to a relative in New Hampshire. The unstated reason for this move, at least in part, was the then general desire of English parents to send their children as far as possible from the new danger of falling bombs, as well as the old one of invasion. Similar thoughts about their families were expressed to Frost by both Smith and Haines, though neither went any further ("I am in one of my darkest moods tonight," wrote Smith, "and cannot trust myself to write freely. But I wish my wife and children were going with you!").

The final ten days were hectic. There was a night or two, with Lesley, at the Haines home in Gloucester, and an overnight dash up to Edinburgh on some unspecified business. There was a quick trip with Elinor to London, again on obscure business, followed by a side trip from London down to the Thomas home at Steep. Here, as time ran out, Frost began to think he would delay his departure to a later sailing, principally in order to have one last get together with all his English friends. In a note to Haines written from Steep he mentions the contemplated change of plan, but then says he has already thought better of it: "All things considered though we doubt if it would be wise to put off the evil day. The Germans have only a little to do with the decision. I will tell you more about it when I see you."

This decision to wait no longer before leaving England may not, as Frost says, have been prompted by the German threat alone, but it is a fact that on February 4, 1915, the German High Command announced that after February 18 the waters around Great Britain would be considered a "war zone," with ships of all nations subject to interdiction or attack by submarines. It was the long-feared naval blockade, and English newspapers specifically warned neutral ships of their danger. Even a glance at the papers early that anxious February is sufficient to call up the fears for his family's safety that must have gripped Frost at the prospect of sailing home in wartime, even with America neutral. All was uncertain, even though the submarine menace at that point supposedly was aimed only at merchant shipping. The German commanders, chivalrous as their comrades in the sky, at first allowed crews of belligerent nations to put off in small boats before the sinking. But just two weeks before the Frosts' scheduled departure a British merchant ship in the Channel was torpedoed without warning, causing the London *Times* to ask angrily and incredulously if Germany had now inhumanly decided "to send ships to the bottom regardless of the fate of crew and passengers."

At the last there was a flurry of farewell notes. One from Smith, received probably on the day he left Ledington, may stand as an example of the several warm friendships Frost was leaving behind:

My Dear Frost,

For nearly a week I have had a premonition that you would sail with the St. Paul on the 13th, and lo! it has come true. And you are doing wisely, I am sure. Whether I really wish that Edith and the Children were going with you is more than I can tell. Sometimes I think it is the only safe course, but in other moods I feel that no immediate danger threatens them. I agree with you so far that I have put away the fear of invasion for a good while to come at least. About starvation—well, I don't know; but that too won't come today or tomorrow. It *might* by Christmas—all depends on what the submarines can really do . . .

I wish above most things that I could come and see you off. But it seems quite impossible. Tomorrow I am booked for Glasgow, & on Saturday I have to read a paper in Edinburgh. It would do me good to take your hand once more. Somehow I think we shall meet again somewhere . . . Now I want you to *wire* goodbye just before you start. Then when you have got safe over *write* at once and let me know where letters will find you . . . Take all our good wishes and don't forget us.

On the morning of February 12 the Frost family left by train from the Dymock station. Next day, after spending the night in Liverpool, they boarded the *St. Paul*. Sometime that evening, recalling that he had received no farewell word from Frank Flint, in what he later called a "melancholy" mood, Frost penned a hasty note on ship's stationery: "I ought to know by the length of your silence that you don't want to write to me anymore—cor silicis [heart of flint]. And if you don't I ought to have pride enough not to ask you to. But no matter. I must at least say goodbye to the man who opened England to me. You are good." Because it was finished too late to get it ashore for mailing, the note was never posted, and for many years it lay in its unopened envelope among Frost's papers. It was this small circumstance that produced the final distortion associated with Frost and England: when the note was eventually opened and published, after Frost's death, its apparently complaining and mildly injured tone convinced some critics that the two men in those last months must have had a serious falling out. Blame for the break—need it be said?—was assigned to Frost. It is a final satisfaction to report, on the authority of none other than Flint himself, that that conclusion must now be set aside. Months afterward, puzzled by Frost's silence in America, Flint made his own inquiry. "Are we still pals?" he asked in opening a long letter he wrote Frost in January 1916, and he closes with "Give my best regards to Mrs. F. Whatever happens I shall always have the memory of your presences & of your childrens."

Under cover of darkness, with passengers lying fully clothed in their bunks and wearing life jackets, the *St. Paul* departed Liverpool on February 13. Outside the harbor the ship joined a convoy under escort of two British destroyers that accompanied them round the north of Ireland. The crossing to New York was made in nine rough but uneventful days. Little more than two months later the British liner *Lusitania*, following the same route, was struck by German torpedoes and went down with the loss of more than a thousand lives.

FROST'S ENGLISH NOTEBOOKS

S URVIVING from Frost's time in England are two small pocket note-books used almost exclusively for jotting random observations. Both are of English manufacture and must have been obtained soon after Frost's arrival in Beaconsfield. In length, the individual entries range from a single word or phrase to a page or more, though most run to perhaps two or three lines. They tumble after one another, in ink or pencil, with abrupt alteration in subject matter, unseparated by any device.

While occasionally the entries coincide with ideas and even actual phrases in Frost's letters (especially concerning his sound-of-sense theories), most appear to concern topics that soon drifted out of view. Definite links to seven published poems are traceable, and these are all included below. As might be expected in a notebook, Frost's punctuation is haphazard, and it has not been corrected in these excerpts. About half the total text of each notebook is given here, comprising those entries which afford a more or less complete thought and are readily decipherable.*

The Morrison Notebook. This appears to have been the first used of the two, but only the initial twenty pages refer to the time in England. The remaining forty pages on which entries appear, judging by internal evidence, were filled after the return to the United States. In 1974 this notebook was given by Kathleen Morrison (Frost's legatee along with his daughter Lesley) to the Frost Collection at Dartmouth College.

The Cohn Notebook. Of the 114 pages of this notebook, ninety-five

---

* The complete texts of both notebooks, along with some forty others Frost kept throughout his long life, are soon to be published by Farrar, Straus & Giroux, edited with commentary by Margot Feldman.

were written on by Frost, and all the entries appear to have been made in England. In 1948 Frost gave this notebook to a friend, rare book dealer Louis Cohn. After the death of Cohn's widow in 1984, it was sent to the Frost Collection at the University of Virginia.

Lawrance Thompson also had access to the Cohn notebook. He made little use of it, however, quoting only the poem "Flower Guidance," and the last four entries as given here, starting with "Life is that which," etc. These four entries he gives as primary evidence in support of what he calls Frost's "guilt" in his customary "daily relations" with his family and friends (*Early*, 427). In that regard see the footnote to those entries below, p. 225.

Morrison Notebook Excerpts

Beggars in England

Pursuit of G.B.S.

Failure of Puritanism. Milton

No stir at the stations

American news in the Times

Bundles of toothpicks for kindling

Joy for a penny

Something of doing everything for its own sake

More foreign news in English papers

The popping of little lighting flame

Schools here are like the streets of Boston; schools with us like streets of Washington.

We see out and out Englishmen so little that we are likely to forget that the English still consider us predominently English. Article in Times.

Mrs. Tynan Hinkson couldn't let her English country friends know that she wrote poetry. Strange they weren't readers enough to know it themselves. The secret sin of writing verse.

Too physical a nature to see both sides to the question. His nature is too vigorous too physical—

If Emerson Had Written a Play.

Marrying was important because need for children let it be.

Brilliance of Shylock's talk shows more intellect and less dignity than in real life. Conflict here.

The bagpipes. A boatload of the Scotch. It does you good to hear that some things are the same as at home.

They think monogamous talk is sentimental.

Criticism is where we say behind the back things to each other's faces.

In looking up trains you have to be on your guard (consciously) against certain things viz getting wrong direction getting Sunday trains. Not so in writing poetry.

Bergson's is a literary philosophy because it uses for everything the idea of every sentence being a fresh start not a sure logical derivation from the last sentence.

On seeing Shakespeare's rhythm done in musical notation by Harriet—all I can say is it's a damned poor tune.

Children in arms not admitted. How can you blame children for being in arms when the whole nation is in arms?

No right prevails of itself except as human beings espouse it.

There is no evil but that was at some time indistinguishable from good. God himself did not know the devil from his good angels.

Extrication. [see "From Plane to Plane," lines 61, 96]

Not as a woman weeps but as a man—against his nature and against his will.

Rub your finger on a smooth surface so as to make it "catch" and vibrate enough for a "note." Just so the speech rhythm on the verse rhythm.

Off-hand judgment is the only kind in human affairs. You may be as conversant as you will with all knowledge in this world the final act of judgment is always a jump.

You must remember that no sentence is quite on the page anyway. The sentence concept that holds the words together is supplied by the voice.

The smoke flowed down the roof and in the open window and up the chimney again.

Something in the sentence that is more effective than any chosen word.

Certain cadences belong to us by birth as certain runs of voice belong to a kind of bird.

Sometimes the donkey pulls the cart sometimes the cart pushes the donkey. Speech rhythm is the donkey.

A ninth wave gathering half the deep and full of voices slowly rose and plunged roaring and all the wave was a flame and down the wave and in the wave was borne [unfinished].

The sentence form almost seems the soul of a certain set of words. We see inspiration as it takes liberties with the words and yet saves the soul. Nothing counts but the increment.

Cohn Notebook Excerpts

A Place Apart [see "Revelation," line 1]

Down among the dead men in Tober Morey Bay

Ricks stand grey to the sun

Dove that perched upon the mast

All night I heard a singing bird upon the topmost tree

Distant lights of London flaring like a dreary dawn

A reeling deck on a rolling sea

Robin robin redbreast

A crooked stile

Milk comes frozen home in Pail

An Hundred Collars [see *North of Boston*]

Nocturnes for Atlantic

Other Lives (Villagers)

Any difference Is a fault

He refused to be hurried by life as by a bad teacher

The Refluent Wave [see "West-running Brook"]

> *Ale does more than Milton can*
> *To justify God's ways to man.* *

* From A. E. Housman's poem (in *A Shropshire Lad*) "Terence," where "ale" is "malt."

Departure from the word laid down must be under stress and impromptu. If imitative it makes the set poetic language.

Youth is afraid that he isn't wanted. All age knows is that he wants.

Hedges the man on horseback can see over. Good roads for the man on horseback. No pavements for the man on foot.

What they are afraid over here can't be done to equalize men is so much greater than over there that I am encouraged to believe all fears are baseless.

Advertisement in Times for someone to see nothing but my good qualities.

Englishmen and Amer. meet as they understand each other from newspapers.

We know nothing about any *whole* improvement in stock brought about by breeding.

War represents what faith we wont be laughed or reasoned out of.

Time has moved the fixed stars.

Literature is not original when it picks up crumbs of whatever is going.

Love has no way or posture.

Heaven without Hell were a house without a cellar under it.

Don't write so much as to fix any stage as a habit.

Spelling may express feelings.

Professorial mind and originality. What new it says is not true, what is true is not new.

As a bird that flies before you and thinks it is pursued. [see "The Woodpile," lines 10–16].

Reproductiveness is not a part of us: we are a part of it.

We see so many strange words never heard in speech when we read an English book we come to think that all book language should be a thing by itself. We don't know that these words are still vernacular in England.

The painter is lucky he can entertain no illusion as to where he gets his lines. He may imagine them but we know in just what sense he may do that. He never fools himself with the notion that he creates them out of nothing.

You must feel that the thing happened that way not for the purposes of the author. Why it should happen so you don't know but it did. It is the didness of it that makes it taste strong.

Once I knew a beautiful woman and we were safe for a long time. There was a strangeness about her eyes and about her forehead and about her upper lip that I never found till in an ill day for her and me (for both of us) I met it in a fearful shrunken face prepared by oiling and drying in the sun by savages for their worship. And her face was beautiful and this not and this made hers not too, slowly drawing it to itself. I could not come near enough to her in the dark at night to forget it.

When it rains up it fills the River Leden [Leadon, in Gloucestershire] sooner than when it rains down.

This rain is as dry as a sandstorm.

He might not be bad in this particular case. But if he is capable of being and I know it I have a right to accuse him.

That a man had eyes and a nose and lips and a lower face and shaved somehow this stone is able to tell without much cutting. It is left flat. Shoulders arms legs—these are suggested. The piece stands erect. There is the statement that it is a man without help of headgear or garment. It is made man by the essential sign without help of headgear or dress.

Take any characterless sentence: The gates will be open between two and five P.M. Now underline any word in it and see how the stress you give it in the sentence suggests another sentence to follow. The *gates* will be open between two and five P.M. You can come into the yard and wait for the door to open.

I have seen people here who frankly sent their husbands to be rid of them. One kind of sending.

A sentence carries a certain number of words and those have their sound but the sentence has a sound of its own apart from the words which is the sentence sound proper. It was before words were. It still has existence without the embodiment of words in the cries of our nature.

The mind or spirit is not really active unless it is finding constantly new tones of voice.

You can always tell a realist from a romantic in this way. The realist will marry some girl he has grown up with and always seen around: the romantic wants a girl from off somewhere—someone that he knew not of.

What a Shakespeare among them all. They were all smut, but he was too various to miss everything in life but smut; or they were all bloody but he was too various to miss everything in life but the blood. And they were all one swelling tone of verse, but he was as various as the tones of speech.

Half our conversation is no more than voting, signifying our adherence to some well known idea in the field. What's the good of it?

Metaphor is not only in thought, it is in the sentence sounds as well. We are playing at other sounds than the ones you would expect in the place. Metaphor is make believe. Metaphor is everything out of its place. It is the whole of poetry in one sense, synecdoche in another.

The calf I was to market.

Exalting God till you make him everything and then blaming him for the evil you can't help seeing.

Thank the poor for keeping up a kind of living very useful to those who have to get along on a little to do great deeds Alfred.

I can't look forward [to] picking a way for a life unlived, except with dread.

When people praise you give them their satisfaction in the matter. Consider where they come in.

He never knew that the pretensions of the unintellectual lords of creation were not absurd, because he was brought up in the New England professor's aristocracy.

After I have poured out words I am left foolish and inclined to talk on though I say nothing unless someone will speak and save me.

Yearning across the barrier. Let man not bring together what God had put asunder.

The essential sentence is some tone of voice, some one of the tones belonging to man, as its set of songs belongs to a kind of bird. That the first function of vowels is to pin these tones to the page definitely enough for recognition. There has been insistence enough on clear images of sight. More important are the clear images of sound. Good writing deals with things present to the eye of the mind in tones of voice present to the ear of the mind.

What a Woman Wants of A Man (No one knows after all these years).

The best mind asks and answers his own questions, not questions asked by others.

The generation fixes on somebody it may be anybody to justify it for neglecting everybody else. Masefield. Tennyson.

Sincerity is an organic compound the formula for which is different for every generation. Seldom a new element enters into this compound. The differences are due to varying proportions of extravagance doubt speech silence sentiment ruthlessness passion reflection etc. One generation finds the balance it holds it by phrases and art for a little while and then goodby.

She would have felt as sad for any ommission in the creed as the child who remembers while in bed that he has forgotten to kiss his mother good night. [see "The Black Cottage," 100–103].

He had so many more children than a mere mother.

Sense of time: who can estimate a minute?

Civilization advances like the fire moving in the soot at the back of the fireplace.—Selectiveness is that which forgets.

Suppose we write poetry as we make a dynamo without ornament well only the great poetry can be written that way.

Men have nothing but vague theory to explain why they are as they are. Idlers in Argentina assigned as reason for Idleness day was too long. They were too poor to work.

Hollis said I could have all the brushwood I wanted to brush my peas. [see "Pea Brush"]

One good thing about Hardy. He has planted himself on the wrongs that can't be righted.

Once you get enough inspiration for a line or two you can finish your poem by logic. But you don't want to.

Certainly some things you can't do without plenty of slaves and subjects.

How may words be made to hold their sounds. Spelling is approximate. They only hold the sounds for those who have heard them: sentences only hold their sound for those who have heard them. The real intonations of Homer's verse are long since lost. That is why we drop into scansion.

Don't you hate or love anyone enough to make fun of him.

We lie as uncomfortably in society as in a bad old bed that rolls us together in the middle.

I would increase everyman's chance not anybody's certainty.

Only a few fairies believe in people I find.

Does Yates [sic] believe in fairies?

They have an air of thinking anything you may say we will have heard before.

Sentence sounds haven't been noticed anymore than perspective once.

It is the common way to think of a sentence as saying something. It must do something as well.

Fatigue like forgetting as an advantage. There's as much hate as love in all getting on.

Curl most significant thing in nature. Things return upon themselves.

Reproductive imagination and transcendent imagination.

It is possible to be just as speculative about people as about God and animals.

A. is speculative I am introspective W. is intuitive.

The poet is himself creative in something that is a resultant of these two, the intonation (sound of sense) and the metre.

No indelicacy to appear in public with the children you have begotten. At the same time you don't care to be seen begetting them.

Suspicion that these tales of magic and the miraculous are some last remains of what some other age was as great in as ours is in science and mechanics.

I am here who have been there. Time, time! It is almost as mysterious that I can be in different places at different times as that I could be in different places at the same time.

Every poet has his regular characteristic displacement, that is to say distance of moving words phrases and things from their place.

Children can't enjoy the joke of an animal standing on its head in a picture because they can't see why they shouldn't turn the picture round and bring the animal right side up (though they should make the trees stand on their head).

The strangeness is all in thinking two things at once, in being in two places at once. This is all there is to metaphor.

Life is that which can mix oil and water (Emulsion). It can consist of the inconsistent. It can hold in unity the ultimate irreconcilables spirit and matter good and evil, monism (cohesion) and dualism (reaction), peace and strife. It o'er rules the harsh divorce that parts things natural and divine. Life is a bursting unity of opposites barely held.*

---

* Thompson's use of this entry (*Early*, 427) is inaccurate. In the second and third sentences he misreads the word "It," though it is clearly written, printing it as "I," and setting up a personal application otherwise absent. He is also misleading as to the final entry of the four he gives in this same place to conclude his chapter. The entry, "Evil clings so in all our acts," etc., does not occur in the notebook in conjunction with the other three entries as is implied by Thompson's placement. It has been moved without indication from its original position seventeen pages earlier (see above, 8, and below, 229). Also, some of the phrases are seriously garbled.

Life is something that rides steadily on something else that passes away as light on a gush of water.

All a man's art is a bursting unity of opposites. He rides them, the opposites. Christ's message almost tears itself apart with its great contradiction.

Ever since man was man he has known the generous thrill of owning a better. There is a better in me than I am. How does he bring himself to it? Christ is one he has taken to do it with.

NOTES AND SOURCES

THESE notes are organized by chapters, and the sequence of citations and comment follows that of the main text. A glance at the page numbers down the left hand margins will quickly locate any item. For quoted matter, the first few words of the quotation are repeated, enough to make identification simple. All sources are given in shortened form and may be fully identified by reference to the bibliography. For those sources often cited the following abbreviations are used:

SL	*Selected Letters of Robert Frost*, edited by Lawrance Thompson. Citations from this volume also provide the date of the letter cited, unless it is given elsewhere.
DCL	Dartmouth College Library
UTL	University of Texas Library (Austin)
UVL	University of Virginia Library
BUL	Boston University Library
PSCL	Plymouth State College Library

Prologue: Over There

For early discussion in America of the fact that Frost had first been recognized abroad—involving the magazine *Current Opinion* and an editorial in the *New York Times*—see Greenberg, "Frost In England." Also see Thompson, *Triumph*, 53–56, and above, 207–208.

5 Identification of the Bungalow: This was first done by a Beaconsfield librarian, D. J. Chandler. Reading in January 1963 of Frost's death that same

month, Chandler went in search of the Bungalow, only to find that no house of that name then existed on Reynolds Road. Later he explained: "it was necessary to obtain the help of the local council's Valuation and Rating Office to trace the building . . . This was done by means of the valuation number, which is never changed, although the building of new houses can alter the street numbers. The entry in the 1914 Rate Book has an entry for 'The Hut' under which is an original pencil entry reading 'formerly the Bungalow.' This is in actual fact the present number 26." (*Beaconsfield Parish Magazine*, March 1963) When Chandler visited No. 26, by then called Maycroft, he was able to inform the surprised owner of the house's unusual literary association. Chandler's conclusions are supported by my own further study of the 1912 *Poor Rates Book* and a 1912 Ordnance Survey map of the area (Public Records Office, Aylesbury). Final proof is to be had in the old photograph, previously unpublished (see the photo section above), which shows the cottage presently standing at No. 26. That this photo was made in the spring of 1913 is shown by a postscript in Frost to Susan Ward, 13 May 1913: "This picture will give you some idea of the size of the children as compared with that of the house they live in." This letter as given in SL 73 omits the postscript, quoted here from a copy in the Newdick papers; the original is at the Huntington.

5   The Frosts' 1928 visit to Beaconsfield: Elinor Frost, in a letter written a few days after the visit, comments tantalizingly: "The weather is so cold now we have to keep a coal fire in the [hotel] grate all day. The smell of coal reminds me so much of the old days at Beaconsfield. It moved me more than the *sight* of the place did, somehow." (Grade, *Family*, 131; italics in original)

6   "Discovering that Reynolds Road"—Thompson, *Early*, 583. Some support for the contention that Frost shrank from entering the Bungalow during his 1957 visit to England is afforded by what happened in the Dymock region a week before. As recalled by the pastor of the Dymock church, who formed one of the greeting party, it was decided that Little Iddens should be Frost's last stop "lest the sudden surging up of the most personal of old memories might be somewhat unpleasant for the octogenarian." At Gibson's former home, the Old Nailshop, Frost was "strangely silent." When he was finally taken to Little Iddens, "there was a definite reaction, a reluctance, it seemed, to enter again upon ground so steeped in hallowed memories . . . Inside the house memories must have flooded in especially when Mrs. Jean Eversham, the married daughter of the house, replied in answer to Frost's inquiry, 'We are six.' In quiet tones came back, 'And so were we.' " (Gethyn-Jones, *Frost*, 2–5) For further on Frost's 1957 visit to Dymock, see Thompson, *Later Years*, 239–241; also *Life* magazine, 23 September, 1957.

7   "Frost told me that he was"—Foster's private journal as quoted in Thompson, *Later*, 8. The entry is dated 8 August 1938.

7   "What a man will put"—SL 141, December 1914.

8   "Evil clings so in all"—the Cohn Notebook, 89 (unnumbered); see above, 225n.

8   Burnshaw on Lawrance Thompson: In his *Robert Frost Himself*, Stanley Burnshaw presents enough clear evidence, from Thompson's own voluminous notes on Frost (UVL), to put beyond doubt what many had suspected, that the biographer, years prior to Frost's death, had entertained a pervasive and growing dislike of his subject. What brought it about is made less clear. Perhaps it was, as Burnshaw suggests, a feeling of inadequacy on Thompson's part when faced with the work of a major contemporary poet, combined with personality differences. Probably to this may be added resentment of Frost's aiding other biographers and writers, in particular Elizabeth Sergeant, whose 1960 biography of Frost anticipated Thompson's by more than two years—see SL 584 for a Frost note mollifying Thompson on that score. Frost himself, it appears, at one point became so alarmed by what he saw of Thompson's attitude that he mentioned the fact in confidence to Burnshaw, then his editor at Holt. "I'm counting on you to protect me from Larry," the eighty-six-year-old Frost is quoted as saying in 1959 (Burnshaw, *Frost*, 6; and see 116, 215). To Burnshaw's suggestion that the arrangement with Thompson (begun twenty years before) simply be terminated, Frost replied that it was too late, that he had given his word. Apparently, Frost expected that Burnshaw, as the Holt editor who was to handle the Thompson biography, would be in a position to control any excesses. As it turned out, Burnshaw claims, he did manage to tone down some of Thompson's commentary in *Selected Letters*, published a few months after Frost's death, but circumstances (none too clearly explained) prevented his having anything to do with the biography. Before Burnshaw, William Pritchard in the introduction to his *Frost: A Literary Life Reconsidered* (1984), had offered a half-dozen pages of balanced appraisal of Thompson's peculiar attitude, effectively baring, if in a general way, both the deficiencies of thought and the strong bias. Even earlier, of course, other voices had spoken up in defense of Frost, but more fleetingly, by mere assertion and in some heat, so less effectively.

8   The Lask review of Thompson's second volume, *The Years of Triumph*, appeared in the *New York Times*, 11 August 1970.

9   "I have nothing left but"—Sutton, *Season*, 185.

Chapter One: Beaconsfield: The Bungalow

15   "The six of us by ourselves"—SL 63, 7 January 1913.

15   The date of the Frosts' arrival in London is derived from the fact that they went that same evening to see Shaw's play, attending, as Frost recalled, the 500th performance (Sergeant, *Trial*, 95; Thompson, *Early*, 393). In reality, it was the 575th performance, advertised as such in the London *Times*, 2 September, p. 6, with a comment from the *Daily Graphic*, "Shaw at his best."

16 "All alone, without a single"—SL 53. In this same letter Elinor provides sundry information about the family's arrival in Glasgow, the trip to London, and the settling in at Beaconsfield.

16 "The streets are full of"—Elinor Frost to Mrs. Brown, 25 October 1912, UVL; also see Crane, *Catalogue*, 246.

17 "He repaired to *T. P.'s Weekly*"—Munson, *Frost*, 61. Another personal reference by Frost to his friend at *T. P.'s Weekly* occurs in a 1947 interview. At the weekly's office, he said, he was directed to "a man sitting at a desk puffing away on his pipe with seemingly great unconcern for all things. This man turned out to be a retired policeman—why retired I don't know, for he didn't look very old." (Ellis, *England*, 10)

17 "He had read in the English"—Thompson, *Early*, 393.

18 "Some place or another"—Lathem, *Interviews*, 37.

19 The Bungalow: Owner of the property when the Frosts rented it was a Miss Helena Staniford, of Ealing, Middlesex (information from deed). Names of the other homes on Reynolds Road in 1912 are taken from a comparison of maps and rate books in the Public Records Office, Aylesbury. Several of the house names mentioned are still in use. Frost's statement in an early letter (SL 63) that the cottage had a "fifteen foot hedge of American laurel more flourishing than any I ever saw in America," was no exaggeration. The tall, leafy, thick-limbed hedge of laurel is still in place, forming one border of the property, and has to be regularly cut back to keep it at a reasonable height (in 1985 about ten feet). Many other homes in Beaconsfield have similar imposing laurel hedges. The "red-osier dogwood" hedge also mentioned by Frost (SL 52) has disappeared without a trace.

20 "That bend when you sit"—Ellis, *England*, 11. On the same page of Ellis is mentioned the kitchen table placed in the living room, as well as Frost's remark that at the Bungalow "We just camped." The Morris chair used by Frost in England was brought home and kept by him all his life. Today it reposes in the library of Middlebury College, Vermont.

20 "We got out of the train"—Sergeant, *Trial*, 93, quoting from the original manuscript. Of the individual composition books kept in England by the Frost children, only those of Lesley have been made available for use in connection with Frost facts, chronology, etc. Those of the other children are still held by the Frost family.

22 "You . . . ought to see how"—SL 99, c. 5 November 1913.

22 "Until it has piled on"—SL 224, 7 November 1917.

22 "One can buy a great"—SL 54, 25 October 1912.

22 "My mother never worked"—Letter of Lesley Frost, May 1969, in Tathem, *Recognized*, 12. Tathem, then a professor at Syracuse University, after several visits to England preserved some information about the Frost sites in his privately printed pamphlet. He was also the first to publish a photo of the Bungalow taken in 1968 (*The Courier*, Syracuse University, November 1968.)

22   "There is no waste"—Elinor Frost to Mrs. Brown, 25 October 1912, UVL.

23   Facts about Beaconsfield in Frost's time are taken from Day, *Recollections, passim*; I have also consulted Taylor, *History of Beaconsfield*, and Warr, *Schooldays*.

23   "By we I mean me and the"—SL 53. The visit of King George to Beaconsfield in December 1912 is in Warr, *Education*, 43. It is also mentioned in the official logbook of Beaconsfield grammar school for 20 December 1912: "Children assembled on the green at 9:30 to meet the King. Holiday by command of the King." In a letter to her father of January 1936 Lesley writes: "So Kipling and the King went almost together. Rather strange, and that they should be the same age too. Do you remember when we went to Old Beaconsfield to see the King?" (DCL)

24   "One would have to go"—SL 63. Other details of Frost's visit to the school are from this same letter. Today the old school building still stands, but it has been made into apartments. Mr. Baker's first name and description were supplied by Kathleen Day, author of *Recollections*, who knew him as a child. Frost's frank appraisal of the children he met in the school is borne out by a passage in Warr, *Education*, 45: "There was certainly a good deal of poverty amongst the cottagers and farm-workers, and we learn of poor conditions of living, ragged clothes, poor feeding, and the sordid home life of many of the children." Frost's report of the way the crowded schoolroom was divided into smaller classrooms is supported by another entry in the school log which complains that "the conflict of voices in a room where 3 classes are being taught at close quarters is very harassing & distracting & imposes undue strain on the teachers." From the original logbook, Maxwell Street School; there is no mention of Frost's visit in the log, which remarks only on official matters.

25   "A big house, all windows"—Mertins, *Walking*, 104. Chesterton's old house, Overroads, still stands on Grove Road. Better known is the house to which he later moved just across the street, Topmeadow, now a retreat for priests. Frost's gift of Chesterton's *Heretics* to Bartlett in 1911 is in Anderson, *Friendship*, 25.

25   The Milton cottage: Located in Chalfont St. Giles, this is now a museum regularly open to visitors, as it was in Frost's day. That Frost was aware of its existence is shown by a reference in an early letter (SL 52) where he says that he is living "within a mile or two of where Milton finished Paradise Lost." Just how he discovered that the poem was *finished* at the St. Giles address is uncertain, but the fact is mentioned in one of the foremost London Guidebooks of the day—Ward, Lock & Co.—in its section, "Trips From Town," p. 256. That this was Frost's source is quite probable, for the same page also mentions the burial of Thomas Grey at nearby Stoke Poges, a fact that Frost too gives in his letter in connection with Milton. One circumstance convinces me that Frost never did visit this cottage: framed on a wall is an ancient receipt, in the amount

of five pounds, representing first royalties on *Paradise Lost*. I hardly think that Frost, had he seen such a fascinating item of literary history, could have resisted making play with it in a letter! The well-known painting of Milton dictating to his daughters, by Munkácsy, is set in the parlor of this cottage, but the picture unduly swells the room's proportions. If anything, it is snugger than the Bungalow.

26　"In England"—The only manuscript of this poem is an inclosure in Frost to Cox, 26 December 1912 (Cox, *Forty Years*, 23). Not published in Frost's lifetime, the manuscript was reproduced in the catalogue of a 1944 Frost exhibition at DCL.

27　"Till they don't know"—SL 63, 7 January 1913. The Shaw meeting was reported in the London *Times*, 27 September 1912, p. 6. For Frost's notebook jotting, "Pursuit of GBS," see above, 218.

27　In January 1913 Frost mentions getting "a card of admission to the library of the British Museum." (SL 63) According to the records of the British Museum (now the British Library), the card was issued to Frost in November 1913. His formal application, which cannot now be found, would have carried a "recommendation of a householder," and at that early period the endorser would probably have been either Mrs. Nutt or his anonymous friend at *T. P.'s Weekly*.

28　Frost and the Henley volume: Thompson, *Early*, 400; Sutton, *Season*, 79. How little some things change in England—browsing in the second-hand bookstores of Charing Cross Road in the summer of 1985 I found not one but two volumes of Henley's poems, both published by Nutt in the nineties.

28　"Take lodgings in the city"—Elinor Frost to Mrs. Brown, 25 October 1912, UVL.

28　"When I leave writing"—SL 52, 15 September 1912. Interestingly, the phrase in this letter about the flaring lights of London also occurs in Frost's notebook: see above, 220.

Chapter Two: Having It out with Myself

29　"As if he had been working"—Tathem, *Recognized*, 4, where the remark is attributed to "a former neighbor," probably Effie Solomon (see below, 241).

30　That Frost initially thought of taking a New Hampshire farm instead of going to foreign parts has not before been suggested. But, as may be seen in his letter to Silver written from Franconia on 13 June 1912, it is a fact. He talks about needing his furniture from the Plymouth house, and continues: "I am living on a small farm that I expect to buy if the vicegerent of my grandfather on earth doesn't fail me. I am going to farm a little. I had two cows come in this week, so that we are swimming in milk already—if you call that farming. At the same time there are great uncertainties." (DCL) Admittedly, the circumstances of this 1912 farming interlude seem to fit better with the return home in 1915 and Frost's settling on a similar small farm in Franconia. But the date of this holograph letter is clearly written as 1912. Since the decision to go abroad was not made until the start of August, it would seem the Frosts spent some two months on that particular Franconia farm.

30   "It became increasingly clear"—Letter of Lesley Frost in Tathem, *Recognized*, 9–10. The quotation, "My father leaned," etc., is from this same letter.

31   "My mind was made up"—Mertins, *Walking*, 101. Regarding the Mertins volume, it should be noted that the direct quotes attributed to Frost were set down from memory immediately after Mertins's many talks with the poet during the thirties and forties. While they may not give Frost's words precisely as he spoke them, they certainly are close enough to invite full reliance on their substance, at least. In fact, in many cases the tone does have a ring of being very close to what Frost actually said. Also, for a good part of what Mertins records, support is available from other, more scattered sources. Mertins, however, seems to have made little effort in the area of independent factual research, so my use of his volume has been carefully measured against the general run of Frost scholarship.

31   "I went to England to"—Untermeyer, *Letters*, 7; Sergeant, *Trial*, 89.

31   "England seemed far"—Ellis, *England*, 8.

31   "But really I am going"—Sergeant, *Trial*, 107. I have not been able to trace the original of this letter, Frost to Ernest Jewell, 6 May 1913. It is not among other Jewell letters at BUL.

32   "Perhaps I ought not"—SL 52, 15 September 1912. The same resentment is echoed several years afterward in an unpublished letter he wrote Alfred Harcourt, then his editor at Holt. It shows that at the back of his mind there indeed existed a hope, veiled even from himself as it may have been, that in England his work would find recognition. "If I ran away from anything when I went to England it was the American editor. Very privately in the inmost recesses of me I suppose my Hegira was partly a protest against magazine poets and poetry. We won't insist on that now, but please remember it when I am dead and gone." A remark further on in the letter makes it clear that he is not so much thinking of his own rejection by American editors, but of "what they have taught people to think was American poetry." (Holt papers, Box 39, Princeton University Library)

33   That the Frosts initially planned to spend only their first year in England, then a year in France, is mentioned by Elinor Frost in SL 54. She adds "if our courage holds out," a reminder of how precarious in so many ways was this whole adventure.

33   "scared"—Sutton, *Season*, 77.

33   "I was always that way"—SL 123; also Lathem, *Interviews*, 37.

34   "could not resist the"—Thompson, *Early*, 396; also Lathem, *Interviews*, 37, and Sutton, *Season*, 78.

34   "I brought it to England"—SL 55, 19 November 1912.

35   "Taking the capital"—Mertins, *Walking*, 106. Same for Frost's references in this paragraph to "cure" and "notes."

35   "Comes pretty near"—SL 66; see also SL 85.

36   "I think I shall run"—Mertins, *Walking*, 107. The Blickensderfer typewriter, it appears, was one of the first "true portables." See G. T. Richards, *History of Typewriters*. The Frosts had bought it about 1900 and were still using it in 1919; see Grade, *Family*, 62.

36   "I went down to London"—Lathem, *Interviews*, 37.

37   "When I told him that"—Mertins, *Walking*, 107.

37   "Little books like that"—Sergeant, *Trial*, 97.

38   "Specialized in certain"—Monson, *Frost*, 62. Also see Baker, "Pumpkin," 119.

38   "The most erratic, erotic"—Mertins, *Walking*, 107; also Munson, *Frost*, 62, and Thompson, *Early*, 40.

39   "I don't think that I"—Unwin, *Publisher*, 233.

39   Mrs. Nutt's novel is entitled *A Woman of Today* (copy in the British Library). Some brief discussion of it may be found in Sokol, "Publication," 230–232, as well as some background detail on the Nutt firm and Frost's dealings with it. The same article was the means of alerting me to the Unwin book. I should state here, however, that I find myself in disagreement with Sokol's conclusions regarding Frost. Mrs. Nutt's probable death in France in World War II is mentioned by Lesley Frost in Tathem, *Recognized*, 10.

40   "I must admit that she"—Mertins, *Walking*, 108.

40   "A pawing horse let go"—SL 60, 25 December 1912. The phrase "great harvest" occurs in Frost's poem "After Apple Picking," which I take to be in some part symbolic of his spent mood after his remarkable, nearly year-long spate of composition had abated in fall 1913:

> *I have had too much*
> *Of apple-picking: I am overtired*
> *Of the great harvest I myself desired.*

He could hardly have written those words at that time, I submit, without being aware of how well they applied to what he had just accomplished in poetry. How the remainder of the poem may fit this concept forms an interesting topic for further study complicated, alas, by the fact that nothing at all is known about the circumstances of the poem's composition. Here I will only suggest that a clue may reside in the conclusion, where Frost admits his concern over the kind of "sleep" he feels coming on, whether it is to be of long or short duration. This may well tie in with the fear he expressed in a later letter (Untermeyer, *Letters*, 29), that his essential powers as an artist had begun to wane; for further on this see below, 259. Since it is not mentioned in either of the two lists of *North of Boston* poems (see below, 248), I conclude that "After Apple Picking" was written in fall 1913, probably October.

41   "Humane realism"—Bogan, *Achievement*, 49.

41   "*Mowing*": Frost many times mentioned that "Mowing" was the first "talk-song" he ever wrote (see Sergeant, *Trial*, 423), and its absence from the booklet of poems he sent Susan Ward at Christmas 1911 (see above, 44) is sufficient to place its composition after that date. That *A Boy's Will* did contain poems written at Beaconsfield is noted by Frost in a letter written from the Bungalow in December 1912: "Very little of what I have done lately goes to swell the first book, just one or two things to round out the idea." (SL 60) That he refers to "Mowing" cannot be proved, but a process of elimination makes it appear certain. The other of the two poems written "lately" was, not surprisingly, the very fine "Storm Fear." This is definitely stated by Frost himself, who called it "the youngest of the lot, the last finished before publication" (Mertins, *Walking*, 106).

42   "A poet must lean hard"—Munson, *Frost*, 110.

42   "The change was sudden"—Lynen, *Pastoral*, 19.

42   "It was his trip to"—Kemp, *Frost*, 85. Similarly, in Sokol, "Publication," 228: "During this [English] period Frost altered his style and material in accordance with new tastes. A result was the writing of *North of Boston*."

Chapter Three: Never Knew a Man I Liked Better

44   "Not the long deferred"—SL 43, 19 December 1911. The same letter supplied "laggard" and "peace offering." The manuscript booklet of poems sent to Susan Ward is at the Huntington Library. Of the seventeen poems in the booklet, five remain unpublished. Best known of the twelve published poems is "Reluctance," in this version, however, showing a much inferior final stanza. The manuscripts of some twenty other Frost poems are at the Huntington (obtained from the files of the New York *Independent*), of which a half-dozen remain unpublished. Of most interest among the published poems are those showing revisions, and of those one in particular is of concern here: "Into My Own" (in this manuscript called "A Wish"). Almost exactly the final printed version, it might well have been used in the *Independent* were it not for a single quite serious flaw in the crucial last line. It reads, "Only more sure *that* all I thought was true," rather than the familiar "*of* all I thought was true." The first is simple youthful arrogance, which entirely defeats the poem. The second, narrowing the assertion to just that portion of his knowledge and beliefs that cannot be questioned or given up, is charmingly self-reliant. The change of that one small word is what probably earned the poem acceptance—it appeared in the *New England Magazine*, May 1909.

45   "I do not say that either"—SL 47, 4 March 1912.

45   "I always feel as if I"—SL 60, 25 December 1912.

46   "I couldn't for the life"—SL 44, 15 January 1912.

46   "He would come hustling"—Letter of Eva Barndollar (nee O'Brien), to Robert Newdick, 26 June 1937 (Newdick Papers). The quotation that ends this paragraph, "he always seemed to be," etc., is also from the Barndollar letter, which quotes several other of Frost's Plymouth students. Mrs. Barndollar also recalled Frost's "nonchalant disregard of meal hours . . . for several weeks after the opening of school, he ate with the teachers and students in the dining room, as his family had not yet moved to town. Many a time and oft we have seen him come sauntering casually into the room and slip into his chair just as the dessert was being placed on the table. The student who acted as waitress would throw a baleful glare in his direction and depart in high dudgeon for the serving room. There the cook . . . would warm up a plate of the first course." Mrs. Barndollar also recalled one morning in class when the newspapers headlined the sinking of the *Titanic* (April 15, 1912), with its appalling loss of life: "The horror of the catastrophe stirred us all, and Mr. Frost seemed deeply shaken by the sea tragedy. We spent the hour in a discussion of the mental and spiritual reactions of those who were aboard the sinking ship. Many of the things he said at that time about inherent and acquired courage and decency and self-control have remained with me through the years."

46   "Who to my own unfamiliar"—SL 45; 10 February 1912.

47   "I had some character strokes"—SL 83; 17 July 1913.

47   Frost and Wordsworth: This, curiously enough, affords a subject still to be explored in Frost biography, but the connection between "The Black Cottage," and "The Excursion" Book I, 434–970, is clear to even a desultory reading. Frost never made much reference to Wordsworth in his career—none at all to "The Excursion"—though he did once or twice admit that Wordsworth was high among those writers who had influenced him (see Lathem, *Interviews*, 7, 24). Probably his most extended commentary on Wordsworth occurs in a talk he gave at Cornell in 1950, entitled "A Tribute to Wordsworth." While saying nothing about influences, at one point he admitted that "Michael" was a poem "I've always admired very, very much." He also mentioned, but couldn't quite describe, a peculiar quality in Wordsworth's poetry that he said greatly appealed to him: "something that I don't think anybody else has as purely as he had . . . I've hunted and hunted for a word for the tone. It's a tone of what I'd like to call Simple Simon met a pieman, you know, that kind of Simple Simony. It's almost vapid, clear down, as if he thought he was getting the innocence of childhood in every word he said." Later in the talk he describes the elusive quality as a "naive accent," and as "that strange banal way," and he ends his comment on the point with:

I think that's essential Wordsworth. That lovely banality and the lovely penetration that goes with it. It goes right down into the soul of man, and always, always there'll be one line in it that's just as penetrating as anything anybody ever wrote. But always this insipid tone, sweet, insipid tone. Now that's the Wordsworth I care for.

Interesting is the way his frustrated groping for the right word leads him to stand on their heads the terms vapid, banal, and insipid, the only instance of such language inversion in his career. The examples he gave that day of Wordsworth's "sweet insipid tone" were three: "Expostulation and Reply," "Anecdote for Fathers," and "The Affliction of Margaret." For the third, he read only the last two stanzas, highlighting certain lines with the comment, "And then she says something that I often—that I suppose many, many people have said in their hearts, not aloud." He then quotes:

> *Beyond participation lie*
> *My troubles, and beyond relief:*
> *If any chance to heave a sigh,*
> *They pity me, and not my grief.*

Revealingly he adds, "Many, many, many, many times I've thought of the way he puts that: 'They pity me, and not my grief.' " He also read "The Solitary Reaper" to his audience that day, but it is not clear from his remarks whether he meant it as another example of that special tone. (Facts and quotations from a transcript of Frost's talk at Cornell, 20 April 1950; courtesy of Gould Colman, Olin Library.) For some additional links between the two, compare Frost's lines "She's glad her simple worsted gray / Is silver now with clinging mist" (from "My November Guest"), with Wordsworth's "By mist and rain-drops silvered o'er" (from "The Excursion," Book I, line 944; on its first publication in the *Forum* Frost's line read "is silvered now"). Also, compare Frost's "Freedom of the Moon," with Wordsworth's "Strange Fits of Passion." It may be only a coincidence that Frost's line from "Tuft of Flowers"—"Sheer morning gladness at the brim"—echoes both the setting and the sense of Wordsworth's line, "to the brim my heart was full" (*Prelude*, IV, 333). There is also, of course, the very similar use made by each man of the word "difference," making it the whole climax of a lyric, Wordsworth in "She Dwelt Among the Untrodden Ways," and Frost in "The Road Not Taken."

47 "Three other books of"—SL 55; 19 November 1912.

49 "What seemed a lack of"—Cox in Munson, *Frost*, 53.

49 "Would chuckle as he"—Sutton, *Season*, 157.

49 Frost's Plymouth year: the signal importance of this one year to Frost's growth as a poet was, so far as appears, first suggested by Peter Davison, in 1974 ("The Self-Realization of Robert Frost, 1911–1912," *New Republic*, 30 March) though he rested satisfied with a few general remarks on the topic. Lawrance Thompson's treatment of the period (*Early*, 369–391) assigns it no particular

artistic significance, strangely missing the special link to the poetry and the new poetic voice. He does note Frost's interest in the unique quality of country talk—not vocabulary and syntax, but "sly inflections and modulations of voice"—yet sees all this only as a kind of aimless personality change: "As a flattering tribute to Hall and other North-of-Boston farmers, Frost had gradually modified his way of talking. He deliberately imitated the manner in which his neighbors unconsciously slurred words, dropped endings, and clipped their sentences. By the time he reached Plymouth, glad to be rid of the farm, he was still perfecting the art of talking like a farmer." (*Early*, 371) As to why Frost might have done this, Thompson ventures no guess beyond the notion of its being a "tribute" to country ways.

50   "Saterday evening Papa"—Frost, *Child*, VI, 9.

51   "He talks all day and"—Sutton, *Season*, 235.

51   John Hall: Everything presently known of Hall is contained in the introduction and notes to Lathem-Thompson, *Poultryman*, which reprints all Frost's poultry articles. My descriptions of Hall's talk are phrases from Munson, *Frost*, 35, which I take to be Frost's own words in his conversations with Munson. Frost's reference to "real, artistic speech" is from Boston *Transcript*, 8 May 1915 (reprinted in Lathem, *Interviews*, 4); Hall is not named but is clearly meant. The *Transcript* passage continues: "Having discovered this speech he set about copying it in his poetry, getting the principles down by rigorous observation and reproduction," facts that come directly from conversations with Frost in early 1915. The only contemporary reference to Hall occurs not in Frost's conversation or letters, but in Lesley's composition books—her distinctive spelling of the man's name is not such a bad guess for a child of six: "a froow days ago we took carol down to gonhols and gonhol had some ducs and we thout that carol wouldnt not no whut they were and when we gut ther we askt him whats that and he saed duculs and we new what that ment it ment ducks and carol likt to look at them and so did i but we likt the little chicins best and by and by we went home . . ." (Frost, *Child*, I 46; undated, but sometime in 1905). In another direct reference to Hall's influence, and very likely using Frost's own words, Munson (*Frost*, 35) states: "The stimulus of this man's talk was greater than the correct speech of college instructors."

53   Excerpts from Frost's poultry articles: Lathem, *Poultryman*, 60–66, 68–71, 83, 84–86; his mistake about the geese (57–59) is in same, 17–21.

57   "partly for the fun"—SL 67, 18 March 1913.

59   "Went down like a felled"—Frost to Flint, 6 July 1913, UTL. The complete letter is in Barry, *Writing*, 82–84. In writing Hall's name in the letter Frost made a momentary slip and wrote "John Kline." But there is no doubt who he means, especially since he is talking about his poem "The Housekeeper," and Hall's name actually appears in that poem. The "Kline" no doubt came from Klein's Hill, a rise which bordered one end of the Frost farm in Derry.

60   "The tone of someone"—quoted in Lynen, *Pastoral*, 90.

60   "a many-sided and complex"—Lynen, *Pastoral*, 90.

Chapter Four: Idling Away an Age

62   "My first clash with realism"—Mertins, *Walking*, 88.

62   "Poetry has been a self"—SL 433, 4 December 1936.

63   "I let my wife sleep"—Mertins, *Walking*, 89.

63   "She seems to have the same"—SL 224, 7 November 1917. Another phrase in this letter referring to Elinor has caused much talk about Frost's supposed callous or ungrateful attitude toward his wife, but again it is a matter of misplaced emphasis. In a long paragraph of praise for Elinor's instinctive high-mindedness, and her unusual fitness to be the wife of a poet, especially his, Frost is rushed into a remark that somewhat distorts the sense of what he is saying: "Elinor has never been of any earthly use to me." From the context it is evident that he has not employed the phrase in any disparaging sense, but is stressing the *earthly*, and has overstated his meaning. A reading of the paragraph with the awkward sentence dropped makes his intention clear enough: Elinor has been of much more value to him as companion and sympathizer than as practical manager of house and family. Later support for that assertion, especially from colleagues and friends, is abundant: see the various comments about the closeness of Frost and his wife collected by Newdick in Sutton, *Season*, 196–197, 216, 332, 335, 356.

63   The poetic silence of 1908–1910: In this connection it is worth noting that there seem to be no Frost letters extant for that whole period. *Selected Letters* jumps from January 1908 to December 1911, and no letters between those dates have turned up in the various collections. The poems published in that period, in addition to "Into My Own," are: "Across the Atlantic," *Independent*, March 1908; "The Flower Boat," *Youth's Companion*, May 1909; "A Late Walk," *Pinkerton Critic*, October 1909.

64   "Suffered a nervous"—Sutton, *Season*, 379.

64   "In a very unhappy state"—Sutton, *Season*, 304.

65   "Strange mixture of hysteria"—SL 246, 31 March 1920.

65   "Jeanie really went into"—Thompson, *Early*, 340.

66   "In 1925, after Jeanie"—Thompson, *Early*, 496. Jeanie was actually committed, by Frost on the advice of doctors, in 1920. For all that is presently known about the sad episode, see Thompson, *Triumph*, 123–134, 557–559; also SL 245–248.

66   "Jeanie was fascinated"—Thompson, *Triumph*, 126.

66   "Intermittent moods of"—Thompson, *Early*, 309.

66   "Lesley was never able to"—Thompson, *Early*, 308.

67   "This anecdote was told"—Thompson, *Early*, 560.

68   "There was once a little"—Frost, *Child*, VI 49.

68   "I was such a bad dreamer"—Frost, *Child*, V 30.

68   "In summer we have to go"—Frost, *Child*, VI 42.

69   "Her conversations with the"—Thompson, *Early*, 340.

69   Hen hawks at the Derry farm: "We sit and watch for a hawlk that coms here very ofen he is a big white hawlk with a little blak on his wings . . . once he came right down betwene the peach tree and the apple tree and the hens made a noise and we yelled." Frost, *Child*, III 41.

69   "About ten years ago"—SL 159, 22 March 1915.

70   "A Blue Ribbon at Amesbury": First published in *Atlantic*, April 1936, but the writing of it in some cruder form is obviously to be assigned to the time when Frost was engaged on his poultry articles some thirty years earlier. The several word variants in the stanza quoted are from the *Atlantic* printing; see Lathem, *Poetry*, 558.

70   "Ghost House"—For a reference to the ruined cottage in Derry that inspired this poem see Frost, *Child*, I 33, III 128. My choice of "Ghost House" as Frost's first poem of merit rests on the judgment that the only other candidates ("Tuft of Flowers" and "Trial By Existence") were not in final form until early 1906. The vague claim that both were written many years before must indicate very early drafts showing nothing like their later finish. Other early poems, such as "My Butterfly" and "Quest of the Orchis" are hardly more than juveniles. "My Butterfly," in fact, is little more than a pastiche of ideas and phrases taken from Francis Thompson's "The Hound of Heaven," along with borrowings from several other poems in the Englishman's 1893 volume. The germ of Frost's "Trial By Existence," written in its first form at about the same time as "My Butterfly," can also be found in Francis Thompson's 1893 volume, in a long poem called "A Judgment In Heaven," and there may be others. These facts, it might be noted, have some importance as bearing on Frost's supposed twenty-year struggle for artistic maturity and recognition. The start of those much-mentioned twenty years is always given as publication of "My Butterfly" in the *Independent* in 1894. But the picture changes drastically when it is realized that composition of "My Butterfly" was not unaided, owing much of both form and substance to the work of another poet, one who was then enjoying great renown and who had, as is well known, captivated the teen age Frost. It is amusing to note that soon after selling the poem to Miss Ward at the *Independent*, Frost suffered some slight pangs of conscience over his composing methods. In a letter to Miss Ward, submitting more poems and discussing "My Butterfly," he slips in the following: "Take my word for it that poem exaggerates my ability. You must spare my feelings when you come to read these others." (SL 20) Some weeks later he writes Miss Ward that he is "greatly dissatisfied" with the poem, and he actually asks "Do you not think it would be well to suppress it." (SL 22) Frost's copy of Francis Thompson's 1893 book *Poems*, which he bought in Boston late in 1893 or early the next year, is preserved at the Amherst College Library. It is clear of any

markings. (See Van Dore, *Hired Man*, 176, for a recent, if passing reference to this link between the Frost and Thompson poems, by one of Frost's longtime friends.)*

71   "Reticence itself is"—Lynen, *Pastoral*, 101.

71   Frost's adaptation of five plays at Pinkerton Academy in 1910 is covered in Thompson, *Early*, 360–363. A program and some tickets for these performances are preserved in the Frost Collection at UVL.

72   To A Moth Seen In Winter—The lines quoted are from the earliest manuscript version, Huntington Library. The published version (*Virginia Quarterly Review*, Spring 1942) was considerably improved. That the poem was written at Plymouth was stated definitely by Frost himself: see Sutton, *Season*, 161, 163.

73   "Someone had complained"—Frost in a letter of 1917, Barry, *Writing*, 70. The correspondent, Lewis Chase, was a critic who had inquired about the possibility of writing a book on Frost, the earliest to show such an interest. Frost was agreeable to the idea—masking what must have been his considerable surprise at such attention so early—but nothing further is heard of it. For another letter to Chase, see Barry, *Writing*, 73–76. Some teaching notes that Frost made at the start of 1912 at Plymouth show that the topic of "speaking tones" had begun to occupy him even then: "Figures of speech sentence forms etc should be discriminated first and first named in their accidental appearance in one's own writing. They are taken from the vernacular rather than from literature." A second note, occurring a page after the first, comes closer to an outright statement about speech tones: "Intonation possibilities of what they read and what they write should be noticed as early as anything." (From an old notebook given by Frost to Robert Newdick, now at BUL; see Sutton, *Season*, 406, 408).

73   Frost's visit to the Ward home in New Jersey: SL 43–44; Thompson, *Early*, 381. See also Francis, "Frost and Ward," *Massachusetts Review*, 1985, 346.

75   "inflexible ambition"—SL 19, 28 March 1894.

75   "Idle away an age"—SL 19. It was no momentary boast, for a month later the eighteen-year-old Frost is assuring Susan Ward, then handling poetry for the *Independent*: "To betray myself utterly, such an one am I that even in my failures I find all the promise I require to justify the astonishing magnitude of my ambition." (SL 20)

Chapter Five: The Shop on Devonshire Street

76   "It is seven weeks since"—Elinor Frost to Mrs. Brown, 25 October 1912, UVL. Same for Elinor's intention to write four letters that day, and for the children's schooling; for the only other of the four letters extant, see SL 53.

77   Effie Solomon: Several present-day residents of Reynolds Road recall Mrs. Solomon talking of her friendship with the Frosts, though unfortunately

*For further on Frost and Francis Thompson, see below, "Added Note," 266.

few details have survived. She died in 1983, aged 92. Tathem, *Recognition*, 4, says that in 1966 she "remembered the Frosts well."

78   "An American poet who"—Drinkwater, *Discovery*, 220. The tone of the book is extremely casual, skimming facts, so that the oversight regarding Frost perhaps proves little. See also Francis, *Talk*, 33; Sokol, "What Went Wrong," 524; Untermeyer, *Letters*, 356; and Smythe, *Speaks*, 131.

78   Mrs. Nutt's original note of 26 October 1912 (a card) is at DCL. A copy of Frost's original contract with Nutt for *A Boy's Will* is at the Jones Library, Amherst.

78   "The day my poetry was"—Lathem, *Interviews*, 22.

80   "I have signed no contract"—SL 55, 19 November 1912.

80   "Traitorously un-American"—SL 56, 19 November 1912.

80   "a fool's contract"—SL 193, 21 September 1915.

81   *A Boy's Will* was originally scheduled for publication in February 1913, but with the delay it did not appear until 13 March 1913. See *The English Catalog of Books*, 1911–1915, p. 529.

82   The Poetry Bookshop: For my principal sources of information see entries in the bibliography under Born, Fletcher, Grant, Munro, Sims. The 1967 book by Joy Grant is a comprehensive and readable account of the bookshop, both at Devonshire Street and at its later site on Great Russell Street. Also of interest in this regard is *Charlotte Mew and Her Friends*, by Penelope Fitzgerald, Collins, London, 1984. For opening day of the bookshop see Grant, *Bookshop*, 62; Mertins, *Walking*, 110; Sergeant, *Trial*, 101. For Flint's background see Hughes, *Imagism*, 153–166, and Fletcher, *Song*, 76–78.

83   "You are not asked to"—*T. P.'s Weekly*, 10 January 1913, 39.

85   "Lay less in merit than"—Fletcher, *Song*, 50.

85   "Was unrivalled in its"—Ford, *Yesterday*, 419.

86   Frost's first letter to Flint, at UTL, is dated 21 January 1913. It is not in SL, but was first used in Thompson, *Early*, 408–409. Flint's answering letter to Frost, 30 January 1913, is at DCL. The enclosure, Ezra Pound's calling card, is listed in the DCL catalogue, but it is now missing.

90   The proofs of *A Boy's Will* were sent by Frost to Bartlett (see SL 65), eventually reaching UVL. They bear a printer's stamped date, 30 January 1913, and the comment "first revise." For this and further information on the proofs see Crane, *Catalogue*, p. 10.

90   "You have no idea"—SL 60, 26 December 1912.

90   "a very bad case"—SL 66; also Anderson, *Friendship*, 38.

91   *The Bung. Hole*: Frost's use of this heading actually antedates Lesley's sprained ankle. It occurs first in a letter to Ernest Silver, 25 December 1912, and is repeated the next day in a letter to Cox, SL 58–60. Neither letter as printed bears this heading but it is quite clear in the originals at DCL. Frost's direct reference to the phrase is in a letter to Cox, 2 May 1913, SL 71.

91   The late hours favored by Frost, both for retiring and for rising, are by

now well known. Writing from the Bungalow in January 1913 to a friend in New Hampshire, he ends: "It is now two o'clock in the morning in Beaconsfield and eleven o'clock at night in Colebrook—time to go to bed in either place." SL 65.

Chapter Six: All Sorts of a Game

92   No. 10 Church Walk: The building is still standing (August 1985), andthe surrounding area, including both church and graveyard, is also unaltered. Further details of the building and Pound's residence there may be found in Hutchins, *Kensington*, 66–74.

93   "Getting reviewed for poetry"—SL 88, 6 August 1912.

93   Frost's first meeting with Pound: Cowley, *Work*, 12–14; Sokol, "What Went Wrong," 525–526; Mertins, *Walking*, 110; Sergeant, *Trial*, 102; Thompson, *Early*, 410; Francis, *Talk*, 32–33; Fletcher, *Song*, 69–72; Smythe, *Speak*, 128; Hutchins, *Kensington*, 70. My own walk from Pound's old flat to the site of the Nutt office on Bloomsbury Street (by August 1985 an empty lot), began at three P.M. Without hurrying but at a good pace, I went through Kensington Gardens and Hyde Park (Rotten Row), exiting at Hyde Park Corner. Rather than going straight along Piccadilly, I cut through some side streets, thinking it would be more direct. But I was slowed by traffic and congestion, and twice became lost. Still, I arrived at Bloomsbury Street at 4:21. That Pound was accustomed to taking such long walks from his flat into London's center may be inferred from his later remark about often going "by foot through Ken[sington] G[ardens] Hyde [Park] to Mayfair and Soho." Hutchins, *Kensington*, 18.

94   "We *must* be taken seriously"—Paige, *Letters*, 10.

94   "We have *got* to be taken"—Monroe, *Life*, 263.

95   "Pouring out an over"—Thompson, *Early*, 411. Frost, when sending a copy of Pound's *Poetry* review of *A Boy's Will* to Cox, explains that he has "scraped out some personalities (very private) which are not only in bad taste but also inaccurate." (Evans, *Forty Years*, 56). The deleted passage is the one that says he had been disinherited by grandfather and uncle. See also SL 84, where Frost decries Pound's "inaccuracies about my family affairs." The bequest of Frost's granduncle, Elihu Colcord, to Sanborn Seminary, Kingston, New Hampshire, was used to erect Colcord Hall in 1912, at a cost of $13,676; information from a letter to Robert Newdick from a trustee of the seminary, 4 July 1939. (Newdick Papers)

96   "Have just discovered"—Paige, *Letters*, 14.

96   "It's our second scoop"—Paige, *Letters*, 16. There are several additional mentions of Frost in Pound's letters of this time (Paige, *Letters*, 17–22), but all are incidental. By spring 1918 Pound is describing Frost as "dead as mutton," and has relegated him to a level with Masters and Lindsay. "Frost sinks of his own weight," he concludes. (Paige, *Letters*, 135)

97   "I had dreamed of a"—*T. P.'s Weekly*, 4 April 1913, 421.

97 "Brilliant and unfailing"—Masefield, *Long*, 141; see also *Yeats and His World*, by McLiamoir and Boland, and the Masefield book, 138–147, for Yeats' apartment and his Monday night gatherings.

98 "a sort of dirge-like"—Goldring, *Lodge*, 49.

98 "To make one of his circle"—SL 70, c. 4 April 1913.

98 "Something unusual"—SL 70. Frost writes further: "I took tea with her yesterday and expect to go there again shortly." The letter is undated but can be assigned to early April.

99 "I am in mortal fear"—SL 70, c. 4 April 1913.

99 Reviews of *A Boy's Will*: *Athenaeum*, 5 April 1913, 379; *Times Literary Supplement*, 10 April 1913, 155; *Poetry*, May 1913, 72–74.

99 "You must do this of"—SL 72, c. 10 May 1913.

100 "Rob has been altogether"—SL 78, c. 3 July 1913.

100 "And yet we are very"—SL 73, 13 May 1913.

103 "Who will show me the"—Frost to Flint, 6 July 1913, UTL.

103 "Ezra Pound manifestly"—Frost to Flint, 23 June 1913, UTL; the complete letter is in Barry, *Writing*, 86–88.

104 Flint's review of *A Boy's Will*: *Poetry & Drama*, June 1913, 250.

104 "I have to thank you"—Frost to Flint, 23 June 1913, UTL.

104 Buckley's review of *A Boy's Will*: *T. P.'s Weekly*, 30 May 1913, 683.

104 "Has recently issued a"—SL 79, 4 July 1913.

105 "a leading literary monthly"—SL 75, c. 16 June 1913.

105 Review of *A Boy's Will* in the *English Review*: June 1913, 505. The editor of the magazine was Ford Madox Ford (then Heuffer), with whom Pound was close friends. In his memoir Ford mentions his first meeting with Pound and recalls that "in a very short time he had taken charge of me, the Review, and much of London." (*Yesterday*, 388) Pound's flat at Church Walk was only a block or two from the *Review* offices at 84 Holland Park Avenue, which it seems he visited almost daily.

105 "None of these three"—*Bookman*, June 1913, 130.

106 "I was so sorry you"—Sinclair to Frost, 6 June 1913, DCL. With the letter, written from 4 Edwardes Square Studios, she enclosed her original unsent note of 4 June, and added: "This proves me a woman of good faith and atrocious memory." Still another note of hers to Frost survives, written 18 July 1913: "Will you lunch with [me] on Wednesday the 30th at the Albemarle Club 37 Dover St. 1:30 to meet Ezra Pound & Miss Mary Moss a fellow-country-woman of yours whom you may like? I hope it may be all right *this* time!" (DCL)

107 "You are indeed a disagreeable"—Flint to Pound, 3 July 1915, UTL. It is a lengthy letter, mostly taking issue with Pound on the history of the Imagist movement.

107 "We're in such a beautiful"—Paige, *Letters*, 13.

107 "apologize for us and say"—Thompson, *Early*, 588, quoting a copy of the letter at the University of Chicago Library.

108   That Frost, at the urging of Pound, dropped "a line or two" from "Death of the Hired Man" is in a letter of Frost's written in 1950, quoted in Thompson, *Triumph*, 597. An interesting first draft of this letter is at DCL. Pound also urged him, he says, to drop the lines "Home is the place where, when you have to go there, they have to take you in." It was of course retained. No clue has yet turned up as to the lines that were dropped.

108   "Among the things that Pound"—Cowley, *Work*, 19. Frost also says, "I was around with him quite a little for a few weeks. I was charmed with his ways. He cultivated a sort of rudeness toward people that he didn't like."

108   "Don't forget that our"—Sergeant, *Trial*, 103.

108   The three Frost-Pound restaurant incidents: Cowley, *Work*, 19–20; Tharpe, *Essays*, III, 214; Munson, *Frost*, 80; Francis, *Talk*, 19–20. Sutton, *Season*, 81.

109   "You will be amused"—SL 84, 17 July 1913.

109   "I think over all we"—Flint to Frost, 23 June 1913, DCL.

110   "If you think it won't"—Frost to Flint, 23 June 1913, UTL. The letter opens: "I had a funny feeling in the region of my dorsal fin this afternoon and when I came to again I had written this debased Whitmanese." See Barry, *Writing*, 85.

111   "I shouldn't take his"—Frost to Flint, 24 June 1913 (an addition to his letter of 23 June to Flint), UTL; see Barry, *Writing*, 88.

111   "Your 'poem' is very"—Flint to Frost, 26 June 1913, DCL.

111   "The only fault I find"—Frost to Flint, 6 July 1913, UTL.

111   "Yet all the time I'm"—Flint to Frost, 15 July 1913, DCL.

111   "You take Ezra sadly"—Frost to Flint, 26 June 1913, UTL.

112   The original manuscript of Frost's free-verse parody ("I suspected though," etc.) is at DCL; the full text is given in SL 85–86. The note in SL says the parody was shown to Flint, who persuaded Frost not to send it to Pound. In support, Flint's postcard of 26 June is cited (misdated in SL to 26 July). But Flint's card actually refers to the earlier parody ("Poets are born," etc.), and in his card Flint says nothing about withholding the verses. A companion observation of Frost's to this parody, quite illuminating, is a passage in a letter to Flint written a year after Frost and Pound had ceased to meet. Consoling his friend after some sort of run-in with Pound, Frost writes: "Pound can be cruel in the arbitrary attitudes he assumes towards one. It pleased him to treat me always as if I might be some kind of poet but was not quite presentable—at least not in London. Some of the things he said and others I imagined drove me half frantic." (July 1914, UTL) The last five lines of the parody make clear what he was frantic about.

112   "I wrote him—I may"—Frost to Flint, 26 June 1913, UTL. See also SL 149. A letter of Pound's about "Death of the Hired Man" to W. H. Wright, editor of *The Smart Set*, 11 August 1913, reads: "As you know the thing I'm most anxious for you to print is that poem of Frost's. I hope the stuff I've sent since won't delay it." (Original at Jones Library, Amherst)

113   "an incredible ass"—SL 96, 24 October 1913. The rest of the passage runs: "I am out with Pound pretty much altogether and so I don't see his friend Yeats as I did. I count myself well out however . . . he hurts more than he helps the person he praises." In later years Frost's sense of obligation to Pound, increased by nostalgia, subdued his dislike of the man, and though he never quite altered his opinion that Pound was "nuts," he eventually allowed him a high place among contemporary artists. The readiest demonstration of this is a letter—apparently never published—that he wrote in December 1932 in answer to an inquiry from an Albert Bobrowsky of New York (the "influence" Frost speaks of here was not, of course, on himself): "Pound has been a great influence. I speak of him and praise him more than anyone else except his own immediate gang . . . he treated me as a friend. He is still my friend and I am his, though we seldom see each other . . . [In England] there was not much he could do for me except back me. He did that most generously in spite of the difference in our schools . . . What then made me cross with him I now think only amusing. I think him the real poet of all this modernismus." (Newdick papers, copy of typewritten original) See also, Grade, *Family*, 160–163, for similar remarks by Frost in 1934. The passing years, perhaps inevitably, again lowered Frost's opinion of both man and poet, especially after Pound's treason in World War II. Still, it was Frost, along with MacLeish, Hemingway, and some others who in 1958 obtained the aging Pound's final release from a traitor's cell.

Chapter Seven: Seeking Ache of Memory

114   Elinor Frost's comments on the weather: SL 77, 82–83. Among English birds the lark especially enchanted her, and at this time a large flock of them had taken up residence in the open field on the far side of the Bungalow. "Every few minutes," she wrote, "one will rise from the ground as if overcome by emotion and soar straight up in the air until one can scarcely see him, singing all the while such a sweet rapturous song, and then let himself straight down again, singing until he reaches the ground." SL 68.

115   The Gardners: The letters of Mary Gardner to Frost are at DCL. That she did in fact attend the opening of the Poetry Bookshop, where Frost met her, is confirmed by a note of hers to William Beveridge: "Will you come to the Poetry Bookshop on Jan 8th between 3 and 6; they are giving a party and Newbolt will read some of his things." Beveridge apparently begged off, for another of her notes to him reads, "It is a pity you can't come and have tea with the poets . . . Do get your poetry at that shop, though, and encourage the Muse." (Both letters, London School of Economics Library, Beveridge Papers) For background on Ernest Gardner see *Dictionary of National Biography, 1931–1940*, 307–308; an instructor in archaeology at London University when Frost first met him, he eventually became the university's vice chancellor. Earlier he had been director of the British School of Archaeology at Athens. In World War I he served as a

Lieutenant Commander with British Naval Intelligence in Greece, and was decorated for his services. Author of several books in his field, he died 27 November 1939 at his home in Maidenhead (obituary, London *Times*, 29 November 1939, pp. 1, 4). One daughter, Phyllis, and his wife had predeceased him. Two other children, Delphis and Christopher, I have not succeeded in tracing. Both Gardner and his wife in later years were connected with the League of the Empire, an organization for promoting the exchange of educational ideas and teachers with other countries of the Empire.

115 "Very kind-hearted and"—SL 79. Elinor writes further: "We have become very well acquainted" with the Gardners, explaining that there are "three children, Lesley's and Carol's ages. We like them all very much, and they have been very nice to us, but they live on the other side of London, in Surrey, and we can't see much of them."

117 "Forgive this unmannerly"—Flint to Frost, 23 June 1913, DCL.

117 "For all the information"—Frost to Flint, 24 June 1913, UTL.

117 "is appropriate to the"—SL 84, 17 July 1913.

117 "What you are good enough"—Lathem, *Send-Off*, 10.

118 "Do you suppose you could"—Frost to Flint, 24 June 1913, UTL. The note ends: "You would advise as metrical expert and he as Philosopher. Or do I ask too much." (The bow to Flint, it should be said, could only have been meant as a courtesy.) Scribbled at the top a P.S. adds: "Be sure not to force Hulme. I wouldn't put him to sleep for the world." Frost's first traceable mention of Hulme occurs in another letter to Flint, 19 June 1913, which shows that the two had actually met some weeks before. If Frost by this time had read some of Hulme's published work, there is no record of the fact, though it is probable, judging by Frost's unusual interest in Hulme's abilities as a literary reasoner.

118 "My ideas got just the"—Frost to Flint, 6 July 1913, UTL. The rest of the passage supplies little further about the meeting: "I don't know but that I have delivered the best of what I have to say on the sound of sense. What more there may be I will be on hand to talk over with you and Hulme at five, Tuesday." One note from Hulme to Frost has survived. Undated, it is most likely of some time in July 1913: "Mrs. Kibblewhite has unexpectedly had to go back to Sussex & so will not be going to the Leibich's at Beaconsfield on Sunday after all. I expect she will go later & I will give her your message. I think a simple explanation of Munro is that he had been dining well. Don't forget to send your poems along as you promised, & come next Tuesday again if you can." (DCL)

119 "I have read your little"—Flint to Frost, 3 July 1913; from a carbon at UTL, and the original is not at DCL. Apparently Frost was not quite satisfied with Flint's rather impersonal comment in this letter, for in writing him a day or so later (6 July), he asks pointedly: "Did I reach you with the poems, did I get them over, as the saying is? Did I give you a feeling of and for the independent-dependence of the kind of people I like to write about?"

120 "I shan't forget the day"—Frost to Flint, 7 July 1913, UTL.

120   "To be perfectly frank"—SL 79, 4 July 1913. The two following excerpted passages on the sound of sense are from this same letter, SL 80–81.

122   "I give you a new"—SL 110–113; 22 February 1914.

122   "Just so many sentence"—SL 140, December 1914.

122   "What bothers people in"—SL 191, 18 September 1915. For further Frost discussion of the "sound of sense" just after he returned to America, see Evans, *Forty Years*, 102–104, and Lathem, *Interviews*, 3–8, 25.

124   "Born in San Francisco"—*Bookman*, August 1913, 189. The reference to Frost's being educated at Boston refers only to his two years at Harvard. The notice ends: "Mr. Frost has completed a second volume for publication this autumn; it is to be called 'Farm Servants and Other People,' and its contents . . . are again drawn, for the most part, from his experiences on that farm in the remote forest clearing." The projected autumn 1913 publication of *North of Boston* is mentioned in several other places, and just why it was held over to spring 1914 is hard to say. At the time of the *Bookman* interview Frost evidently told the magazine that he had already completed the manuscript for the new volume, and that would have been ample time for fall issuance. Perhaps the postponement (to 14 May 1914) was a marketing decision which saw a fall volume as treading too closely on *A Boy's Will*: two books of verse by a newly discovered poet appearing in the space of seven or so months would certainly have been overdoing the debut.

125   "lots of Americans as I"—Frost to Flint, 19 June 1913, UTL.

125   "I have been in such a"—Frost to Flint, 26 June 1913, UTL.

125   "Please don't show these"—Frost to Flint, 16 July 1913, UTL.

125   "While tramping the muddy"—Sergeant, *Trial*, 116.

125   "Birches"—Frost never said anything about when this poem was written, and there exists no direct evidence on the point, but two documents help to fix at least the date of its completion. In a letter to Flint, 6 July 1913, Frost lists eight poems as ready for publication. "Birches" is not among them. Another list, in Frost to Bartlett, 7 August 1913, includes twelve titles as being ready, and one of these is "Swinging Birches." While the poem must have been started some little while before this mention, it could not have been much before, since Frost makes a point of the "muddy yard" at the Bungalow during the writing. (The first letter is at UTL, and see Barry, *Writing*, 82; for the second letter, see SL 89.) A possible oblique reference to the writing of "Birches" may be contained in one arresting sentence of a letter Frost wrote on 17 July 1913. Discussing the contents of *A Boy's Will* with Thomas Mosher, he remarks, "In Mowing, for instance, I come so near what I long to get that I almost despair of coming nearer." (SL 83) As he was writing those words it seems that he was indeed, with "Birches," in the very act of "coming nearer" his long-sought poetic goal. Solely on instinct, I am inclined to carry the point a bit further—does the "despair" he mentions in that sentence perhaps reflect the initial throes of inspiration, before the lines of "Birches" began to flow? "Birches" is one of the

dozen or so poems about which Frost was accustomed to say that he had written it quickly, "with one stroke of the pen," or some such words. This claim drew the particular attention of Lawrance Thompson, and he devotes a good deal of space (*Early*, 594–597), toward refuting it. Of "Birches" he says that it required "many strokes and re-strokes of the pen," a verdict he bases on study of "the first draft" of the poem, preserved at Jones Library. But the manuscript at the Jones contains only the opening five lines of the poem (and no other manuscript of it has yet come to light). While these five lines do show several word changes, they really offer no proof against Frost's claim to having occasionally written rapidly and with a sure touch, which surely is all he intended by his "one stroke." When a writer, especially a poet, talks of the exhilaration of writing at high speed, he does not mean that he composes without having second and even third thoughts in the process. He means that the second thoughts themselves are thrown up and handled with rapid certainty.

126   "Two fragments soldered"—Frost in a letter of 1950, quoted in Thompson, *Triumph*, 598. A draft of that letter (DCL) has it slightly different: "Birches is two fragments I saw the affinity of put together so long ago I have forgotten where the joint is." When he joined the two separate fragments the best he could do for a transition was to insert the three lines:

> But I was going to say when Truth broke in
> With all her matter of fact about the ice storm,
> (Now am I free to be poetical?)

Those lines appeared in *Atlantic*, August 1915. For reprinting in *Mountain Interval* the following year the strangely flaccid third line was dropped. Exactly when the two fragments were first joined together cannot be said, whether in July 1913 along with the writing of the main fragment, or as late as spring 1915 back in the U.S. The fact that the poem was not included in *North of Boston* argues that it was not completed in time, that is, by January or even February 1914. On the other hand, an interesting case is made by critic John Kemp (*Frost*, 135-142) for the poem's having been deliberately omitted from *NOB*, on the ground that its more assured tone and outlook did not fit the ambivalent, tentative mood established by the volume's other poems. Kemp sees "Birches" as the poem which signals the start of Frost's switch from authentic artist-as-seeker to his later and lesser role of Yankee Bard. Though it is rather fine-drawn at places, his argument does seem to have elements of value for the study of Frost's subsequent career.

126   "as a lump in the throat"—Untermeyer, *Letters*, 22. It is a peculiarly affecting thing to hear Frost, forty years after writing the poem, tell an audience that the line in "Birches" that meant most to him was, "When I'm weary of considerations." He went on to explain, "That's when you get older. It didn't

mean so much to me when I wrote it as it does now. I've made some of the worst psychological mistakes in the world so don't listen to anything I say." (Cook, *Voice*, 51) One short passage in the poem, surely among the best known in all Frost's work—

> . . . *Earth's the right place for love:*
> *I don't know where it's likely to go better.*

would seem to have a definite connection with another brief lyric written about now, the twenty-line "Bond and Free." Contrasting Love and Thought, this poem concludes that, while Thought fittingly "cleaves the interstellar gloom," Love happily and properly remains in "earth's embrace." Whether "Bond and Free" was actually written that July admittedly is uncertain, but that it was present to his mind at that time is beyond question, for he copied it into a letter to Cox of 10 July 1913. (See Evans, *Forty Years*, 26; the same letter is given in SL 81–82, but there is no mention of the enclosed poem.) Also of interest is the subsequent rewriting of "Bond and Free" for inclusion in the 1916 volume, *Mountain Interval*. Where the first version seemed to value and praise Thought over Love, the final version reverses the process. Perhaps of equal pertinence is the fact that it was Frost himself who linked these two poems in his volumes, always placing "Bond and Free" just preceding "Birches."

127   Lesley Frost's two compositions about birch swinging are in Frost, *Child*, II 2, 5; V 82. The following, in no particular order, are some of the more obvious links between Lesley's compositions as a child and her father's poems (I omit quotation marks from the poem titles to simplify the reading): Hyla Brook, IV 10, V 78; Rose Pogonias, I 54, 16–17; A Prayer In Spring, III 27; After Apple Picking, IV 66; Fireflies In the Garden, IV 10; Storm Fear, V 30, IV 59; The Vantage Point, V 10; The Bonfire, I 26, 31; The Generations of Men, III 28; Two Look At Two, V 1; The Line Gang, V 13–17; Cow In Apple Time, I 14, 49; Need of Being Versed In Country Things, III 128, V 69–70.

128   "Based on an actual"—Lathem, *Interviews*, 109.

128   "I always drew for my"—Cook, *Dimensions*, 143.

128   "a little circle that"—Lathem, *Interviews*, 109.

128   "I am not a realist but"—Cohn Notebook, 77, unnumbered. See above, 217. He made a similar remark three years later in explaining his technique to an interested critic. When he was younger, he says, "I was afraid I hadn't imagination enough to be really literary. And I hadn't. I have just barely enough to imitate spoken sentences . . . I'm what you would call reproductive. I like best (in my poetry at least) not to set down even an idea that is of my own thinking." Letter of 29 April 1917 to Lewis Chase, in Barry, *Writing*, 70.

128   "We write of things we"—SL 141, December 1914.

129   "He said he had spent"—Sutton, *Season*, 230.

130   "Stopping by Woods on a Snowy Evening"—The story behind this poem was revealed by Frost only in 1947 when, after a lecture at Bowdoin College, Maine, he privately responded to a young questioner, a student named N. Arthur Bleau. Later, when Bleau published the story (Tharpe, *Essays* III, 174–177), it was supported by Lesley Frost in a note to Bleau's essay. She had known the story for many years, she said, but had thought her father had meant to keep it private. No specific date is given for the incident, but 1905 seems certain: Lesley says the little horse involved was called Eunice, and a calculation from Frost, *Child* (I 20, II 40, IV 53), shows that Eunice was acquired in early 1905, and was sold before December 1906. Also, it seems natural to link the incident with Frost's final resolve, formed no later than January 1906 and under financial need, to go back to teaching. I may say, further, that Bleau's story provides, for the first time, a reasonable explanation for that rather puzzling third line: "He will not see me stopping here." Personally, I had always wondered why a man sitting in a halted wagon and enjoying the beauty of a snowfall should care if anyone saw him.

131   "On the Sale of My Farm"—This poem, never published by Frost, was included in the manuscript booklet sent to Susan Ward in 1911; the manuscript is at Huntington Library. The complete text may be read in Thompson, *Early*, 368.

131   Frost's visit to the Derry farm in 1938 with the dead Elinor's ashes is recounted in Thompson, *Triumph*, 495, 507–508, on information directly from Frost. He was acting at Elinor's own request. See also, Sutton, *Season*, 387–388.

Chapter Eight: Dry Stone Walls

132   "I hope that I have not"—Mary Gardner to Frost, 3 August 1913, DCL. The note is headed "Kingsbarns, Fife." Another note, from Ernest Gardner to Elinor Frost, shows the trouble the Gardners took to arrange things for the holidays: "After writing the letter to you, we found the lady in the cottage had another offer, but she said she would accept yours in preference if you would make it the last fortnight of August. So we telegraphed, and when we got your answer we told her you would take it. We are glad, as we may be leaving about 28 Aug. and we want to be here while you are. Do come by the boat on the 16th if you can." (DCL)

133   A copy of Mrs. Gardner's volume, *Plain Themes*, is in the British Library, London. It contains thirty-one poems, all quite short, only one of which had been previously published, in the *Westminster Gazette*. Obvious is the way her daughter's excellent woodcuts tend to overpower the poems. In 1924 she published a second volume of poetry, entitled *Broads*, and according to Elinor Frost (SL 79) she was also author of a Greek grammar.

134   "Well, I haul off"—SL 90, 30 August 1913.

134   "These Gardners are the"—SL 90, 30 August 1913.

134   The cave incident: The only record of this is in Frost's letter to Bartlett written from Kingsbarns 30 August 1913. That he was still in some heat when he wrote it can be seen from its opening: "'To relieve my feelings just a word from Scotland on the funny holiday we are having with the Professor Gardiners [sic]. They are a family I got entangled with at the opening of the Poetry Shop in High Holborn last winter." The excavation history of the Kinkell and Constantine Caves is in *Proceedings of the Society of Antiquaries of Scotland*, vol. XLIX, Fifth Series, Edinburgh, 1915, 233–255. Further particulars may be found in E. MacKie and J. Glaister, *The Wemyss Caves, Fife*, University of Glasgow, 1981; and in Francis Diack, *The Inscriptions of Pictland*, Aberdeen, 1944, 34–42. One of the authors of the article in the *Proceedings*, A. J. B. Wace, is linked to Gardner through his several articles in *Journal of Hellenic Studies*, of which Gardner was for a time co-editor. My choice of Constantine's Cave as the one visited by Frost, rather than Kinkell Cave, is based on the fact, pointed out to me by Professor James Kenworthy of St. Andrews University, that no animal carvings were found in the latter.

135   "his own archaeological"—Thompson, *Early*, 425. Thompson sees Frost's behavior in both incidents at Kingsbarns as comprising "one fierce display of superiority," with all the unpleasantness of the holiday arising out of "the darker Scottish side of Frost's moodiness." That Frost was at fault in the cave incident to some degree may be readily admitted without calling on heredity and formal psychology to explain his reaction. Sufficient is a remark of John Bartlett's: "I never knew a person who was more sensitive to slights, rebuffs, acts of unfriendliness than Frost. He seemed to carry the scar of them longer" (Munson, *Frost*, 50).

137   "and it has just struck"—Mary Gardner to Elinor Frost, 15 December 1913, DCL. An additional mention of the Gardner's, while the Frosts were still in England, occurs in a letter of Edward Thomas to Frost, 19 September 1914: "I shall be glad if I hear Mrs. Nutt has got a job for you & Mrs. Gardner a cottage I can cycle or walk to this autumn & winter." (DCL) The Thomas home at Steep, in Hampshire, was some twenty miles from the Gardner home at Tadworth in Surrey, so this may mean that Frost was about to ask the Gardners to look out for a cottage for him in their locality, or had already asked. If so, it argues friendlier relations between the Frosts and Gardners after Kingsbarns than has been thought. (For more on Thomas's reference to "a job," which would have required Frost's living nearer London, see the notes below, 263.) There is no sign, however, that the two families were ever in touch after 1913. When the Frosts visited England in 1928 they saw many of their old friends, but not the Gardners—though it seems they may have been expecting to. Elinor wrote home: "We haven't communicated with the Gardners yet, or heard anything about them." (Grade, *Family*, 129)

137   James Cruikshank Smith: Born in 1867, at his death in 1946 Smith was senior chief inspector of schools in Scotland. For further information see obitu-

aries in London *Times*, 9 November 1946, the *Scotsman*, 8 November 1946, *Glascow Herald*, 8 November 1946. Smith's wife was Edith Philip, of Dundee, sister of Mrs. Jessy Mair. His four daughters, all good friends of Lesley Frost, are now deceased. For more on all the Mairs, Philips, and Beveridges, see *Shared Enthusiasm*, by Philip Mair, son of Jessy Mair. The Mairs home at Banstead, Surrey, was only two or three miles from the Gardners' place at Tadworth. For Smith's rescue of Frost in the swimming incident at Kingsbarns I have brought together references in Cox, *Swinger*, 12; Evans, *Forty Years*, 84; Sergeant, *Trial*, 111. That first meeting between Frost and J. C. Smith, it should be said, presents something of a minor problem. I have taken their meeting to be the natural result of Frost's being at Kingsbarns with the Gardners, who were friends of the Mairs, and therefore of Mrs. Mair's sister, Edith Smith, and her family, also then at Kingsbarns. But Frost in a letter three months later (December 1913 to Gertrude McQuesten) writes as follows: "We had a jaunt in Scotland in the summer that we could ill afford. We were some time near St. Andrews . . . with literary friends, but the best of it all was the new friends we made by chance on the beach. They were literary too—or at least one of them was . . . edits Shakespeare and Spencer and knows by heart all the great poetry in Greek Latin and English. He has introduced me to an entirely new set of people . . ." (BUL) The coincidence of meeting someone by accident, whom he would have been expected to meet in the regular course, while giving reason for pause, is of course quite possible. It agrees with what Frost later told his biographers (Sergeant, *Trial*, 111; Thompson, *Early*, 604).

138   "And there are dry stone"—SL 94, c. 15 September 1913. There is nothing further in the letter about these walls.

138   "Of course I recognized"—Smith to Frost, 24 November 1913, DCL.

139   "Thinking of the old wall"—Thompson, *Early*, 594, quoting a talk by Frost at Wesleyan in 1936. Frost adds that he wrote the poem while feeling "very homesick" for his old wall in Derry.

141   "on the way ofer we fond"—Frost, *Child*, II 14.

142   The old country saying about good fences was probably encountered by Frost more than once during his days on the Derry farm, both in talk and in print. It occurs in *The Old Farmer's Almanac* for 1906, a copy of which is in the Barrett collection of Frost materials at UVL (nothing in this copy actually links it to Frost himself, and its provenance has not been explained; the statement in Crane, *Catalogue*, 255, that it bears a Frost signature, is incorrect). Under the entry for April, p. 13, the column of commentary ends with an admonition to "Fix up the fences before you turn out the stock. Good fences make good neighbors." Perhaps I should record here my disappointment with reference to the other poems in *North of Boston*. I had hoped to uncover specific background on "Home Burial," "The Mountain," and "A Hundred Collars," in particular, but none have yielded anything of themselves beyond the few bare facts already known.

142   "I don't think anyone"—The source of this quotation I have unfor-

tunately mislaid, and it has eluded rather feverish attempts at recovery. My hope is that some kind reader will be able to place it for me.

143   "With all the work he"—SL 115, 23 February 1914. The two letters of Smith to Frost of fall 1913 are at DCL. The second is dated 24 November.

145   Reviews of *A Boy's Will* in fall 1913: *Nation*, 20 September, 924; *Dial*, 16 September, 211; *Academy*, 20 September, 360. Regarding the identity of the effusive *Academy* reviewer, Lawrance Thompson hints (*Early*, 426) that Frost himself suspected that the writer may have been a woman.

Chapter Nine: A Poet and Nothing Else

149   "All I say is don't let"—SL 58, 25 December 1912.

149   "You mustn't take me too"—SL 98, c. 5 November 1913.

149   "My dream would be to get"—SL 103, 8 December 1913.

150   "Forgive me for keeping"—SL 92, 14 September 1913.

151   "Shall you by chance be"—Hodgson to Frost, undated but about 1 October 1913, DCL.

151   "The strangest accent of"—SL 94. In this letter, dated c. 15 September 1913, there are some further details about Frost's visit to Yeats. In Thompson, *Early*, 413, the events of this visit in fall 1913 are mistakenly assigned to Frost's initial visit to Yeats the previous spring.

151   Frost's first meeting with Robert Bridges, and his discussion of Bridges prosodic ideas, is in Frost to Cox, 19 January, SL 107.

153   "These Englishmen are"—SL 96, 24 October 1913.

153   The issue of *Poetry & Drama* in which Frost wrote his marginal comments is at UVL. The full text may be read in Crane, *Catalogue*, 145–148; also, less accurately, in SL 103–106.

154   "But Godfrey Mighty it's"—Frost to Flint, 10 December 1913, UTL. In this letter Frost explains, perhaps not quite seriously, that he is "all tired out" because of "all I have written to keep (sixteen pieces) and all I have written to throw away. I do make such hard work of it all." The reference is to the contents of *North of Boston*, the manuscript of which by that time had been given to the Nutt firm.

154   "Our means forbid"—SL 101, 8 December 1913.

155   The excerpted lines of verse (". . . two babes," etc.) are from "Good Relief," a poem never published by Frost, but included in a 1929 anthology compiled by Lesley Frost. Manuscript at Jones Library, Amherst. That the lines quoted refer to Frost's children is my own conclusion. For the full text see Thompson, *Early*, 430.

155   "I have no friend here"—SL 121, 26 March 1914. There is no formal biography of Wilfrid Gibson; the best source for particulars of his life and career remains *The Dictionary of National Biography* (1961–1970), 430. He is also mentioned at length in many of the books by and about his friends and col-

leagues; see especially, *Rupert Brooke*, by C. Hassall, and *Discovery*, by John Drinkwater. For Frost's references to his interest in Gibson and Abercrombie together, see SL 96, 98.

156   "I'll be here at 7:30"—Gibson to Frost, 4 August 1913, DCL.

156   "I gladly took from"—Thompson, *Early*, 439, 599.

157   "Gibson is my best friend"—Frost to Gertrude McQuesten, undated but early December 1913, BUL. Also, Frost to Marie Hodge of Plymouth calls Gibson "a much greater poet" than Ezra Pound (Oct. 1913, BUL).

157   Gertrude McQuesten: So far overlooked in Frost biography, Miss McQuesten was a teacher at Emerson College of Oratory in Boston. She and Frost first met while Frost was on the faculty of Pinkerton Academy, Derry, where Miss McQuesten gave at least one lecture and reading, probably in 1911. (In a letter to her of December 1913 Frost says, "Let's storm something high in the name of Hildreth Hall, Derry N. H. where you and I first talked poetry and the poets." BUL) Her parents' home was in Plymouth, N.H., and there Frost met her again in 1911–1912 when he joined the staff of the Normal School, and where Miss McQuesten's invalid mother became "especially fond of Mrs. Frost" (Nettie McQuesten to Robert Newdick, 15 September 1938, BUL). In 1914 Miss McQuesten and her sister Nettie spent the summer traveling in Europe, including England, and were invited by Frost to visit Gloucestershire. He hoped to have her give readings for the Dymock poets, and later take a turn at the regular readings at Poetry Bookshop, so his English friends could "get an idea of the right American style" of reading poetry (Frost to McQuesten, November 1914, BUL). In the end her itinerary, disrupted by the war, did not permit a side trip to Ryton. The interest of this forgotten friendship of Frost's centers on Miss McQuesten's position as a speech teacher ("instructor of voice," including "literary interpretation"), just at the time when Frost was groping toward his new conception of the use of the spoken word in poetry. For further on Miss McQuesten, who died in 1931, see *Emerson College Alumni Bulletin*, November 1931; *Emerson College Magazine*, January 1913, 84, and February 1909, 164–166. An article by her on "Technique in Vocal Expression" is in *Emerson College Magazine*, November 1905, 40–46. At her death it was said of her that "she interpreted the best—Shakespeare and Tennyson, Browning and Kipling,—and the stories of the New England she knew and loved so well." (*Emerson College Alumni Bulletin*, November 1931) At present no further information is available, either about Miss McQuesten herself, or about her friendship with Frost.

157   "There were the friends we"—Mertins, *Walking*, 117.

157   "I shall have to run into"—Frost to Gertrude McQuesten, undated but early December 1913, BUL.

158   "To be with Wilfrid Gibson"—SL 110, 15 February 1914.

158   "The important thing to us"—SL 124, 18 May 1914.

159   "We had a lovely"—Irma Frost to Beulah Huckins, 1914, PSCL.

160   J. C. Smith's long letter of 31 January 1914 is at DCL. If Frost declined to read his poems for Smith's Edinburgh group, as it appears he did, he still made the effort to be present at the meeting, held sometime in March. Writing on 26 March 1914 to Cox he mentions some traveling he did "the other day," and he says "It thrilled me enough merely to see the names on the stations. I got as much out of seeing Dunfermline town from the train as from straggling round Edinburgh Castle for a day." (SL 121) Smith's remark about Frost "trying a prose tale" probably indicates only another effort to earn some quick cash by writing for the magazines. So far as is known, nothing came of it.

162   The Bungalow: The sublet tenant after Frost was a Dr. R. F. Fox, who took possession as of 1 May 1914. The cottage's owner, Miss Staniford, sold the property in August 1915, and since then it has changed hands a half-dozen times. The present owner, Mrs. Joan Clarence, bought it in November 1962 unaware of its link to a famous poet. See notes above, 228.

162   "We've been thinking of you"—Gibson to Frost, 25 January 1914, DCL.

163   "We have just this moment"—Mrs. Gibson to Elinor Frost, 25 February 1914, DCL. On 12 March Gibson wrote Frost: "All thanks for your letter (which was, of course, written before the telegram) I find we cannot get the key to look over the cottage near here until Saturday afternoon. But I'll write to you about it as soon as possible." (DCL)

163   "We mean to do the city"—SL 121, 26 March 1914.

163   "We are staying in"—Lesley Frost to Beulah Huckins, 1914, PSCL. Irma's card is to the same, also at PSCL.

163   "This being my birthday"—SL 121, 26 March 1914.

Chapter Ten: Ledington: Little Iddens

165   Little Iddens: The rental fee and the age of the cottage are given in a letter of Elinor Frost, SL 126, and are corroborated elsewhere. The cottage and its surroundings appear to have been very little changed (September 1985), except for the erection of another house just up the road which now blocks the view of Little Iddens from the east. The one-hundred-acre working farm on which the cottage is situated was and is called Henberrow, now the property of Gordon Churchill, a resident of the farm for sixty years. When Little Iddens was being used as a holiday cottage, in the seventies, part of the attraction, according to a tiny printed brochure, was the fact that it was "once the home of the American poet Robert Frost." During the time of my visit, Little Iddens, a private dwelling once again, was not open to visitors, so my description of its interior is based on information supplied by Philip Churchill, by the holiday brochure, and Thompson, *Early*, 447. The name Ledington is given varied spelling in Frost literature (Leadington, Leddington), and the reason is that all three forms actually appear on signs and documents in the area.

166   "Think of me still"—Frost to Flint, 18 May 1914, UTL.

167   "I will concoct plans"—Haines to Frost, 31 May 1914, DCL. The letter continues: "I enjoyed my visit yesterday immensely and only wish I had either come earlier or that the train back had not come so soon. Tell your wife that not the least of my regrets was my lost bread and butter."

167   "a very fine looking man"—Mertins, *Walking*, 132.

167   "No one doubts that he is"—SL 123, 18 May 1914.

168   "Whatever he did he made"—Farjeon, *Four Years*, 88.

168   "The Frosts did not live"—Farjeon, *Four Years*, 89. Concerning the Frost children, she says that Carol picked fruit in the surrounding orchards "with tireless care from morning to night, for the sheer love of doing it . . . In his absorption Carol seemed to be the very embodiment of Robert's apple-picking poem. He came second to Lesley, a tall girl of noble promise, her mother's chief standby in the domestic chores. The two younger girls were generally occupied with something. Life, materially meager, satisfied these children."

169   "Complete nervous prostration"—SL 127. She says it happened "three weeks ago" and the letter is dated about 20 June 1914. Continuing, she explains that "the household and teaching and the excitement of meeting so many people constantly, has been almost too much for me . . . But I pulled out of it and am feeling considerably better now."

169   Review of *North of Boston*: London *Times*, 28 May 1914, 262.

169   "Your damnfool publisher"—Pound to Frost, 3 June 1914, DCL. It is a postcard, addressed to Frost care of the Poetry Bookshop. It also says that Ford Madox Ford had not gotten a copy.

169   "I couldn't refuse to"—SL 149, 2 January 1915.

169   "is good stuff, the very"—Abercrombie to Frost, 16 June 1914, DCL.

170   "Yours was the first praise"—SL 193, 21 September 1915. Frost's reaction to Abercrombie's review at the time was expressed in a letter of late June 1914 to Haines, in which the real source of his pleasure is revealed in one casual sentence: "It was a generous review to consider me in all ways so seriously." (DCL) The complete letter is in SL 127.

172   Reviews of *North of Boston*: *Pall Mall Gazette*, 20 June 1914; *Outlook*, 27 June 1914. Both are quoted here from a 1914 advertising leaflet prepared by the Nutt firm, PSCL. See also Munson, *Frost*, 117–124.

173   Gibson's poem, "The Golden Room," was published in *Atlantic*, February 1926; the excerpt quoted here is from Thompson, *Early*, 454. One line in the poem claims, "Twas in July of 1914 that we talked," but the evidence shows that the day was actually Wednesday, 25 June. (See Thomas, *Bottomley*, 235, for instance, where Edward Thomas in a letter dated 27 June 1914 says, "We saw Rupert Brooke at Gibson's on Wednesday.")

174   Further reviews of *North of Boston*: London *Times*, 2 July 1914, 38; *Egoist*, 1 July 1914, 248; *Bookman*, July 1914, 183.

177   "I saw enough of his"—Frost to Haines, 2 April 1915, DCL. For a further extract from this angry letter see above, 201.

177   "Poor dear Gibson! Whatever"—Frost to Flint, 24 August 1916, UTL.
Gibson's boasting about his lack of prosodic knowledge is in Grade, *Family*, 19–
20. Frost's dislike of Gibson's artificiality is reported by Cox: "His friend in
England, Wilfrid Gibson, was writing about working people and their wives—
miners, for example. Gibson admitted that he had never been near a coal-mine.
He wrote of what they must be like. All conjecture. Robert shook his head,
smiling." (Cox, *Swinger*, 8) See also a veiled reference to Gibson's artificiality of
technique in Frost to Edward Garnett, 12 June 1915: "The more or less fishy
incidents and characters are gathered to the idea in some sort of logical arrangement, made up and patched up and clothed on." (SL 179.) Also, a letter of Frost
to Untermeyer has this: "Take it easy and don't upon any consideration look for
copy—as dear old Wilfrid Gibson does wherever he goes. Once we were coming
home from some country races, what they call point-to-point races, when he
asked me uneasily 'I didn't see a thing there I could use, did you?' He counted the
day lost and only asked consolation in learning that I had lost it too." (Untermeyer, *Letters*, 10) Frost's opinion of Gibson's best-known poem, "Solway Ford,"
is also on record: "It is a good poem. But it is oh terribly made up . . . And then
look at the way the sentences run on. They are not sentences at all in my sense of
the word." (SL 151, 2 February 1915.) Frost's revulsion from his initial high
regard for Gibson as poet could not have gone much farther.
178   "I keep far enough away"—Cook, *Dimensions*, 16.
178   "He's always differentiated"—Sutton, *Season*, 220.
178   "You see I haven't led"—Cowley, *Work*, 29. About his life in England
Frost adds: "My instinct was not to belong to any gang, and my instinct was
against being confused with the—what do you call them?—they called themselves Georgians, Edwardians, something like that." When the interviewer
asked if there had been much of a "gang" feeling among the literary people in
London, Frost replied, "Yes, oh yes. Funny over there. I suppose it's the same
over here . . . I had an instinct against belonging to any of those crowds." This
negative way of expressing the fact was later put more positively, especially in the
years just after the return from England. By 1923 he could end an interview
with the *New York Times* with the perfectly sincere if offhand statement "I am an
ordinary man, I guess. That's what's the trouble with me. I like my school and I
like my farm and I like people. Just ordinary, you see." (Lathem, *Interviews*, 53)

Chapter Eleven: The Only Begetter

179   "The war is an ill wind"—SL 131, 20 August 1914.
180   "Life is once more one"—Frost to Haines, 5 January 1915, DCL.
180   "Strange, complex temperament"—Thomas, *World*, 158.
180   "The closest I ever came"—SL 220, 22 October 1917.
180   "The only brother I ever"—SL 217, 29 April 1917.
180   "He more than anyone"—SL 220, 22 October 1917.

181   "He is quite the most"—SL 126, June 1914.

181   "Through the little door"—Eckert, *Thomas*, 96. In a note to Eleanor Farjeon, 5 October 1914, Thomas says he is meeting "an American" the next day (Farjeon, *Four Years*, 37); see also the note on Hodgson, above, 254.

183   "I wish you were near"—Thomas to Frost, 19 February 1914, DCL. The inquiry about lodgings in Beaconsfield is in Thomas to Frost, 30 January 1914, DCL.

183   "I knew from the moment"—SL 126, 27 April 1917.

183   "I tell you I should"—Thomas to Frost, 3 May 1915, DCL.

184   "I wish I could write"—Thomas to Frost, 19 May 1915, DCL.

185   "I believe he has taken"—Heilbrun, *Garnett*, 136. Joining in this pre-Frost judgment of Thomas's true bent were at least three other Thomas friends: Garnett, Bottomley, and Rhys; see Thomas, *Portrait*, 248.

186   "the most our congeniality"—Frost to Grace Conkling, 28 June 1921, UVL; same for "I dragged him out," etc.; also, partially in Crane, *Catalogue*, 249.

187   "had about lost patience"—Eckert, *Thomas*, 150, quoting a letter of Frost to H. R. Brennan, 1926.

"The calf I was in the"—Untermeyer, *Letters*, 29. That Frost for a while, at least, made a deliberate practice of overhauling his youthful romantic lyrics, recasting them in the techniques of his mature strain, seems definitely confessed in this letter. The remark about the calf, for example, is followed by a teasing but at bottom sober admission: "I am become my own salesman. Two of my phases you have been so—what shall I say?—as to like. Take care that you don't get your mouth set to declare the other two (as I release them) a falling off of power, for that is what they can't be whatever else they may be, since they were almost inextricably mixed with the first two in the writing and only my sagacity has separated or sorted them in the afterthought for putting on the market . . . I tell you Louis it's all over at thirty . . . now my time is my own. I have myself all in a strong box where I can unfold as a personality at discretion." The strong box may have been real or may have been metaphorical. But that it denotes a collection of early manuscripts, the now rejected lyricism, can hardly be doubted. While the best evidence for this, the manuscripts themselves, have mostly disappeared, one or two remain, and already on record are the two versions of "The Black Cottage," with the earlier having been accidentally preserved at the Huntington Library (see Thompson, *Early*, 592–593). A second may now be suggested, "The Oven Bird," again with the early version, entitled "Midsummer Birds," at the Huntington. Frost's anxious response in 1929 to the news that the Huntington had acquired so many of his youthful manuscripts, and his quick disowning of them followed by an openly expressed wish to have them destroyed, itself forms no slight part of the evidence. (For Frost's relations with the Huntington, see Sutton, *Season*, 110–112, 140–180, *passim*; SL 354–356; Thompson, *Early*, 532.) All of this, obviously, bears directly on Frost's deep concern, a year or more after his arrival back home, that his creative powers had waned from their first intensity, leaving him with a mastery of technique but dulled sensibilities. That he never surpassed, and all too seldom equaled the best of the poems in *North of Boston*, is perhaps comment enough.

187 "The loveliest book on"—SL 124, 18 May 1914.

188 "I may as well write"—Farjeon, *Four Years*, 81. The remark forms only a quick break in a chatty letter about the comings and goings of friends. The next sentence after the remark reads: "Yet I would almost as soon be on Dartmoor with Bertie and David." Also pertinent is Thomas's later admission to W. H. Hudson that "I had done no verses before, and did not expect to, and merely became nervous when I thought of beginning." Eckert, *Thomas*, 150.

188 "One thing and another"—Farjeon, *Four Years*, 83.

188 "The Frosts are all over"—Farjeon, *Four Years*, 83.

189 Edward Thomas's three reviews of *North of Boston*: *Daily News*, quoted here from Farjeon, *Four Years*, 77–78; *New Weekly*, 8 August 1914, 249; *English Review*, August 1914.

191 "It was almost the best"—SL 131, c. 15 August 1914.

192 "dazed"—SL 171, 22 April 1915. The complete sentence reads: "If I was a man dazed by the reviews that happened to me last summer and the friendliness of the English, what am I now?"

192 "no book of verse has"—SL 132, 20 August 1914.

193 "Whatever the words the"—Farjeon, *Four Years*, 90.

193 "a self-appointed over"—Farjeon, *Four Years*, 89. A lighthearted description of the banquet given for the poets at Glyn Iddens is in Farjeon, *Four Years*, 91–94, but there are no further details of Frost's part in the evening. The focus is on the unintended humor provided by the kind but simple-hearted host and hostess.

194 "Three meadows away lived"—From "This England," *Nation*, November 1914, quoted here from *Selected Poems and Prose of Edward Thomas*, Penguin Ed., 161–164. Out of the thoughts and actual phrases of this essay Thomas shaped, some two years later, the eight stanzas of his poem "The Sun Used to Shine," in which he describes the walks he took that summer of 1914 with Frost through the Dymock countryside:

> The sun used to shine while we two walked
> Slowly together, paused and started
> Again, and sometimes mused, sometimes talked
> As either pleased, and cheerfully parted
>
> Each night. We never disagreed
> Which gate to rest on. The to be
> And the late past we gave small heed.
> We turned from men or poetry

To rumours of the war remote
Only till both stood disinclined
For aught but the yellow flavorous coat
Of an apple wasps had undermined . . .

The remainder of the poem, written after Thomas had been in the army for a year, sadly laments the passing of such happy times.

195 "Ill with thinking"—Thomas to Frost, 31 October 1913, DCL.

196 "I saw too little of"—Thomas, *Bottomley*, 238.

196 Frost's letters to Edward Thomas: Of the nine letters extant, three are in *Selected Letters*. Six others are in the Thomas Collection, University College, Cardiff, Wales, and have only recently been published (*Poetry Wales*, vol. 22, no. 4, 1987; also in Thomas, *Wing*, 307–318). Five of the nine were written in 1915, and four in the latter part of 1916. There are no letters for the first seven or so months of 1916, when Thomas was still in England, and there are none for the first three months of 1917, when he was in France. Admittedly, Frost was an intermittent correspondent (see SL 263, where Frost confesses that "I should have written him twice as many letters as I did write"). But with Thomas, and in these circumstances, it is not likely he would have let so much time go by without writing. Of course, letters for these two periods may yet turn up.

196 "I am in it and no"—Thomas to Frost, 15 December 1914, DCL. Still with the original letter are typescripts for some fourteen poems. But Thomas, *Portrait*, 256, says that the original enclosures numbered no more than nine, including one poem not now present, "Up in the Wind."

197 "Frost hasn't said any"—Farjeon, *Four Years*, 108.

197 "The goodness is in Lob"—SL 164, 17 April 1915.

197 "I got a letter from you"—Thomas to Frost, 3 May 1915, DCL.

198 "your last poem 'Aspens' "—SL 185, 31 July 1915.

198 "Your talking of epic and"—Thomas to Frost, 5 March 1916, DCL.

198 "Your letter of Feb. 24"—Thomas to Frost, 16 March 1916, DCL. For further information on Thomas's poem, "Rain," see *Selected Poems and Prose of Edward Thomas*, Penguin English Library, 1981, 292.

199 "admiration for the poet"—SL 263, 20 January 1921.

200 "snooping in the hedge"—Sutton, *Season*, 298. The date of the game-keeper incident can only be given as mid-October. See Thomas, *Bottomley*, 240, and Farjeon, *Four Years*, 99–100.

200 "Damned cottager"—SL 142, December 1914. Thomas's joking reference to this phrase as good advertising is in this same letter, which Frost wrote to Harold Monro, another close friend of Thomas's.

201 "T. coming up the g's going"—Sutton, *Season*, 298. Newdick's notes on the long conversation in which these facts came out are dated 26 July 1936. They open with the phrase, "He told me the gamekeeper business."

201   "You mustn't tell me"—Frost to Haines, 2 April 1915, DCL. Abercrombie's role in the gamekeeper incident is found in a letter of Frost to Abercrombie, September 1915, where he discusses his contractual difficulties with Mrs. Nutt: "I wish you could settle her for me by yourself the way you settled the gamekeeper." (SL 193; also, Sutton, *Season*, 298, and Thompson, *Early*, 467). It is possible that further information about this whole incident will be found in the records of the Beauchamp estate, but presently these are not open to public inspection (letter from Countess Beauchamp, 22 June 1987).

202   "if he wanted so much"—Thompson, *Early*, 468.

202   "I only hope that you"—Thomas to Frost, 31 October 1914, DCL.

202   "I dread them as much"—Thomas to Frost, 23 May 1915, DCL.

202   "I can ride a motorcycle"—Thomas to Frost, 22 January 1917, DCL.

203   "We spend nights without"—Thomas to Frost, 2 April 1917, DCL. According to Edward Thomas's war diary, the chimney incident occurred on 15 March: "Huns strafe I sector at 5:30. We reply and they retaliate on Arras and Ronville. Only tired 77s reach O.P. A sunny breezy morning. Tried to climb Arras chimney to observe, but funked. Four shells nearly got me while I was going and coming. A rotten day. No letters for 5 days." (*Selected Poetry and Prose of Edward Thomas*, Penguin Ed. 276; the full war diary is available as an appendix to *The Childhood of Edward Thomas*, Faber & Faber, 1983.) The chimney itself is described in a letter of Thomas to his son, sent a few days after the incident: "There were iron rings all the way up and one I knew was loose, but I didn't know which. One bad feature was that you were always hanging *out* a bit, because the chimney tapered. It has been hit three times but only with small stuff. Now I suppose it is likely to survive as the enemy is further off." Thomas, *Portrait*, 287.

204   Further to the gamekeeper incident: Edward Thomas's daughter, Myfanwy, has recently made a brief but curiously inaccurate reference to this unfortunate little drama, apparently calling on family memories. Describing a day when Frost and her father were "turned out of a wood by a gamekeeper," she casts Frost in the rather strange role of accuser against his friend: "My father, being a true countryman, understood that the gamekeeper was doing his job, albeit in a surly manner, but Frost was near to calling him a coward for not squaring up to the gamekeeper and knocking him down." (Thomas, *Wing*, 14) If this is the version of the incident current in the Thomas family, it must be said it could only have been reached in ignorance of the true import of the letters and facts given herein.

204   "I had a friend who died"—Cook, *Voice*, 72.

Chapter Twelve: Telling It with a Sigh

205   "Under present political"—Lathem, *Send-off*, 15. The full facts of Frost's American debut, with correspondence, are available in this 1963 pamph-

let. Mrs. Holt had earlier (7 August 1914) written to Frost in England expressing her pleasure in *North of Boston*, but without identifying herself (SL 130). No
doubt she expected Frost would recognize the name, since she ends, "I hope I am
not taking too much of a liberty in writing this note, but probably you will not be
displeased to know of our interest." At the same time she gave her copy of *North
of Boston* to the Holt editors, urging its publication. Two readers endorsed her
opinion and the first letter to Mrs. Nutt was on its way by 2 September 1914.
That Frost did not recognize the Holt name until he received from Mrs. Nutt the
news about the completed contract seems certain. Thompson, *Early*, 460, says
he thought the letter was from a "Vermont farmer's wife," because it was headed
"Four Winds Farm, Stowe, Vermont."

205   "Now we can go home"—Thompson, *Early*, 469, quoting an interview
with Frost in the *New York Times*, 21 October 1923.

206   "a quiet job in a small"—SL 138, October 1914. The executor of
grandfather Frost's estate, Wilbur Rowell, apparently prompted by the concern
of Jeanie Frost (SL 145), wrote Frost on 30 December 1914 offering to advance "a
proportionate share" of the annuity for 1915 (UVL). I judge that this offer was
declined, mainly because of the loans Frost soon arranged among his English
friends. Further correspondence with Rowell makes it appear that Frost did
accept an advance on his annuity soon after reaching home (UVL). Only the loan
given Frost by J. C. Smith is reflected in the surviving correspondence. On 11
February 1915 Smith wrote Frost, "Yes, I got your [?former] letter & note of
hand. But there must be no talk of interest between you and me. Repay me when
& as you can; but no interest!" (DCL) Before Frost decided on seeking loans for
his return passage, it appears he thought seriously of taking a salaried position,
perhaps editorial work for Mrs. Nutt. So much seems definitely indicated by his
letter to Haines of mid-September 1914: "There's some likelihood of my being
called nearer London on business. While I'm not out for money, and in fact ran
away from the filthy stuff when I crossed the deep, I begin to feel as if I ought to
be earning a little again provided I can do so with dignity, that is, without asking
for the chance. But I will tell you more about this when I know more myself.
Nothing may come of it." The correspondence has nothing further, but for some
oblique evidence that Frost actually did begin looking for a place "nearer London" see a remark in a letter of Edward Thomas to Frost, 19 September 1914,
quoted above, 252.

206   "I believe I have made"—SL 148, 2 January 1915.
207   "The book is epoch-making"—SL 151, 2 February 1915.
207   "I fear I am going to"—SL 147, 2 January 1915.
207   "It is a sinister thing"—*Poetry*, December 1914, 127–129.
208   "I don't see that it is"—SL 148, 2 January 1915.
208   "half-heated English homes"—Frost to Haines, 30 September 1914,
DCL. The letter is headed, "20 Braid Avenue, Edinburgh," which was Smith's

address. In another letter to Haines (October 1914, DCL), Frost mentions that in Edinburgh he was "under a doctor's care," and that he came home hurriedly "on a summons" because of sickness in his family.

208   "If I was sure I was"—Frost to Haines, 5 January 1915, DCL.

208   "I admired Elinor so"—Thompson, *Early*, 458.

209   "We think of home all"—SL 149, 2 January 1915.

209   "We are very quiet in spite"—SL 137, October 1914.

209   "There are soldiers swarming"—SL 144, 23 December 1914. An earlier Frost letter, 30 August 1914, to Gertrude McQuesten, written when the fighting was less than a month old, was more flippant: "Today recruiting parties have been scouring the countryside for young men who haven't answered the call to arms. They have to speed the enlisting to keep ahead of the wastage at the front. Some of the young men have to be made to realize that it is a great war. No fear but that they will want to fight when they see the need. A cartload of them swept out of this hamlet tonight—one a man who has a boy as old as Carol . . . The horse was going fast and they waved their hats with an intimacy advanced by the thought of their sacrifice. The place seems lonelier." (BUL)

210   "Today I felt a terrible"—Mrs. Nutt to Frost, 19 September 1914, DCL. Frost's war sonnet, entitled "Suggested By Talk of Peace At This Time," was included in a letter to Edward Thomas, 7 December 1916 (Univ. of Cardiff). It was first published in *Poetry Wales*, V. 22, No. 4, 1987. Thomas's opinion of it was expressed in a letter of 31 December 1916, DCL.

211   "At the bottom of"—Thompson, *Early*, 458.

213   "I suppose my little"—Frost to Thomas, 26 June 1915, Cardiff.

213   "The Road Not Taken"—The original of this poem, at first called "Two Roads," was sent to Edward Thomas apparently in early April 1915. The letter containing Thomas's initial reaction is missing, but that he failed, not surprisingly, to grasp the poem's oversubtle intent is clear from his letter of 13 June 1915 in which he apologizes for his error, explaining it as a lapse of attention. He ends, however, with an oblique defense of his first opinion: "I read 'The Road Not Taken' to Helen just now & she liked it entirely, & agreed with me how naturally symbolical it was." (DCL) The original manuscript of the poem (owned by Howard Schmitt of Hamburg, NY) shows several differences from the final version, especially in line 10—"Had gone to them both about the same," which was improved to "Had worn them really about the same"—and in a much less graceful third stanza:

> *And both that morning equally lay*
> *In gold no step had sullied yet.*
> *I marked the first for another day*
> *At the same time knowing of old my way*
> *I knew that I should be sure to forget.*

The improvement in clarity, tone and a certain suggestiveness is quite marked in the final version; see above, 212.

213   "It is all very well for"—Thomas to Frost, 13 June 1915, DCL.

214   The final move of the Frosts, from Ryton back to the Chandler farm in Ledington, took place before mid-January 1915. A letter of Frost to Haines, 5 January 1915, is headed "Ryton Dymock," and says "we are on the move at last after all the threats." Another letter to Haines, 3 February 1915, is headed "Oldfields Ledington," which was the Chandler farm. Both letters at DCL.

214   "I am in one of my"—Smith to Frost, 22 January 1915, DCL.

214   "All things considered"—Frost to Haines, c. 8 February 1915, DCL.

215   "to send ships to the"—London Times, 1 February 1915, 10. For the warnings to neutrals see Times, 5 February 1915, 1.

215   J. C. Smith's last letter to Frost in England is dated 11 February 1915. (DCL) Because of the closeness in dates of the letter and of Frost's departure from Ledington, it is possible the letter missed him in England and did not catch up with him until he settled in Franconia that summer.

215   "I ought to know"—Frost to Flint, 13 February 1915, DCL. The reason the farewell note was not sent is explained in a later letter of Frost to Flint, 24 August 1916, which also reveals Frost's mood as he was about to depart England: "I keep somewhere about me a very melancholy letter I wrote you the night we lay in the Mersey River at Liverpool to send ashore before we sailed. No mail was permitted to go ashore, so you never got the letter. Sometime when we meet again, here or there, we will open it together to see just how melancholy I was that night when I thought of myself as leaving you behind me. It is sealed in an envelope of the American liner St. Paul." (UTL) As can be seen, the short note itself doesn't really seem to carry the depth of melancholy here remembered, and perhaps Frost is thinking more of how he felt at the time, rather than of what he put down on paper. The fact that he and his young family were about to cross the ocean in conditions of extreme danger probably added its share of depressed feelings that night.

216   "Are we still pals?"—Flint to Frost, 31 January 1916, DCL. During Frost's first return visit to England in 1928 the two men met again, and in his last known letter to Frost twenty-five years later, Flint recalled that meeting: "I shall never forget that last evening I was with you in Hampstead. I saw your tears when you got into the cab in College Crescent. Dorothy—my Dorothy—fell in love with you; but she always did with the Americans I introduced to her. And I can still see you with your overcoat over your shoulders—unused to our English draughts . . . All I wanted to say is that, in this country, there is at least one Englishman that loves you and I think I can say one Scotswoman—Dorothy." (28 June 1952, DCL) Lawrance Thompson, in treating the 1928 reunion of the two, does not quote or refer to this letter, and his description of their meeting manages to make it all seem somehow faintly unpleasant (Triumph, 340). Frost and Flint met for the last time when Frost went over in 1957 to receive degrees at Oxford and Cambridge.

216   The SS *St. Paul* and the Departure from England: SL 157; Lesley Frost in Tathem, *Recognized*, 10; Sergeant, *Trial*, 148; Thompson, *Early*, 474. For the first leg of the journey around the north of Ireland the *Lusitania* itself was in the Frosts' convoy, a fact recalled by Lesley Frost as late as 1969: "The *Lusitania* sailed beside us and we were both blacked out." The *Lusitania* sinking occurred on 7 May 1915.

The day Frost arrived in New York, 22 February, he had the pleasure of finding that his American recognition had already begun. Stopping at a news-stand after leaving the ship, he unexpectedly came across a long and favorable review of *North of Boston* in the *New Republic*, written by Amy Lowell. Later in the day, at the offices of his American publisher, Henry Holt, he was handed a check for $40, payment for use of "The Death of the Hired Man" in the *New Republic* two weeks before. (Thompson, *Triumph*, 3–6; Sergeant, *Trial*, 150–153). Less than five months later his growing reputation was given an enormous boost when *The Atlantic Monthly* published a highly laudatory and discriminating article on *North of Boston* by leading English critic Edward Garnett. This crucial article was a direct result of the good offices of Edward Thomas, a close friend of Garnett. In fact Thomas read and commented on the article in draft (Lathem, *Send-Off*, 4, 11, 18–19; SL 169–170). Frost and Garnett had not met in England, a missed opportunity that Garnett later regretted (Thomas to Frost, 1 June 1915, DCL).

Added Note

Frost and Francis Thompson
(see above, 240–241)

During his stay in England, curiously enough, Frost seems to have repented of his youthful enthusiasm for the poems of Francis Thompson. In a letter of fall 1914, for example, he actually denies to Thompson, by omission, any significant place in the poetry of the nineties. Talking of Walter De la Mare, he remarks, "The nineties produced no single poem to put beside his 'Listeners.' Really the nineties had very little on these degenerate days when you consider. Yeats, Jonson [for Lionel Johnson] and Dowson they had, and that is about all." (SL 93)

When Frost reached England in fall 1912, Francis Thompson had been dead just five years, but still alive and active in London's literary circles were Wilfred and Alice Meynell, Thompson's rescuers and literary sponsors. Frost, as it appears, made no effort to meet them despite having direct access through several mutual friends, including Eleanor Farjeon. He did have brief contact with Viola Meynell, daughter of Wilfrid and Alice, when in fall 1914 she asked permission to use his poem "The Pasture" as an epigraph in her novel *Columbine*. Her note of thanks to Frost (DCL) makes a point of saying how much his poetry had come to mean to her. In some degree, perhaps, it may be taken as peculiar that Francis Thompson's name never came up between them, for Viola had known Thompson well, as a child was the subject of some of his poetry, and later wrote a book about him.

It does seem that for a time Frost shied away from any recognition of Francis Thompson's influence on his early poems, several examples of which were in *A Boy's Will*. The explanation of this reticence is probably to be had in the fact that it occurred while Frost was in the throes of perfecting his new voice and style, and needed to free himself entirely from past constraints. It would be hard to think of two poets more unlike than the Francis Thompson of "The Hound of Heaven," "The Making of Viola," and "A Corymbus for Autumn," and the Frost of "A Hundred Collars," "The Axe-Helve," and "The Witch of Coos."

The record shows, however, that after his return from England Frost was soon openly speaking in praise of Thompson again: see Sutton, *Season*, 39, 213; Cox *Swinger*, 10; Cook, *Voice*, 38–39; Barry, *Writing*, 75, to name a few instances. A prime example of his true feelings in the matter is his repeated telling how as a youth on a trip to Boston he spent all his return carfare for the Englishman's then just published 1893 volume, containing "The Hound of Heaven," and had to walk the whole twenty-five miles home to Lawrence: "If I could meet that poem again for the first time," was how he put it more than once, "I'd walk the same miles and find them easy underfoot." (*National Geographic*, June 1955, 774, as quoted in Cook, *Voice*, 39. The account in Thompson, *Early*, 198–200, dates this incident at least a year too late.)

Throughout his long career Frost often used the phrase "sight and insight" as a shorthand description of his preferred way of understanding the world. This phrase too seems to have been picked up from Francis Thompson. It occurs as a section title in his *New Poems* of 1897.

SELECTED BIBLIOGRAPHY

Included here are all the printed sources drawn on for this book, as well as some whose contribution was more general. Sources of unpublished material, letters and other documents, are given at appropriate places in the notes. Unless it is otherwise stated, or is obvious from the citation, the place of publication for books in each case is New York City. University Press books are designated U.P.

Anderson, M., *RF and John Bartlett: The Record of a Friendship*, Holt, 1963.

Baker, C., "Frost On the Pumpkin," *Georgia Review*, Summer 1957.

Barry, E., *RF On Writing*, Rutgers U.P., 1973.

Bax, C., *Some I Knew Well*, Phoenix House, London, 1951.

Bogan, L., *Achievement in American Poetry*, Regnery, 1951.

Born, A., "Harold Monro And the Poetry Bookshop," *Antiquarian Book Monthly Review*, April 1980.

Burnshaw, S., *RF Himself*, Braziller, 1986.

Cook, R., *The Dimensions of RF*, Rinehart, 1958.

Cook, R., *RF: A Living Voice*, Massachusetts U.P., 1974.

Cowley, M. (ed.), *Writers At Work*, Viking, 1963.

Cox, S., "The Sincerity of RF," *New Republic*, 25 August 1917.

————, *RF: Original "Ordinary Man,"* Holt, 1929.

————, *A Swinger of Birches*, New York U.P., 1957.

Crane, J., *RF: A Descriptive Catalogue of Books and MSS. In the Barrett Library, University of Virginia*, Dawson, London, 1974.

Davies, W., *Later Days*, Cape, London, 1925.

Davison, P., "The Self-Realization of RF, 1911–1912," *New Republic*, 30 March 1974.

Day, K., *Recollections of Old Beaconsfield*, The Beaconsfield and District Historical Society, 1969.

Diack, F., *The Inscriptions of Pictland*, Spalding Club, Aberdeen, 1944.

Drinkwater, J., *Discovery*, Houghton, 1933.

Eckert, R., *Edward Thomas*, Dent, London, 1937.

Ellis, F., *RF In England 1912–1915* (M.A. Thesis), Columbia University, 1948.

Evans, W. (ed.), *RF and Sidney Cox: Forty Years of Friendship*, University Presses of New England, 1981.

Farjeon, E., *Edward Thomas: The Last Four Years*, Oxford U.P., 1958.

Fletcher, J., *Life Is My Song*, Farrar, 1937.

Ford, F., *Return to Yesterday*, Gollancz, London, 1931.

Foster, R., "The Two Frosts and the Poetics of Confession," *Centennial Essays*, Vol. 3, 1978; see under Tharpe, below.

Francis, L., "RF and the Majesty of Stones Upon Stones," *Journal of Modern Literature*, Vol. 9, 1981–1982.

———, "RF and Susan Hayes Ward," *Massachusetts Review*, Summer-Autumn 1985.

Francis, R., *RF: A Time to Talk*, Massachusetts U.P., 1972.

Frost, L., *New Hampshire's Child: The Derry Journals of Lesley Frost*, New York U.P., 1969.

Garnett, E., "A New American Poet," *Atlantic Monthly*, August 1915.

Gethyn-Jones, J., *Dymock Down the Ages*, Privately printed, 1951.

———, "RF—6th June 1957," *The Courier*, Syracuse University, No. 32, 1957.

Goldring, D., *South Lodge: Reminiscences of Violet Hunt, Ford Madox Ford, and the English Review Circle*, Constable, London, 1943.

Grade, A., *Family Letters of Robert and Elinor Frost*, New York U.P., 1972.

Grant, J., *Harold Monro and the Poetry Bookshop*, Routledge, London, 1967.

Greenberg, R., "Frost in England: A Publishing Incident," *New England Quarterly*, September 1961.

Grieder, J., "RF on Ezra Pound 1913," *New England Quarterly*, June 1971.

Haines, J., "RF In England"; see under Thornton, below.

Hall, D., "Vanity, Fame, Love and RF," in *Remembering Poets*, Harper, 1978.

Hassall, C., *Rupert Brooke*, Harcourt, 1964.

Heilbrun, C., *The Garnett Family*, Macmillan, 1961.

Hughes, G., *Imagism and the Imagists*, Biblo & Tannen, 1931, 1973.

Hutchins, P., *Ezra Pound's Kensington*, Faber, London, 1965.

Jeffares, N., *W. B. Yeats, Man and Poet*, Routledge, London, 1949.

Kemp, J., *RF and New England*, Princeton U.P., 1979.

Lathem, E., *RF: His American Send Off*, Stinehour Press, Vermont 1963.

———, *Interviews With RF*, Holt, 1966.

———, and Thompson, L. (eds.), *RF: Farm-Poultryman*, Dartmouth, 1963.

———, *Collected Poetry of RF*, Holt, 1975.

Lynen, J., *The Pastoral Art of RF*, Yale U.P., 1960.

MacKie, E., and Glaister, J., *The Wemyss Caves, Fife*, Glasgow University, 1981.

MacLiammoir, M., and Boland, E., *Yeats and His World*, Viking, 1971.

Mair, P., *Shared Enthusiasm*, Ascent Books, Surrey, England, 1982.

Marsh, J., *Edward Thomas*; Elek, London, 1978.

Masefield, J., *So Long to Learn*, Heinemann, London, 1952.

———, *Some Memories of W. B. Yeats*, Cuala, Dublin, 1940.

Mertins, L., *RF: Life and Talks-Walking*, Oklahoma U.P., 1965.

Miller, L., "Design and Drama in *A Boy's Will*," *Centennial Essays*, vol. 1, 1974; see under Tharpe, below.

———, "William James, RF, and The Black Cottage," in *Centennial Essays*, vol. 3, 1978; see under Tharpe, below.

Monroe, H., *A Poet's Life*, Macmillan, 1938.

Moore, J., *Life and Letters of Edward Thomas*, Heinemann, London, 1939.

Morrison, T., "The Agitated Heart," *Atlantic Monthly*, July 1967.

Mullins, E., *This Difficult Individual*, Fleet, 1961.

Munson, G., *RF: Sensibility and Good Sense*, Doubleday, 1927.

Newdick, R., "RF and the Dramatic," *New England Quarterly*, June 1937.

———, "RF and the Sound of Sense," *American Literature*, November 1937.

O'Donnell, W., "RF and New England: A Revaluation," *Yale Review*, Summer 1948.

Ogilvie, J., "From Woods to Stars," *South Atlantic Quarterly*, Winter 1959.

Paige, D., *The Letters of Ezra Pound*, Harcourt, 1950.

Poirier, R., *RF: The Work of Knowing*, Oxford U.P., 1977.

Pound, O. (ed.), *Ezra Pound and Dorothy Shakespeare, Their Letters 1909–1914*, New Directions, 1985.

Pritchard, W., *Frost: A Literary Life Reconsidered*, Oxford U.P., 1984.

Sergeant, E., *RF: Trial By Existence*, Holt, 1960.

Sims, G., "Alida Monro and the Poetry Bookshop," *Antiquarian Book Monthly Review*, July 1982.

Sinclair, M., "The Poems of F. S. Flint." *The English Review*, January 1921.

Sisson, C., *English Poetry 1900–1950*, Methuen, 1981.

Smythe, D., *RF Speaks*, Twayne, 1964.

Sokol, B., "What Went Wrong Between RF and Ezra Pound," *New England Quarterly*, December 1976.

———, "The Publication of RF's First Books," *The Book Collector*, Summer 1977.

Squires, R., *The Major Themes of RF*, Michigan U.P., 1963.

Sutton, W., *Newdick's Season of Frost: An Interrupted Biography of RF*, New York U.P., 1976.

Tathem, D., "RF In England," *The Courier* (Syracuse University) 30, 1968.

———, *A Poet Recognized: Notes On RF's First Trip to England*, privately printed, 1969.

Taylor, A. (ed.), *The History of Beaconsfield*, Beaconsfield and District Historical Society, 1983.

Tharpe, J. (ed.), *RF: Centennial Essays*, Mississippi U.P., 3 vols., 1974, 1976, 1978.

Thomas, E., "How I Began," *T. P.'s Weekly*, 31 January 1913.

Thomas, H., *World Without End*, Heinemann, 1931.

———, with Thomas, M., *Under Storm's Wing*, Carcanet, 1988.

Thomas, M., *One of These Fine Days*, Carcanet, 1982.

Thomas, R., *Letters From Edward Thomas to Gordon Bottomley*, Oxford U.P., 1968.

———, *Edward Thomas: A Portrait*, Oxford U.P., 1985.

Thompson, L., *Selected Letters of RF*, Holt, 1964.

———, *RF: The Early Years*, Holt, 1966.

———, *RF: The Years of Triumph*, Holt, 1970.

———, *RF: The Later Years* (with R. Winnick), Holt, 1976.

Thornton, R., *The Recognition of RF*, Holt, 1937.

Untermeyer, L., "Edward Thomas," *North American Review*, February 1919.

———, (ed.), *The Letters of RF to Louis Untermeyer*, Holt, 1963.

Unwin, S., *The Truth About A Publisher*, Allen and Unwin, London, 1960.

Van Dore, W., *RF and Wade Van Dore*, Wright State University, Dayton, 1986.

Wace, A., et. al., "Cave Excavations in East Fife," *Proceedings of the Society of Antiquaries of Scotland*, XLIX, Fifth Series, vol. 1, Edinburgh, 1915.

Waggoner, H., "The Humanistic Idealism of RF," *American Literature*, November 1941.

Warr, E., *The Early Education of Children in Beaconsfield, 1854–1904*, Beaconsfield and District Historical Society, 1968.

———, *Early Schooldays in Beaconsfield*, Beaconsfield and District Historical Society, 1968.

Whicher, G., "Edward Thomas," *Yale Review*, April 1920.

———, "Out for Stars," *Atlantic Monthly*, May 1943.

INDEX